Time to be Holy

TIME to be HOLY

Reflecting on
Daily Life

SWAMI SIVANANDA RADHA

Timeless Books
publishers of timeless wisdom

1996

TIMELESS BOOKS

PO Box 3543

Spokane, WA 99220-3543

- 1-800-251-9273

In Canada: Timeless Books, Box 9, Kootenay Bay, BC V0B 1X0
- 1-800-661-8711

In England: Timeless Books, 7 Roper Rd., Canterbury, Kent CT2 7EH
- (011-44) 1227-768813

Printed in the United States of America

Editor: Karin Lenman

Cover illustration and interior design: Margaret White

Typesetting: Joyce Ansell

Library of Congress Cataloging-in-Publication Data:
    Radha, Swami Sivananda, 1911–1995
        Time to be holy : reflecting on daily life/Swami Sivananda Radha.
        p.   cm.
        Includes bibliographical references and index.
        ISBN 0-931454-84-0 (cloth: alk. paper)
        ISBN 0-931454-81-6 (paper: alk. paper)
        1. Spiritual life--Hinduism.   I. Title.
    BL 1237.36.R325   1996
    294.5´44--dc20

                                                        96-14329
                                                        CIP

Published by

Timeless Books
publishers of timeless wisdom

Contents

Other books by the author:

The Divine Light Invocation
Kundalini Yoga for the West
Mantras: Words of Power
Radha, Diary of a Woman's Search
In the Company of the Wise
Seeds of Light
Hatha Yoga: the Hidden Language
From the Mating Dance to the Cosmic Dance
Realities of the Dreaming Mind

Also published by Timeless Books:

Glimpses of a Mystical Affair

Introduction

Time to be Holy is a treasure house of practical and inspiring seed-thoughts on spiritual life as they were presented during satsang by Swami Sivananda Radha. In these talks Swami Radha's purpose was to help people deepen their reflective process, using her words as a starting point, so that each could discover the power of reflection as a transformative spiritual tool in his or her life. Now in book form, her words can offer that same opportunity to many more people.

Satsang, a devotional gathering, is held each day at Yasodhara Ashram. It is a time of prayer, reflection and chanting, a time to see the personal challenges of life from a different perspective—a time to be holy. The word *satsang* means literally "in the company of the wise"— the wise being those who seek a deeper meaning in life and who sincerely want to make progress toward their own ideals.

Although satsang is a rejuvenating experience at any time, it was an extraordinary blessing to be there at those times when Swami Radha was present. I was one of the many people who had the privilege of this experience and it left an unforgettable impression on my mind. Our time together would begin with all of us chanting, letting the thoughts of the day recede and creating a space in the mind. It was usually during the time of our preliminary chanting that Swami Radha would arrive. Upon entering she would offer the salutation of *namasté* to all of us— "the Divine in me salutes the Divine in you." Then she would walk over to the altar and offer her *pranam* to the Divine. As she did this, the atmosphere of the whole room would be transformed. It took on the quality of what she was expressing in that moment—something I can only describe as a profound humility. It was clear she knew who she was in the highest sense—what her relationship was to a Divine Power. And in that moment she opened a door so that all of us could share in this experience. It wasn't that her gesture was grandiose or dramatic—for that was not her way—but something of the depth of her understanding seemed to be directly communicated to us, and we were all uplifted by it.

In these talks she would often be addressing people from very different cultural, economic and spiritual backgrounds, so she needed to express the most profound truths in a way that everyone could understand. Her talks always reflected her keen perception and deep compassion. By using examples from daily life—frequently her own experiences—she showed how spiritual ideals like faith, selfless service, surrender and love could be approached on a day-to-day basis. A feeling of intimacy was created, and it was not uncommon afterwards to hear people remark, "I felt as if she were talking directly to me and addressing my personal concerns."

Swami Radha repeatedly emphasized the importance of taking time for daily reflection to penetrate the deeper significance of life's events. Through my own reflections I came to understand that some of the hardest challenges of my life were not simply random misfortunes or hard luck but opportunities that brought to the fore intangible qualities of commitment, responsibility and dedication and made them accessible to me for my later use. The more I looked at the patterns of events in my life, the more I saw the workings of an invisible intelligence that seemed to have arranged for certain situations at just the right time so that I could learn more about myself and direct my strengths more consciously. By gaining this perspective I was able to take more responsibility for the unfoldment of my life and not to blame others for what had happened.

Daily reflection can contribute to a sense of harmony and well-being within ourselves and in our outer relationships. Perhaps the best example of its effectiveness can be seen at Yasodhara Ashram itself. The residents of the Ashram live and work together. They also write personal papers on a variety of topics to gain a deeper understanding of themselves and the purpose of their lives. As a result, Swami Radha's Ashram is one of the longest established spiritual communities in North America and has not become bogged down with personal politics or ethical shortcomings—problems that typically arise in groups or communities.

How was it possible for one woman to kindle the flame of spiritual awareness in so many people, myself included, and to teach them how to keep that flame going for themselves? What was it that drew all of us to her? I was immediately drawn to the fact that she encouraged self-reliance and independence and was not interested in taking the credit herself for her students' achievements. She would say, rather, that if they are better people, it was not through her grace but through their own personal efforts in working on themselves. She was there to encourage, to set the example, to offer opportunities, to ask questions and to inspire, but she could not do the work for her students or simply say the right words to make them enlightened.

I met Swami Radha in 1978 when she was introducing her book, *Kundalini Yoga for the West,* at Sheridan College in southern Ontario. It was her quality of true humility which made such an impression on me and drew me to her. At that time I called it her way of being "ordinary" even though she clearly embodied something extraordinary. Most of the people I had known in prestigious positions up to then had an aura of self-importance and impatience around them which functioned to keep others at a distance and to discourage anyone from occupying too much of their time. It amazed me that a great spiritual leader of Swami Radha's stature did not have this sense about her. She was very approachable and moved with ease and grace among all present.

In that first meeting I was also struck by her groundedness, her practicality and her knowledge of both the everyday world and the world of the spirit. When she opened her briefcase to retrieve a copy of her book, I saw that her reading material included copies of *Scientific American.* It was clear to me that she did not see spiritual life as something separate from life in the world, and I wondered then about the special kind of genius she possessed to be able to live both ways. She encouraged me not to leave my job to go and live at an ashram since life itself has a way of teaching us no matter where we are, as long as we make the effort to understand through daily reflection the lessons being offered.

As her Ashram grew and developed, she never forgot the offerings that each person had brought to its unfoldment. She would often bring it to our attention, for example, that the first Prayer Room would not have come into existence if the family of Margery Eyre* had not donated the funds to pay for its completion. She remembered and often mentioned those who had built the various buildings, those who had donated money so that specific projects could be completed, and those who worked outside the Ashram and offered their salaries to help pay the daily expenses. In this way she showed us how to overcome the mind's ever-present tendency to take everything for granted. Her example also demonstrated to us that we must never ignore sincere offerings, no matter what the people who made them might do in later years.

Through her teachings I have come to understand how life in fact does offer me many opportunities to grow in character and human greatness. And through her patience and compassion I have been increasingly able to face my fears and insecurities and cooperate with my heart's desire.

Satsangs are held daily in the beautiful Temple of Divine Light, dedicated to all religions, at Yasodhara Ashram—everyone is welcome. Its simple yet elegant design graces many of the pages of this book. Swami Radha had had a recurring image of the Temple in her dreams for most of her life. When the physical building was finally completed it seemed

---

* Margery Eyre was the wife of a prominent member of the British parliament, who lived her life according to the guidance of an inner spiritual teacher. She is the author of *The Revealing Light* and *The Seeker and the Finding.*

to function as a lens—gathering her rays of Light and focusing them in this one spot. Today, even though her physical form is no longer with us, it is still possible to read her messages from those earlier satsangs and to come in tune with her essence in the Temple.

Time to be Holy—Reflecting on Daily Life is a special gift to you from a true Guru. It carries the living quality of her satsang messages—the "secret oral teachings" passed on from an accomplished yogini to those who would ask, How do we transform the quality of our daily lives and apply the lessons that life brings us? May all who encounter this book be inspired to take her words to heart, to think in depth about the questions she raises and to set aside some time each day to be holy.

—Swami Hridayananda

Take Time to be Holy

Ignorance is kept alive because we are
all so busy with so many activities. Take time off
to think, to reflect. This is your time to be holy. When
you pause to think this way, you will realize that in
spite of what you know and what you can do, you still
get anxious and you still have your moments of worry.
If you take a moment to ask, "Why do I worry?
Why am I upset?" most of the time you will be able to
rebalance yourself pretty quickly.

It's all right to be busy, but don't be so busy that
you don't have time to think. For years I was very busy
with the Ashram—meeting people, corresponding,
traveling. I refrained from taking recreation because I
realized it wasn't the pleasure, the fun, that kept me
in balance. It was my periods of thinking, of reflecting, that kept me balanced. Instead of participating
in entertainments, I gave that time to thinking in
depth. That was my time to be holy.

Take time to be holy. Make that one of your key
sentences for conducting your future life. This kind
of thinking is more important than meditation for
the very reason that meditation will be more fruitful
after you have gone through this process of reflecting. It will prevent unnecessary thoughts from going
into the subconscious and bothering you from there.
Once you have completed your process of thinking,
then meditate.

—*Swami Sivananda Radha*

Swami Sivananda

My Guru, Swami Sivananda, was a great master and was very well-known in India. When I met the late president of India, Dr. Rajendra Prasad, after my initiation, he said, "One day you will know what a great soul Swami Sivananda is and how fortunate you have been."

My attraction to Swami Sivananda was not because of his miracles or psychic powers. Many people came to Gurudev because they wanted to see miracles. They would ask me, "Have you witnessed any? Have you ever seen anything?" People like to see miracles, but miracles don't make people more spiritual. Swami Sivananda never demonstrated any and he even told the few people who knew about the experiences that I had in India to keep silent about them. He never did anything to advertise, or make his Ashram known, or attract people.

He attracted me by his greatness of character. For example, he had many or-

phans in the Ashram, but he never used them as a work force. He tried
to find families to adopt them so these children, whose parents had died
of starvation, would have a good life. And for many years after they had
left, he would try to find out how they were.

He would say to a visitor, "Where do you live?"

If the visitor said, "Delhi."

He would say, "Go and see such-and-such family. Find out about
little Anil, and tell me how he is."

He would always inquire to make sure that the people who had
taken these children in would treat them well. He could have used them
to become sanyasins, or even as workers to help in the Ashram, but he
did not.

I knew one little boy there who wanted to be a great yogi like Gurudev was. One day he disappeared and it was thought he had run away,
but he hadn't. He had built a tree-house so he couldn't be found and
sent to a family, because he wanted to stay in the Ashram with Gurudev
Sivananda.

My attraction to my Guru came also because I saw his teaching in
action. If somebody really needed him, he was ever ready. At any hour
of the day, any hour of the night, he would be there. The swamis guarded
him so that people wouldn't take too much advantage of him, but they
did not guard him to the point that no one could see him.

That does not mean that I didn't see that Gurudev was very human. I had to deal with my own criticisms—for example, "How can he
be a medical doctor, and serve milk from dirty cups that the dogs have
licked?" There were many things that could have given me a solid basis
for criticism. But then I had to sit down and ask myself, "Did I come
here to sit in judgment? What do I really want? Why don't I sweep
everything else away, and go after what I want from him?"

Once this decision was made, I was able to receive his teaching
very quickly. I never put up any struggle after that.

Swami Sivananda's birthday is the eighth of September. That certainly was a blessed day. I don't think anybody can estimate how great
his influence was both in India and in many other countries. His message has gone around the world. The work that is done today by his
disciples and the work we do here is all an extension of his work.

The Spiritual Search

My Guru would have called all of you who seek a life of Higher Consciousness "gods and goddesses." The way he used that term it means exceptional people, people beyond the average. True spiritual leaders think that the masses, with their strong attachments to pleasure and to life itself, have no chance for spiritual attainment because they're satisfied with what they have. They never think of seeking anything greater than what serves their immediate needs, even in the fields of their personal interest. So from that angle, people on the spiritual path can really be considered exceptional people because they are seeking something more than the daily gratification of their desires.

Most people don't want to reach further. Let me explain that with an illustration. If a great violinist were to come to a town to give a concert of Bach, and I invited the whole population, how many people would want to come?

Some would say "Oh, I'm playing bridge tonight," or "We're having a party," or "I'm busy in the house," or "I'm working tonight, I really can't make it."

Others would say, "I don't have any money." And if I said, "Well, I will give you a ticket," they would say, "But I don't have a car. How do I get there?" If I said, "I will take you there and bring you back home," they would say, "Well, I don't think I can make it."

They are not interested in anything that is a bit demanding and does not immediately gratify their senses. The senses are indeed the windows through which we perceive life, but this seeking of immediate sense gratification, without ever making a change or reaching out further— that is what prevents them from having spiritual development.

It is not that the teachings are not available to everybody. They are. But you must want them. You must turn to the teachings, keep coming back to them, and keep asking yourself, "Why was I born? Why am I here? What is the purpose of my life? What should I pursue? How far should I go? What is my place in relation to the universe?" These are the things that are important. It doesn't matter what words you use to formulate those questions—that's very individual, that's the way you speak, the way you see things. It's that you *ask* those questions, and that you seek contact in life with a power greater than yourself, some Light greater than that visible to human eyes, *that* is what sets you apart from the masses. You are on the path to realization of the Self, realization of your own divinity. It makes no difference whether you are a woman or a man.

Keep asking questions. Try to go further. Remove your obstacles—your personality quirks and your personality aspects, which you often take for real, and give power to. The only thing that has power in you is your inner being or inner Light. You may call this inner being *soul*, if you like, or *Higher Self*—the term you use has to be meaningful to you, so choose your own words.

There is an underlying unity in all the teachings. What separates us most times is just man-made doctrine. We should remember that even in the Christian faith the saints came first, with the process by which they had found God-Realization. The monasteries and the doctrines were built around them later, and that's when the divisions were created. All people who have had experiences of God-Realization have no divisions among themselves. Their experiences are individual, but they know the truth they have realized is all one. It is doctrine that divides us. When people from other groups come here, I say, "If you want to bring the picture of your Guru to satsang tonight, that's fine," because I don't want any divisions like that here.

Disciples often create division also. Some of them get possessive. I say to my students, "Don't get into this, ever, because the divine work is one. We all have to do the same thing: to develop compassion, to develop understanding, to develop the Light within. Whether it is the light of understanding, or the light of love, or the light of healing, it is *that* which we have to attain to."

When I came back from India, I was looking for a place to stay for a while to sort out my mind. The people at the places I went to would say, "Yes, we accept anybody, whatever your background. But when you come to us, you must accept our belief system." Many of them told me, "But Sivananda isn't our Guru. You must accept our Guru." Some of the Christians said, "No, you are too outlandish. You will create too much commotion, and with your orange robe you will attract too much attention." So I couldn't stay in any of those places.

I am glad for these experiences. They were very painful at the time, because I felt there was no place for me, but they showed me what can happen when divisions are created. My Guru had said I should start an ashram and some centers. I decided that in this Ashram, I would not demand that people change their religion. I would just see if I could help them to become better Jews, or Catholics, or whatever. I made that a principle at the Ashram in the mountains, and I have kept to that ever since, because doctrine is *not* what spiritual development is about.

Yoga is not a religion. It's a technique that helps you to concentrate, that helps you to keep healthy (because you need your healthy body to find God-Realization). It means, in simple terms, to know God—and to know the God within. Yoga is a technique to help you clarify. If you are a devout Christian, what are you really saying when you say the Lord's Prayer? Do you really *know* what you are saying? It is this greater clarification that is the yoga process. All my students are trained this way: don't try to change what people already have. Try to help them improve on it and bring the Light into it.

When people say, "Oh, Zen is very interesting. It appeals to my intellect," I say, "Fine. But you must study the history of Zen and study the culture where it developed." Because each culture puts its own stamp on a tradition. Buddhism in Japan is barely recognizable as the Buddhism which originally began in India. It was changed in China, too, and in Tibet, simply by the surroundings. The Tibetans lived in the mountains with terribly cold weather and short periods of natural growth. They had to develop fields thousands of feet up the mountains. Working at that height is difficult and it builds a very different body and stamina.

When I was in India, I visited some Christian churches and bought some Christmas cards. They are very different from our Christmas cards because the Indians have made something very different out of Christianity. In North America, we have done something else with it, and it does not look like the Christianity of the Middle East.

What really matters is your own personal self-development. You must develop so that, whatever tradition you have, you can see with greater clarity and understand with less confusion. Then you can know how your mind works and how to focus your attention. Changing your tradition is not what I or my students have in mind. Only take what you have and increase that. In business, to make money you need some money to begin with. In spiritual life, it is somewhat similar: you can use what you already have and increase your awareness from there. That process always leads you to greater knowledge. You can also build on your own creativity. For example, if you are a musician, you could take music to a great height just by adopting the principles of Mantra. A poet could do the same thing, using poetic talent to become almost a prophet.

You can be what you are and go on from there. Just find out what you are. Ask yourself, "Who am I? Where do I want to go? What do I want to make out of this life? When I get older and I know that death is approaching, can I say I have lived a worthwhile life?" If you can say yes, you will have a very peaceful death. If you have a goal in life, your life will be richer than if you are just tottering and stumbling around, not knowing where you are going. When you have a goal, you know that stumbling is a necessary part of your journey, and you will pull yourself up by your own bootstraps and go where you want to go. If you ask yourself what kind of person you are now, and what kind of person you want to be physically, mentally/emotionally, and spiritually, you can get the tools through yoga to achieve that goal. But *you* must decide on the goal. Nobody can do that for you.

The yoga that I learned from my Guru helps people to answer their own questions, helps them to find out what kind of life they want to live. You don't have to give up what you have. You can pursue the life that you have already and the commitments that you have taken on in life. All you need to do is deepen what you have and clarify where you are going. That is all up to you. Some of you are probably aware quite clearly that you need to develop more deeply, and some may have just an idea that there is a need and maybe it will become clearer in the future. There is no particular urgency, except perhaps that life is becoming increasingly complex, and so you may wish to seek something of a greater and much deeper value in yourself. If the teachings can help you to uncover this, then they have served their purpose.

However, if you really want the Divine, that has to be number one.

It *really* has to be number one. People have sometimes asked me, "How did you do it with all the work you had to do?" The work has to be related to the desire for the Divine. You have to constantly keep people in the Light. Otherwise you can't do it. If the work is one thing, and your spiritual practice is something else, then you can't do it. If you think you have worked hard, then you were working from your human personality. If you give your hands and head and senses and say, "Here, use them," then you can do it.

I had never been able to give lectures or sing before an audience. But I could, once I was able to surrender and say, "Well, I have no control over this, but I will call on Divine Mother. Let her do it. We'll see."

If you can make that shift at least every now and then (the more often, the better), you will feel all right. And there won't be much question of, "Did I do the right thing?" Just bring the Light back to yourself. Make all the actions a service.

Illusions

The West and the East are so different. In my journal of the time I was in India,* I give a glimpse of what it meant for me to go there. It wasn't just the travel itself that was such a big step. I was forty-four years old, and I had to quit a very secure job in which I had some seniority. My boss had talked to me as if I were out of my mind, because when I came back from India, I would be forty-five and I would be unemployable by the regulations of the company in those days.

But something in me wanted always to know: What was the purpose of life? Why was I born? Why was I here? Looking around and seeing what goes on in life had convinced me there must be something else. I saw people falling in love, getting married, having babies, divorcing, then looking for new partners and starting all over again. Children did not provide fulfillment for them either. So what else could there be?

A couple of my friends had got married more than once, and I saw that their problems didn't change because *they* had not changed. Each one attracted and married the same kind of personality again, so they had the same problems again. It seemed to me that the cost—the emotional cost, the years, all the effort people put into living—was enormously high, and there was so little gain. I could see what was going on in other people's lives, and I decided that I was not going to pay that cost. By that time I had already been twice widowed and I did not want to have another relationship. I felt that somehow destiny had put me into this situation to wake up and do something else. And that something else was a continuous questioning of the purpose of life.

There was a small group of people in Montreal who followed the teachings of an Indian Guru. They did not have much money and they needed a place to meet. They asked me if they could meet once a week in my studio in which I practiced dancing.† I said they could, and they met

---

* Swami Sivananda Radha, *Radha, Diary of a Woman's Search* (Spokane, USA: Timeless Books, 1981, 3rd printing 1990).

† I had been a professional dancer in Europe and I often offered my services for charity performances in Montreal because they would raise quite a bit of money.

there for about a year. They tried very hard to persuade me to join them. I said, "Look, I left all this behind. I have no particular faith in any religion nor in any god. After the things I saw during the war and during the Hitler time when babies were killed, not just by the Nazis, but sometimes by their own grandmothers taking their food and milk, I have no particular faith in any religion. I'm just not a joiner." I put them off for many months this way.

Eventually, I was persuaded by a woman who was very determined. She just did not give up. So one day I decided, "Okay, I will spend one evening with them to see what they do and then I can tell them why I don't want to join. Right now I can't really say anything because I don't quite know what they do."

They always had a picture of their Guru on the altar. The group leader said, "Just look at his picture and close your eyes and see what happens." They were not at all prepared for what did happen. For the next four hours I totally disappeared. I was physically sitting there, but I had no awareness of where I was, what was going on, nothing.

This was one of the times that I met Swami Sivananda in meditation. He spoke to me in a language that I did not understand. Later on, when I was in India, he confirmed this by telling somebody that he had called me from the West and he had spoken to me in Tamil on purpose. He said, "She didn't like it, because she couldn't understand Tamil."

So, it was with great effort that I arrived at the Ashram in Rishikesh. I had to give up a job, I didn't have much money, and then there I was in a room somewhere on a hillside in India. The walls of the room were literally dripping. Because of the monsoon, the humidity was so great that everything was wet. If you washed your hair, you didn't need to worry about drying it. It wouldn't dry. Clothes wouldn't dry. Someone brought me a tray with hot tea and milk and biscuits and gave me instructions about living in this place. There was a little porch of very strong chain-linked metal. I was told, "Make sure you always close the door, because the monkeys will come in and take anything they can get."

There are many such stories in the *Radha* book of my initial cultural shocks and adjustments to the circumstances. The Sivananda Ashram today has all the facilities—electric light, bathrooms, running water—so it's very convenient now. But then, there was only one building that even had electric light.

I had to decide to forego the way I was used to living, and to renounce all my ideas of how one ought to live, and to accept my Guru's teachings. But I had already gone through six and a half years of war which were a very good preparation, because many times during the war water or electricity or heat didn't function because of the bombings. I was very sick a couple of times in those years. It was just a miracle that I survived a lot of things.

That experience helped a little in India. But that people would have a house and not take care of it, that they would leave it dirty and dilapidated, and not have proper bathroom facilities—all this was absolutely beyond me. I knew Swami Sivananda was a medical doctor and still these things were not taken care of. I soon found out that most of the time women didn't stay there. They would come for a day or two and then leave, moving back into a hotel because they didn't want to take the difficulties of that very, very primitive life. I had to make up my mind whether I cared for the comforts of life, or whether I wanted the teachings. If I wanted the teachings, that was the price I had to pay, and I decided that I was willing to pay the price. If anybody asked me today, I would say, "I would do it all over again."

Have your comforts if you can, but don't make too great an effort to have them and don't cling to them. When you are living the spiritual life, you must be able to walk out on comfort any time. It must not make any difference to you where you are, what you do, where you sleep. Our houses are pretty safe and comfortable in North America. Most of them are carpeted, so even if you sleep on the floor you're not sleeping on a stone slab.

In India what I thought was a huge table turned out to be a wooden platform for me to sleep on. No one could sleep on the floor because all sorts of snakes, rats, and insects crawl there. In these conditions, you experience what it is like to live in a world with other creatures and share the world with them. Some creatures are very nice and charming, and others not so nice, and some are really hostile. Many of those characteristics we have, too.

If you look at what is going on all around you, you will find out how much effort life takes. If you have experienced enough pain, disappointment and disillusionment, you will discover that most of your pain comes because you have approached a situation through unnecessary embellishment of your hopes and illusions. With your hopes and illusions you embellish even something so simple as thinking tomorrow morning you will have a wonderful breakfast. What if all of a sudden the electricity is shut off so you can't have your favorite coffee, or an egg cooked in the particular way you like it? Everything is upside down. Is this going to ruin your day? What if your wife comes home late from work and hasn't done any shopping for food, and has forgotten to turn on the heat, or your husband says he has a business meeting and you're not sure what that business meeting really is?

You have illusions about things, and illusions are never, ever fulfilled. If you think you will be fulfilled if you can just achieve this social status, or that income bracket, there are always people who have more, whose social status is higher, whose influence is greater, and whose income is more. There is always somebody who has more.

If you have won part of the race by finally getting into a particular group, socially or financially, what have you got? You're not satisfied because you become aware that this group is not really all that much better. You should be in the next one. *There* things will be better. You can go on and on this way, constantly in a race because desires and illusion go hand in hand. One desire creates another, and then all your time and effort goes into the fulfillment of desires.

Then I come along and say, "Why bother?" If you want to belong to an exceptional group, belong to the yogis, who seek Higher Consciousness where there are no false promises, only clarification and the realization of how much of your power is illusory. Can you make this change? Can you stop living in illusion? From my experience I say, "Yes, you can." Find out what you truly desire, and if it is Higher Consciousness, then go straight for it. No sightseeing trips.

I never went on sightseeing trips in India, and I was there a total of three times. I knew why I was going. I knew what I wanted. Sightseeing would have taken away my focus. I did my sightseeing in Italy and Spain.

I went to India only to get Higher Consciousness because that is where there is the theoretical knowledge of it, the scriptural texts which show the way, and the people who have attained it. I wanted to meet people who were ahead of me on the same royal highway even if they hadn't attained the highest consciousness, because I could learn from them, too.

Today, Swami Sivananda and most of the other great souls have left the Earth, but their teachings remain, so their messages about making different choices for a different life are available to everybody. Unfortunately, these teachings are counteracted by the biological forces of nature in people. But sometime, in some lifetime, everyone will have to make the effort to break away from these forces. Otherwise you will remain in the grip of instinct. Nature always wants to use you to reproduce—the purpose of marriage, really, is the propagation of the human species. If you try to do something else with marriage, you will have nothing but disaster. You see that over and over again. Only a very few children are truly wanted. Most parents have just resigned themselves to parenthood. Nearly all the measures to prevent pregnancy just injure people's health. Because we deny the purpose of sex, we are living against Nature. I have known only a very few couples who have successfully made something spiritual of their marriages.

If you go on the spiritual path, you live against Nature, too, but with a very definite purpose that has nothing to do with self-gratification. Your purpose on the spiritual path is to achieve a very different state of mind—the pearl of great price. Everybody has to decide as an individual whether to pursue that pearl. If you decide you want it, you have also to be willing to pay the price. That price is your own self-gratification, self-glorification, self-importance, and the heaps of desires that you probably can't fulfill anyway.

Look at your imagination. The power of imagination is very great. You use your imagination to anticipate events. You create illusions which don't come about. If they did, every marriage would be happy. Every child would be received as the gift of the Divine. Every life would be wonderfully in harmony with all the cosmic forces. But if you look around, you see this is not the case.

So, go in search of the pearl of great price. Find it.

Selfless Service

THE GOAL OF YOGA is to achieve true union with the Light—knowing that the Light is within, and acting on that knowing. My Guru, Swami Sivananda, used to say that selfless service was the way to achieve this. "Selfless service will make you divine," he would often say. He would tell people to concentrate on that instead of intellectualizing about concepts like Liberation, the Absolute, or Atman. The Bhagavad Gita says the same thing, too, over and over—selfless service is the way to the Divine.

No work is too lowly to be done in Divine Mother's service, and none is too lowly for you to learn from. Often when people are asked to work in the kitchen, they think, "Oh, I'm only in the kitchen." *Only?* I learned some of my most important lessons in the kitchen. I did all the Ashram cooking in the early years, and I did it on a stove which had no heat controls. I had to give up all my ideas about the wonderful meals I was going to prepare. The stove could handle only the simplest cooking, and even then it sometimes burned the food or didn't cook it through. So I learned a lot about pride and letting go of results.

You can learn everything you need to know about yourself in the kitchen. That's where you learn to get along with people. It's where you can learn to serve with care and attention by learning how to cook with love. Food cooked without love does not get eaten.

If you have a great need for recognition, the kitchen is a place where you can get a lot of that. Chop a whole cord of firewood and nobody notices. Nobody will comment on how well you cleaned the guest lodge, or praise you for perfect bookkeeping. There is a lot of work like that done in the Ashram. On the other hand, in the kitchen, you can get lots of praise. Some people have spent enormous amounts of money on expensive ingredients because they were really soaking up the praise they got for their cooking. In their search for praise, they were wasting money which was in short supply in the Ashram, and they were creating gluttons. You can learn a great deal in the kitchen about how far you will go to be praised.

If praise comes to you, give it back to the Divine, because your ability to do a good job has come from the Divine in the form of intelligence and the Light of understanding.

Sometimes people become sidetracked trying to understand what the Bhagavad Gita means by action and inaction. They think that action disturbs contemplation, but the fact is that very few people can contemplate. Who can be single-pointed for three, four, five hours? There are people who can trigger themselves into a trance, but trance is not contemplation or meditation. Even what we think is inaction really isn't because the mind is constantly active, even in sleep. Also, as long as you are alive, you have to eat. Eating is action. So you have to act *because* you are alive. You may as well act to the best of your ability, and dedicate as much action as possible in the most selfless manner to the purpose and glory of the Divine. Rather than going around in circles, place the whole question of action and inaction in the Light. You will have much less worry about it and you won't need to do fantastic mental acrobatics to explain it.

Swami Radha speaking during construction of the Temple of Divine Light, September 1989.

To practice Karma Yoga, the yoga of selfless service, the yoga of action without desiring the fruits of the work, you have to know your motivation. Then, in order to be successful, to reach your goal, you have to be complete and sincere in your dedication. Without sincere dedication, nothing specific can be achieved. We all have many personality aspects which often counter what we intend to do, but if your motivation and your dedication are right, in the end you are bound to win the battle—the battle in which you conquer yourself.

Letting go of your attachments to work and to its rewards will not happen immediately, but if you are sincerely trying, you will probably have some success within a week. As a small beginning, you might try giving a service of some kind to someone as an anonymous gift. Also, think about what selfless service means to you. Reflect on this deeply and often. In the end, you will see that being attached does not give you the rewards you think it will. If you list the debits and credits of your attachments, you will see that you're in the red.

Selflessness is an attitude that you bring to your work, and everyone, individually, has to make a decision about that attitude. If you say, "I really don't want to do this work. It's a *real* sacrifice," then this is where you are and this is where you have to start. Sacrifice whatever there is. If you think your work is too difficult or tiring or boring, make it an offering to the Divine. This will help you to achieve personal harmony inside. You have to drive out negative thoughts quickly, because if they become a habit, you won't find *any* work that is agreeable. That can be very troublesome.

I did all the housework at the Ashram in the beginning. I had never done any housework before, and I had certainly never cleaned bathrooms. I vomited for the whole of the first week that I cleaned the Ashram bathrooms. Then one evening when I was going into the prayer room for satsang, as I put my hand on the doorknob, I heard what seemed like a voice saying very clearly, "It's a privilege to serve those who seek the Most High." So, there was my reward: the work itself—it's a privilege to do this service.

If you have work you find disagreeable, do the Divine Light Invocation and put the work in the Light. Then make it an offering in your mind, or lay it before whatever symbol of the Divine you are using. Say, simply, "I give this work."

The idea of getting rewards for work is a trap that will swallow up the benefits of your efforts to be spiritual. Jesus said if you expect rewards on Earth for what you do, you may get them, but you can't then have rewards in heaven, too.* He also said there is much work to be

---

* Matthew 6:1, 5.

done in the Lord's vineyard, but very few want to do this work because they don't get paid. When you work for the Divine, you don't get paid in dollars and cents. But if you learn perfect surrender, who is to say that isn't a reward in itself?

Surrender

SURRENDER IS ALL that you want to get from work, and the first thing you have to surrender is selfishness. You cannot do only the work that you know everyone will praise. You have to do the work whatever it is, not because you like doing it, but because it is there to be done. Divine Mother gave it to you. You do it. You can never be truly a handmaiden of Divine Mother unless you do it to the very best of your ability—and don't try to get out of it by dumping it on somebody else or leaving it undone.

Your surrender must have depth. You may let people wash the dishes or type letters their way instead of your way, but that is not surrender. That is only beginning to understand that there are many other useful ways besides your own. You may see that letting other people do work their way gets the job done faster, but that is still not surrender. That is only the beginning of making tiny little inroads on your own rigidity, on the idea that your way is the only way.

Surrender has to be done with discrimination. It makes no sense to move a lake from one valley to another by carrying the water one cupful at a time over the mountain. You have to think about what you are doing. God gave you intelligence. Use it. Go to the very edge of your mind, to the point where your mind can do no more and begins to run in circles. That's the time to stop thinking. When the mind has exhausted its capabilities, that's when the message will come. Surrender, and the answer will emerge.

Obedience and doing the work from a sense of duty, that is not surrender, either. When I came back from India to establish an ashram as my Guru had instructed, my fear and lack of self-confidence were so great that in the beginning I did all the work simply out of obedience to

Swami Sivananda. The next phase was duty. That lasted for several years. I felt it was my duty to carry on what I had started. Then one day in meditation I had an insight that work done from a sense of duty is not surrender. But the work is no different. Only the attitude is different. If you are working from a sense of duty, fulfill your duty as well as you can, but offer the work. Make that your gift, because it's the only thing you really can bring to the Divine.

A duty is not done selflessly if all the time you are doing it, you are looking forward to when you will be off duty: "Oh, great, in three days, I have a day off." If you want to move ahead in your spiritual development, you have to go beyond duty.

Also, you cannot make duty into surrender by saying, "Oh, well, I don't want anything anyway," because that can be just indifference or sour grapes, not true letting go. You have to be clear when you are letting go, and when you are being indifferent. Discrimination is very important in surrender.

If you are not sure that you are truly surrendering—if you are not sure that you still mean it when you say "Thy will be done"—you simply have to sit down and take time to reflect, or ask for a dream. Drop everything else, sit down, and figure out how you can clarify that uncertainty to yourself. Every time you doubt that you are still able to surrender, it's very important to put that in your diary so you won't forget it. Then you must find ways to clarify your uncertainty. You don't just live with it and say, "Oh yeah, I know, but just for today it's okay." *Do* something.

Explain the idea of surrender to yourself in many ways. When you light a candle, you can see that the candle has to surrender to your action and to the flame. It has to burn down. It can't say, "No, I don't want to." Ask yourself, "What am I surrendering to?" If you are surrendering to the Light, make sure it's the Divine Light, not some colored or black light.

People who live in the Ashram may think at times they are surrendering to me or to the Ashram or its policies and regulations, but really the Ashram is only the battlefield on which they battle their own problems and difficulties. It is here only to provide them with the opportunity to practice surrender. If it becomes really tough, I tell people, "Ask the Divine for a breathing spell, but don't be foolish and pack and go. There is no great lesson in packing and going. Anybody can do that. If you feel like doing that, acknowledge those feelings. Don't hide them in the closet. Don't make ghosts out of them. But don't act on them."

When it comes to surrender, there is often less struggle for a woman than there is for a man. I did not have many of the struggles that a man undergoes, particularly if he has made a name for himself. Men go through life always with the undercurrent in their mind, "I am superior. I can do this and I can do that and I can do the other." Unless a man has developed the feminine part in himself, he feels very superior to any woman because he has greater physical strength and he is usually physically taller.

If you are a woman and you feel badly about your position, think also of the advantages you have on the spiritual path. To surrender to the Divine is, from my experience with what I have seen of the struggle of men, considerably easier for a woman. A woman doesn't usually need to nourish intellectual pride. If she feels like crying, she cries. A man too often feels, "No. Men don't do this," or "That is beneath my male dignity."

Women don't have that problem. But a woman must be careful to surrender to the Divine and not to the desires of her feminine nature. Look at all your desires. Don't surrender to them. Don't scheme the fulfillment of those desires.

You will go through phases in your efforts at selfless service, but the important thing is to *do* it. The quality of your work and the quality of your attitude will improve if your dedication is complete.

Why is surrender essential? Because you can't always know when your self-will is active. There may be just a tinge of greed or desire in your attitude to the work—and just a tinge is too much. Let go and say, "Well, I will wait and work and when the time comes the answer will be given." You will see that it will be given.

Every now and then review how you are doing with surrender and obedience. Put a list on the inside cover of your diary and tick it off. When you come to the bottom of the list, put up a new list and start all over again, because it is so very easy to slip up. You have to keep your mind on the many things that have to be incorporated into your spiritual practice.

Self-will and work done selfishly keep you in bondage. The biggest enemy of your spiritual development is stubborn resistance and self-will. The Buddhists have given perhaps the most detailed description of how to control the mind, and it's mainly control of self-will. You have to keep asking the questions: "What am I doing with this life? Am I really making the best use of it?" Those are the questions everyone has to ask himself or herself. No teacher can do more than present you with them and advise you how to apply them. These questions have to be ingrained, they have to become part of you so that you can help yourself. A teacher can give you the opportunity, but what you do with the opportunity is up to you. As a teacher, I can stimulate, coax, and sometimes give you a little shove, but you have to do the walking. I cannot just pick you up like a stone and fling you into the lake. That wouldn't work.

So, let go of self-will. Work done selflessly in the service of the Most High—and that Most High is also in part within yourself—is what will get you to your destination. Selfless service will bring you into contact with that Guru within and that will make you independent.

Selfless service is also your protection in these times when the obstacles to Higher Consciousness can have a devastating dimension. Krishna in his last message to the world says, "Whenever people suffer at the hands of others, I will destroy evil." To the evildoers, he says, "If you remain hard-hearted, I will destroy you." Today there are millions of people suffering at the hands of others. How do you protect yourself in such times? By practicing selfless service, for that is what will make you divine. It is the road to return to the Light, to your inner being.

Selfless Service Will Make You Divine

To work "WITHOUT SELF" means to work without seeking any personal gratification. You are not working to attract compliments, or to satisfy the ego's pride, or to achieve identification through your work. Selfless service is work performed as well as you can do it, because Divine Mother needs it done, whether or not anybody notices you doing it. That's not easy, but selfless service can take you beyond your small s self. Your work can become sattvic or pure. Doing the work because it needs to be done will purify the mind, taking you beyond birth and death.

If you have likes and dislikes about the job before you, or if you think it's beneath your social status or educational level, you are not doing selfless service. Forget those considerations. Have no attachment to your reactions. Try to get over and through them as fast as you can. It is this non-attachment that will give you the knowledge of selflessness. Otherwise, your understanding remains only intellectual and you will take whatever Light comes to you and your feeling of satisfaction as rewards. Then your emotions will get the better of you and you won't be able to let go of self-gratification.

It helped me to think of myself as Divine Mother's handmaiden. Anyone—man or woman—can be Divine Mother's handmaiden. Or you may wish to think of yourself as Lord Krishna's assistant. With the attitude that you are serving the Divine, you can protect yourself from becoming attached to what you are doing. Then you can see everything that comes to you as a contribution to your learning process. If you become aware also of the mistakes of others, you can decide how to avoid making those same mistakes. This way, you find your path to the Divine within yourself.

When I first came back from India, I worked very hard to understand Karma Yoga and the renunciation of the fruits of work. I thought of myself as Divine Mother's handmaiden, because that gave me something tangible and personal, something I could relate to in my daily reflections. I would look over the day and clarify my degree of selflessness. Where was I the handmaiden of Divine Mother? Where was I gratifying myself? I would note these in my spiritual diary.

If you do this kind of clarification, it will help you to achieve inner equanimity. You will not be exhilarated because you received praise, or upset because somebody criticized you. Criticism will mean very little, as long as *you* are clear that your selflessness was as complete as you could make it on that particular day.

It is very important to combine selfless service with spiritual practice and reflection. There were some missionaries in India who worked with people who had leprosy. Some of them became ill. I could not understand why this would happen to such good people. In answer to my

question, Swami Sivananda said, "Work and reflection are your right and your left eye. You need both to see properly." If either is missing, he said, you are only a do-gooder. That is a place to start, but spiritual development comes only if you bring spiritual practices and reflection together with your service.

There are many ways of running away from the work we need to do. We may fear criticism, or wish to avoid unpleasant people, or allow ourselves to sink into bad moods, or hide in ideas of duty. Fearing criticism, for example, is the other side of seeking praise. In your work, you want to please Divine Mother. You don't have to please anybody else. Fear of criticism in spiritual work is something you have to overcome because it puts you into a straightjacket. It is also a difficult habit to give up once you get yourself into it. You have to have courage, and you have to learn to accept even unjust criticism. It is self-serving to abandon your work because you are afraid of criticism. You are making yourself more important than the work. If you do that, naturally you won't receive any of the blessings of doing selfless service.

If you run away into your work, that is not selfless service, either. People often come to an ashram and find themselves behaving in ways they never did before. They are irritated by those around them, they become impatient, bad-tempered, because suddenly they are in an environment where they can no longer hide their negative personality aspects. Many people then take refuge in work. They make it their hiding place. They don't come to satsang. They don't do spiritual practice, or they do so little they do not get to a point of concentration.

Your work is not selfless if you try to avoid the people who irritate you. You cannot run away from such people. You shouldn't even try. You will make great progress by staying where you are and working out your problems. If you pack and go somewhere else or try to hide in your work, your problems will stay with you and you will still have to work them out.

When you find yourself in a bad mood, it may be that you have not done the best job you could and something in you knows that. You have been trying to sneak out a back door and even though no one saw you, something within knows and is unhappy. Pull yourself out of that negative mood, out of that depression, by taking immediate action. Find out what you have left undone, what you did from selfish motives, or where your desire for recognition was disappointed. If you seize the mood quickly before it goes too deep, you can begin to cut it down, perhaps to half a day, then to a couple of hours, then to half an hour. Be as aware of your moods as you can.

Service given without any expectation of self-gratification or praise or recognition—that is true selfless service. Do all actions and all work selflessly in the service of the Most High and remember that the Most High is also in part within yourself. Have faith in your Divine within and that will get you there. But without selfless service, you will not come in contact with the Guru within, and then you will become very upset and frustrated because without that you will never succeed on your spiritual path. You will depend on this and that and the other—on things outside yourself. Become independent. If you surrender your self-will and put your will without self into the service of the Divine, you will get there. But self-will and selfish work will only keep you in bondage. Let it go.

And never think you are too small, too insignificant, or too ignorant. Divine Mother needs many kinds of workers. All she asks is that you do the work.

Control

To get to your own true Self, you have to learn how to control your personality aspects. This is no easy matter. Each personality aspect has its own ego. I learned this horrendous fact from my Tibetan Guru. I didn't know how many personality aspects I had or how they worked. I wondered if they would converge, or if they were all in just one aspect of ego. The answer is no. They all have separate egos, and they are all at war with each other.

Many people have a great desire for control, and it makes them do horrible things, not just on the world scene but in daily life and even in spiritual centers. Such people have a whole army of personality aspects over which they have little control. But instead of learning to control them, they try to control other people. They do not realize that these personality aspects create a great barrier between them and their inner Light.

This need for control comes from a merciless ego. No tiger or lion could ever be fiercer than that kind of ego.

Your attempts to control others can be very dangerous. You can spend three hours in meditation and then give in to this powerful desire to control somebody else's life and lose all the effects of the meditation—even if you had an experience of divine ecstasy. It's gone. You destroyed it just by giving in to the desire to control the life and the surroundings of somebody else.

Of course, it's much easier to project your desire to control outwards, because the more you control everybody else, the less time you have to examine how your own personality aspects need to be controlled. And the more you believe it is others who need to be controlled, the less responsibility you will have to take for your own actions.

The desire to control is very powerful. Even little babies have it. They know how to get their will, how to control their mother, their father, or the whole family. Everybody is focused on them. They can't even talk yet, but by humming and screaming and crying and singing to themselves, they control their surroundings very precisely.

You can try to exercise that same kind of control in your spiritual life. What you are doing then is trying to control the Divine. Do you think that just because you go to satsang from eight to ten every night, or because you chant for two hours every day, you are so important that Krishna had better be there? It just doesn't work that way. It takes surrender and humility to bring the Divine to you. That's the only way, and sometimes that surrender requires a lot of patience. The Divine comes in its own time.

Intellect, Knowledge, and Action

KNOWLEDGE AND ACTION are two different processes of yoga. Both demand control of mind. In the Third Discourse of the Bhagavad Gita, Arjuna asks Krishna, "Which is the right path? One time you say *knowledge*, another time you say *action*, and now you say *neither*."

All human beings are born to act. Even babies do. As long as a person can move, *some* action and some use of the senses will take place. Speaking is an action; so is seeing. To understand the action of seeing, think about these expressions:

—*I see,*
—*the act of seeing,*
—*what is seen.*

It is one thing to act, but we have to *understand* what we do. We can't just act carelessly because there is nothing we do that does not have a result of some kind. We must understand the responsibility we have for our actions and their consequences, and how we affect the lives of other people by everything we do. Everything is interaction.

Knowledge comes only through personal experience because without that we have only information. Information is not knowledge. My own Guru was very insistent on this point. You must be aware, too, that the experience of people in various walks of life is bound to be different.

In the West, we often think of intellect as a storehouse of knowledge, but intellect is not understood that way in the East. When my

Tibetan Guru said he was not interested in disciples except those of superior intellect, I took that remark in the same way any Westerner would have done. It was some time before I understood. To him, intellect was something to be used to learn from the mistakes of others. Then you don't have to make those mistakes yourself. All the Ph.D.'s in the world won't do that for you.

Now, is there anything beyond the intellect? Certainly. But there is no clear-cut word for it, because there is no agreed-upon meaning for such terms as *samadhi* or *nirvana* or *Higher Consciousness*. Everyone who claims to be an authority has his or her own particular interpretation. This is knowledge that comes only through personal experience, so I suggest you find your own meaning. You have a right to find your own interpretation, and the sooner the better.

Setting a Selfless Example

THE THIRD DISCOURSE OF THE GITA speaks about action. "The Yoga of Action" is its title. But it emphasizes *selflessness*. It is selflessness that must govern the action. Why? Because otherwise we create new samsaras.* We will become attached to the action, to the fruits of the action, and we will have to be reborn.

So, when my Guru said, "Selfless service makes you divine," he knew what he was saying. And by reflecting on this, we can know it and recognize the importance of selflessness.

Action done in selflessness is nourishing. You nourish yourself and you nourish the other person. When this kind of interaction, interpenetration, takes place, an exchange of energy occurs between people.

Whatever you do, do it without self. Do it with selflessness. Then you can take your portion. If you take what's rightfully yours, if you take

---

* Samsara may be understood as a pattern of mechanical behavior which develops in the mind and which has to be broken before new ways of behaving and thinking can be established.

only what you need and don't misuse what is available, there is no wrong action committed. But if you take more, if you become grubbing and greedy, you deny nourishment to others, and then you have reason to worry.

Not sharing what you could share makes you a thief, so share even if sometimes it seems like a sacrifice. In other words, give whatever it is even if you really don't want to. That's better than not giving it at all, because selfishness and greed make you a hard person—unforgiving and without compassion. The finer elements of your emotions do not develop if you can't be generous. We have a saying: "You can only make money if you have money. Money creates money." It's the same thing with blessings. You can't give blessings if you don't have them. So first you have to become eligible, so to speak, for the divine blessing. Then share it. Then be a blessing to others. Try to kindle that Light in other people. That will strengthen your own knowing of your Self, and make it clearer to you. It will also help others, and that's the greatest good you can do. That creates blessings for you, and doubles and triples them.

In the Third Discourse, the Gita says the ability to work is not your own. You have not given yourself life. You take for granted the life force that is in your body, that you use to act. It makes your hand move, it makes your eyes see, it makes all your senses and your limbs work. You think, "It's mine." But if that essence, that life force, that pranic energy, leaves the body, then what? You cannot give the prana to yourself. You cannot get it back. You can get to know and move the pranic forces in your body if through practice and knowledge you have gained an understanding of them. But even your life is not really your own. It was given to you, and so you ought to share what you have in life.

Knowledge helps you do the greatest good. The highest knowledge is knowledge of the inner Self, the inner Light. Even if you are not Self-Realized, something in you knows there is an inner Light. And once you recognize this, then the greatest good you can do is to help others find it in themselves. Why is it called the greatest good? The Gita explains that very clearly: because it frees you from the rounds of birth and death. So, do not do things that will strengthen the weaknesses in others just to make them like you better, or be nicer to you, or give you gifts, or smile at you, or accept you. That is like an indirect stealing from the Divine.

Through selflessness we can also help each other pay off our debts. While in India, I resorted to putting all my burdens down, and saying, "Well, Gurudev can carry this," because he had done so much practice by the time I met him. It was as if he was helping to pay off my debts. We can do that at any time for each other. We can help each other pay off debts by prayer and meditation for each other, including putting people into the Light. You can even tell the people you are doing this for, because it helps them to know somebody is thinking of them.

Lord Krishna instructs Arjuna that he must fight. He must be the example and set a high standard. He must show courage and honor because, Krishna says, "If you don't set the standard, how will the other people know what to do?" In one edition that I read, it said, "The masses, how shall they act? The masses, like children following the example of parents, follow the example of leaders."* Many people learn by imitation. "So," Krishna says to Arjuna, "even though you know me (that means Arjuna already has Realization), assuming this, you still must act."

It's like the saying, "Before nirvana, chop wood, carry water. After nirvana, chop wood, carry water." You still have to act and set the example.

---

* Bhagavad Gita, Third Discourse.

For a number of years when we had satsang on Gurudev's birthday, I did not participate in the ceremony, until one day that passage from the Gita about setting the example popped into my mind. I thought that I should salute his picture, too, even though salutation of the picture didn't mean much to me because I was meeting him in meditation. But it occurred to me that I should set the example, so I started joining in all the celebrations. This verified to other people that I have never stopped giving my Guru the respect and the honor that I gave him when he was alive. Very rarely do I give a talk in which what he has said or given to me isn't somehow mentioned, because we must always recognize and give credit where credit belongs.

You can set an example and be an inspiration even to people you don't know. You can't always know where that inspiration may go. For a long time, I received a Christmas letter every year from people I had never met. They lived somewhere that to my mind was an uninhabitable region, an outpost. They used to say, "Just to *know* that the Ashram is there has helped us through many trials and tribulations."

Now, who sets the example for you to follow? First of all, it is the Divine by whatever name or form. Krishna, Siva, Buddha, Jesus, God, Divine Mother in 108 names—the Divine sets the example by keeping this world alive, by keeping us alive. And that probably takes work of some kind, perhaps not in the context that we see and understand "work," but certainly the Divine is very busy.

I met a yogi once at a waterfall, where the water of the Ganges made a big splash and beautiful foam. He was sitting there clapping his hands, saying, "Marvelous, marvelous, marvelous. Great achievement, great achievement."

And I thought, "Now, what's this all about?"

He was trying to give recognition to the life force. This water had been coming down like this for years and years and years, and there was plenty of water in the Ganges, so he did not have to depend on that waterfall. It was an example of generosity from the Divine. I don't know to what degree he put this example to work in his own life, but he was trying to give recognition to something besides that from which he could benefit.

The Gita says, "Only the ignorant are attached to what they do. The wise act for the welfare of others."*

We know of many great people, like Buddha or Jesus or Gandhi or Albert Schweitzer† who have done that.

Gopi Krishna is another example. Once he had had the experience of Higher Consciousness, his life was dedicated. From the age of seventeen to the age of thirty-seven, for twenty years, he would meditate every day for about half an hour on the image of a golden lotus on top of his head. Because he had a wife and young children, he had to go to work. He earned very little as a clerk for the government, and so had to be very careful with money. Most of the time he had to walk from home to work and back. Yet he did marvelous work. What we know is only what he wrote about Higher Consciousness, but he did a great deal of other work. He started an organization for young people in India to do away with the dowry. In India, some parents almost died of starvation because they had to give everything to their daughters as dowry to get them married. I remember him telling me that when his daughter came of age, a young man asked if he could marry her. Gopi Krishna said, "Yes, if she wants to marry you, it's fine, but there will be no dowry." The young man said he knew that and accepted it.

So the wise live and act for the welfare of others. That is selfless service. But what can you do if you *are* attached to your work and you are struggling to do it selflessly? The scriptures say that you can fulfill yourself in devotion in offering your work. By offering your work to the Divine you will achieve purification, and eventually you will attain the wisdom that is necessary to dedicate life to selfless service entirely.

So, many blessings for selfless service.

----

* Bhagavad Gita, Third Discourse, verse 25.

† Albert Schweitzer was a Christian clergyman, accomplished musician and medical doctor who decided he would live an intellectual, academic life until the age of thirty, and then give the rest of his life to helping others. On turning thirty, he gave up his academic career and went to Africa as a medical missionary where he ran a hospital in the jungle for many decades. He was awarded the Nobel Peace Prize in 1952.

Self-Knowledge

You have to know whether your service is truly selfless, whether it is a true offering. You have to know what your emotions are and where they come from. This kind of knowledge comes from self-inquiry. You must ask, "Why am I here on earth? What is the purpose of my life? Why was I born in the first place? What is this whole life drama about? What is knowledge?" Study. Understand. You must understand those things, or you will sweep them under the carpet. What you stunt, what you suppress, what you ignore, will just explode some other time in a different way. You must use proper understanding to release those pressures so they won't need to explode.

Self-inquiry leads you to self-knowledge, because it increases your understanding. The more you understand, the more questions you will ask. Some questions you will have answers for. Sometimes you will have more questions than answers. But in due time, the answers are bound to come, by intuitive perception—not by sense perception, but by intuitive perception.

Through your self-inquiry, and your offering of selfless service, all your sins will be discounted. You may look back and say, "My God, all the mistakes I have made!" But you may have made only a few mistakes that are truly sin. Most were probably made in ignorance. You would have done better if you had known more. For the mistakes which were not made in ignorance, pray for forgiveness.

The fire of knowledge lets you see what was done in ignorance. Ponder that point very carefully and deeply because it is the key to your ability to forgive others. If you see that what they have done to you was done by them in ignorance, you will be able to forgive them. You can't ask somebody who hasn't even one dollar to give you a hundred dollars. And you cannot expect somebody who knows nothing, and is living in darkness and ignorance, to act in wisdom, love, or consideration. These words are missing from their dictionary, and have to be acquired through inquiry. Nevertheless, whether they acted in ignorance or not, always remember that you will be forgiven in the proportion in which you are able to forgive. Both Eastern and Western teachings say this. Jesus says you should forgive seventy times seven because you need that much forgiveness yourself.* Most of the time, we are so self-absorbed and so wrapped up in our self-importance that we don't realize how much forgiveness we need.

Discrimination leads to knowledge and knowledge leads to liberation.

---

* Matthew 18:22.

The Senses

WE PERCEIVE the world around us through the senses, which often give us misleading impressions. Certain things attract our senses more than others, and we value these things more highly, because we get more gratification from them. That applies even to feedback: you want to have something echoing back, mirroring back, in order to decide whether you will pursue a certain course of action or change course.

Arjuna is told by Lord Krishna in the Fourth Discourse of the Bhagavad Gita to let the higher mind control the lower mind, and to let the Higher Self control the lower self. When the higher mind controls the lower mind, you can begin to investigate what it is you perceive through your senses, and how much you can trust your senses. You are often deceived by them.

It is explained in Tibetan Buddhism that you may see something which is green in color, and you think it's a tree, but as you come closer, you may see it is just something painted green. Or you may see a rope and think it's a snake, but you discover it's only a rope.

But the question of perception goes further. You need to ask, "What *is* a rope?" A rope is made up of lots of fibers twisted tightly together. What happens to the rope if you untwist it and take all the fibers apart? Is the rope gone? We need to question what we see in people the same way. We think beautiful people are also beautiful on the inside until we experience that this isn't always so. Many a woman has believed a well-built, tall man would be really good protection for her, only to find he is more fearful than she is herself.

We have many, many sense impressions. We look at a food and think it's wonderful, only to find out it tastes terrible. How many times have you tried, for instance, eating a piece of cake that's so beautifully decorated but tastes of nothing. It's wet and sweet, and that's about it.

You use your sense perceptions to make judgments and to discriminate. But how much can you trust your senses? Are your perceptions just illusions and imagination?

Some people say one or all of the five senses should be sacrificed. This is a mistake. The senses need to be purified, not sacrificed. At

Sivananda Ashram we would pass our hands over the fire, then touching each sense organ, we would say:

"May I see only what is pure,
—smell only what is pure,
—taste only what is pure,
—hear only what is pure,
—touch only what is pure,
—think only what is pure."

At Yasodhara Ashram, we do a similar thing, passing our hands over the flame of the candle and saying "May all my sense perceptions be purified by Divine Light" as we touch our eyes, ears, nose, and mouth and then bring our hands together.

In the Third Discourse of the Bhagavad Gita, Krishna tells Arjuna to kill desire because all desires arise from the senses. However, the real villain is the mind which interprets things, colored by the emotions and by attachment. The eye can see, but it is the emotions which color what is seen, and mind interprets from there. To have real clarity it seems we have to strip ourselves of all color, of all attachments. If we can do this, then there is also no pain.

If you can say "May all my sense perceptions be purified by Divine Light" with the power of all your emotions so that you really mean it, you will not be deceived by your senses. Pain is caused when your senses are colored by the emotions that mislead you. Disappointment comes, and then pain, because of the attachment to sense perception.

It seems to be a very cruel way of living at first, but if you can pursue it, even for little bits of time, you will gain another breath of freedom each time. And one day you will say, "My goodness, *why* did it take me so long? I could have let go of all this pain." It takes this long because you have to let go of the opposite, too. Today somebody says, "You're wonderful, oh, you're wonderful," and you are happy. Tomorrow somebody says, "You know what they *really* think of you?" and you are miserable. You have to let go of both pain and joy.

The Divine Light clears your sense perceptions and that frees you from deceiving yourself. That same Light will, if you give enough time to thinking about it and reflecting on it, also dispel all the clouds of doubt. Doubt is a big issue in our lives. We say, "Well, how do I know I'm doing the right thing? How do I *know?*" Look at every day in your reflection time from that particular angle, and you will find out.

The senses should be refined to the point that they serve the Most High in the best way, and become the tools through which the Most High can reach us. If the senses are truly refined, you will be able to really see, to really hear, to really feel the divine presence. You will have a taste for divine life. You can even smell divine presence.

The five senses are the windows of life itself; they guide you through life, and they have got you where you are now, but they cannot take you any further. So if your mind is in the right place, what you do next is sacrifice the *benefits* that you have had from your five senses. If you sacrifice your dependency on them—which is like a dependency on anything else, whether it is wealth, or asanas, or another person—that sacrifice will bring you closer to your essence.

You have to figure out how to get yourself there. You can go by a very direct route, or by a winding way. You can do lots of sightseeing on the way—but sightseeing may be so attractive to the senses that you may forget where you wanted to go. Don't forget.

Listing to the Divine

WHEN I WAS IN INDIA, Gurudev Sivananda told me that he would always be with me. He would be in front of me, he would stand behind me, he would be beside me. A few months after I had returned, a publication arrived from Sivananda Ashram. I leafed through it very quickly to see what was new. Suddenly, I saw myself in two pictures. This was rather peculiar, because I had often been in Gurudev's kutir when he was choosing pictures for the next issue and he would say, "No, no. One of these pictures has to go. Nobody appears twice in one publication."

What could be the reason for these two pictures of me? I went through the publication, page by page, from the beginning. And suddenly I caught it. I saw four pictures of Sivananda with me. In the first one, he was standing on my right side, in the second on my left, in the third behind me, and in the fourth picture we were sitting on the floor cross-legged with him in front of me. Without even sending me a letter, he confirmed what he had said to me: that he would be all around me if I needed him.

Before I left India, I made an agreement with Gurudev—really it was more of a promise that I extracted from him, because I was terribly worried about being able to do what he had asked of me. I can't remember having any confidence in myself at that time at all.

I said, "When I chant the Krishna Invocation for ten minutes, will you come?"*

He thought for awhile, and he said, "All right. But don't overdo it."

There is a different kind of communication between people when they put their goodwill into understanding each other. When there is surrender to the divine work, when there is surrender of one's own will, of one's own concepts and desires about how things should be done— when one can anticipate the activity of one's own mind and put it all

---

* For the Krishna Invocation Mantra, see Swami Sivananda Radha, *Mantras: Words of Power* (Spokane, USA: Timeless Books, 1994), p. 68.

aside—then receptivity is at its best, and communication is possible without words, even over great distances.

After I had been in India one or two months, Gurudev would ask the swamis to bring a big cushion. He would have it put on his left for me to sit on, and then he would say, "Cover your face." I would pull my veil over my face and then a stream of communication would come that is very hard to put into words. But I noticed it was only possible if I put aside all my anticipation of what he was going to say or what it might mean.

You just have to be receptive.

Years later I read an explanation of the difference between prayer and meditation: prayer is your petition, it is you asking for help. Meditation is just listening. Nothing but listening for what may come back.

Listening is very difficult for most of us. But there are circumstances in which listening is more appropriate than action. When you have a proper understanding of that, you will discover the results of just listening. But if you think, "Should I do this? Should I do that? This may not be so good. Maybe I should do that. Why can't I do this?" you are just getting into a war with your personality aspects. Then there is no way you can receive an answer. Also, if you have already decided what answer you want to hear, that is all you will hear because you are not listening, and that is no true answer.

When you can't listen because your emotions are running high and stilling the mind is almost impossible, pranayama is the only solution. Either slow down the breath, or do the 4-16-8 breath.*

You can also do the pinpoint of Light visualization,† but when your emotions are running high, the pinpoint of Light visualization requires too much concentration, so several other things have to be done first. I often suggest chanting, expressing the emotions in the sound of your own voice and breath. When your breath has calmed down, do the 4-16-8 breath. After this, when you are a lot quieter and calmer, you can

---

* For instructions in this pranayama, see Swami Sivananda Radha, *Kundalini Yoga for the West* (Spokane, USA: Timeless Books, 1978), pp. 216–217.

† Swami Sivananda Radha, *Guided Meditation* (Spokane, USA: Timeless Books), audio cassette.

slow down the breath more. Then do the Divine Light Invocation to give yourself the proper identification, even if you just go through it in your mind while you are sitting. When you have done all this, you can do the pinpoint of Light visualization.

This may take a couple of hours, if you are really very upset. And, of course, your mind will become active again, start warring again, so you will have to repeat the process until you are in full control of the mind.

The identification with the Light is the most important part. The visualization of yourself filled with Light is the most effective, powerful, and potent exercise because your problem is that you suffer constantly from wrong identification. You are constantly telling yourself, "I'm not good enough. I need this person's approval, and that person's." Look only for the approval of the Divine.

When I wasn't really sure about something, I asked that the Gurus I had met be the example or the channel for an answer. You can do that, too, but eventually you have to learn to still your mind and your emotions, so that you can hear that still, small voice within yourself. That will give you the right answer.

All these practices are necessary for dealing with the emotions in an appropriate manner. At the same time, invoke the divine presence and keep yourself in a receptive mood. Ask, "What is it that I should do?" You must learn not to overemphasize little problems for the sake of self-importance. You must emphasize only what counts.

And do not expect that you need only to whisper, and the Divine will come. You must remember that you cannot command the Divine. You can't say, "I want the answer tomorrow, because I will feel miserable as long as I don't have an answer."

We can ask the questions, but we cannot demand an answer, certainly not within a time that we determine. It is important to remember that. Put your question out. Repeat it as many times as you want. Then sit in silence, keeping your palms turned up, and have the thought in your mind that you want to receive. Even if it's only a feeling of peace, something will come if you are truly receptive.

But nothing will come if you want to have only the answer that you have already decided on. A woman came to me who wanted to divorce her husband. She had already made up her mind, but she asked me if she should. There was no point in my saying anything. Still, I tried.

I said, "Well, why don't you have a dialogue with each other. Maybe things can be worked out?"

She had no intention of working things out. She just wanted to have assurance from me that she had made the right decision.

This is precisely how most people approach the Divine, but it doesn't work. The answer will only come if you are ready and *willing* to receive what is given. Nothing will come if you only want a confirmation of what you have already decided.

You cannot always easily assess the repercussions of your own decision, but if the decision comes from the Divine, harmony will be re-established in your life.

Live in harmony.

Mind and Sense Perception

I DIDN'T FEEL that six months in India with my Guru was enough time, but that was all I had. Little did I know then that actually the path is an ongoing process—that it has no end. As long as you are in a human body, as long as you breathe, you move on. Things only become more subtle, more refined.

When I was in Italy, Padre Pio made the statement that he was the greatest sinner in the whole monastery. I was really shocked. I said, "Well, if *he* says that, with all the saintly evidence about him, what chance is there for other people?"

It was only as the years went by that I could see how the mind functions, and how many subtle thoughts pass through the mind un-noticed. And then I began to understand what he meant. I began to wonder if my thoughts left a trace anywhere. If they did, what effect would they have? What would happen? Could I control that effect?

For a number of hours a day, I did a practice of watching the mind. I examined the contents of the mind, and tried to find out how I could deal with them. I had times when I was quite discouraged that I could not see the end of my mind. I could not collect and be aware of all the thoughts that were passing through it. I could remember only some, the ones that somehow affected feelings or emotions, or the ones put to-gether by thought associations. But with many other thoughts, I had no clue where they went or what happened as a result of them.

I also observed my meditation, and for some time I even thought that I really could meditate well, and was very happy about this. But by chanting five hours of Mantra every day, I had learned (unknown to myself) how to trigger some sort of trance. And trance is *not* meditation. In true meditation you are very alert. The idea of trance exists in many Eastern cultures. However, I doubt that the English word *trance* means the same thing.

So, there is a lot to learn about the functioning of one's own mind.

For example, Gurudev used to say, "Bear insult, bear injury." There is plenty of that. One day somebody may send me a beautiful card of the inside of a cathedral, and write, "To the teacher who has helped me to build the Cathedral of Consciousness." I could get very happy and excited about this, but what do I do if the next day somebody comes to me and says, "You have just wasted my time. You have used me here in the Ashram as a work force. I haven't learned anything"?

This sort of thing happens to us all the time. If you let yourself be elated by the one and hurt by the other, you are constantly on a teeter-totter, going from one extreme to the other. The closer you are to one end of the teeter-totter, the more up and down, down and up, you go. Where is there a more quiet point? As you move closer to the center, you do not go up and down quite so much. If you can move very close to the center, the movement is very slight, and maybe you can handle that much. When you finally come to the center, you may stand on your teeter-totter with one foot on each side of the center, and then you can control the up and down movement.

Why is that important? Because otherwise you go from great ecstasies of happiness (which is only an emotional and ego happiness) down to great pain where you think you are going to die. Of course, you won't. That pain comes from the ego which is fighting because it doesn't want to die. But the ego has to die. So, learn to bear insult, to bear injury.

One time Sivananda was highly critical of me in front of all the Western visitors. He said, "I have heard Germans are very industrious and dependable, but I have been waiting for a whole week for the work I gave you. And I haven't even had any information from you on how it's going!"

I raced through my mind to find out what this could be, because

Gurudev's work was number one for me. I never kept him waiting for anything. I would start immediately on his work and put everything else aside, even my practices. This was a particularly difficult situation, because these Western visitors were very critical of me for letting a man who was not even white, as they said, treat me in such a way. To be humiliated in front of them was very hard to take at first.

However, I held back my emotions, and I waited for a whole week, thinking all the time, "What is it that he is trying to teach me? Can I find out by myself?"

But I couldn't find it. So I said to him, "Gurudev, you taught me a lesson I have not understood. Is it all right if I ask you, or is it still ego?"

I was just learning in those days that ego is a very powerful force. For most of our lives, we survive by the interference and control and dominance of the ego. But on the spiritual path, ego doesn't help at all. It is destructive, because it keeps you away from the spiritual.

He said to me, "What are you talking about?"

I recalled the whole situation to him. And then he said, "In this country, one scolds one's own daughter to teach one's daughter-in-law a lesson."

I thought, "I am his disciple, his devotee, but I am not his daughter. Where is his daughter-in-law? I don't understand." So I asked Venkatesananda, "Swamiji, what did he mean?"

He said, "He gave you a wonderful message. I watched your reaction. It was a good thing that you didn't object to that criticism. Next to you was Parvati, and the accusation was meant for *her*. But she is not as close to his heart as you. He knows you are strong enough to take that unjust criticism, and he expects Parvati to be sensitive enough to say, 'No, he really means me.'"

There is a different way of teaching in India. If people were not sensitive to that, Gurudev could be very harsh with them right in front of everybody.

But there are many opportunities where we can get the message without needing harsh treatment, if we will only listen. The refinement of our sense perceptions is extremely important. We are all very sensitive—very touchy—about things that go against our wishes and beliefs, or our will, or our expectations and illusions. Then we are upset, we are in pain, and we cry.

Surrender is the only answer to that. And surrender starts with listening to what is said—in the family, in the classroom, at work. In teaching yoga, if you don't hear what students say, you aren't teaching. You are only trying to superimpose your perception of the teachings and not allowing any room to hear the teachings. That kind of teaching is a seed that has dried out and won't root, because the power—the energy—of the seed has been taken out by that attitude.

You cannot make yourself the instrument of your own will and emotions, and then say, "Well, *God* told me to do this, or say that."

To refine your perceptions, pay attention to your dreams. But remember, *one* dream is not sufficient. You do not surrender without discrimination. If you think you've had a message, very humbly ask the Divine to give you that message two more times, just to be sure that it isn't your ego that asserted itself, unrecognized, giving you a feeling of elevation and making you think you really had a divine inspiration.

The daily diary with a daily reflection is an absolute must. Then every week check through your diary. Every month read the whole month through, then take a weekend, or whatever time it takes, to go through your diary for the last two months, and then for three months. This will show you where you have been given warnings not to listen to the false prophet of the ego.

To assert yourself is one thing. To dominate, to domineer, and to control, is something else. You need a lot of self-investigation to know the difference. When you find an area in which you see that your control is emerging over and over, *that* is the area where you must surrender. And surrender comes through listening.

Hear what the other person says. Don't immediately criticize in your mind, and oppose just because you have a different opinion. If you are only asserting your conviction and your opinion to that individual, then what? If the person walks out and won't listen to you, you feel hurt. Your dignity and your self-worth feel injured, and yet where is self-worth to be found? Only in that inner Light, in that true divine being.

You cannot find self-worth in your personality aspects. They are just a bunch of traitors, screaming and throwing tantrums, and competing with each other. You can be a good wife and a bad doctor. You can be a marvelous teacher and a bad husband. You can think you are a saint when really you are only a pretender. Know the truth about yourself, and in the process of finding the truth about yourself, you will get to know yourself. That is not easy.

Saint Paul said, "Daily I die."* He wasn't talking about his physical body. He meant the powerful, self-asserting ego that says, "That's the way *I* want it. That's the way *I* see it. Now *don't* oppose me!" That ego has to die, and it's like a Hydra—you cut off one head, two others grow. You cut those two off, and four others appear. You are surprised, but this is only because you have never bothered to notice them before.

Dilip Kumar Roy said once that after he had given up everything and come to Sri Aurobindo's ashram, he found that he didn't like *anything*. He seemed to be obnoxious and stubborn and resistant and procrastinating. This was because he had never paid any attention before. When you are in an ashram, it is like being in a greenhouse. The gardener waters the plants and cares for them. But if there are mealy bugs or red spiders, he takes very strong measures to save the plants. Some of the leaves may be damaged when he does this, but that cannot be avoided.

Become aware of *all* your personality aspects, how they struggle and fight with each other, and how each one wants to be in the front, to be the star in the act that you are playing on the stage of life. It is good to make a list of them. Then watch one of them for a week, and see what it's doing. You may become aware that it is not only your personality aspects that are jealous of each other and fight with each other and want to be on top. You may also find that your sense perceptions are in competition.

Seeing and hearing can be in conflict. You may hear somebody with a wonderful, melodious voice, but you may *see* something about the person that you do not like. Are you attracted by that wonderful voice? Or are you turned away by what your eyes see? When your two senses are in competition, you can fall right between them. Now, these

---

* 1 Corinthians 15:31.

are only two senses. You have three more. And you have the mind besides, which is the interpreter of all your experiences.

What you see may not be what is really there. You see somebody and have a wonderful impression. That person looks so saintly! How could you doubt what you are seeing!

I once met a Catholic nun who had a round, heavy build. She did not have a cultured face and beautiful hands. But the young nuns around her looked like little madonnas. This was because they hadn't started learning about themselves yet. The pain of self-awareness had not yet carved any lines into their faces. They were not as innocent as they looked—they were just ignorant.

We are very ignorant of ourselves, so we are easily influenced by a beautiful image. "Here comes the swami!" we think. "He looks wonderful—like a hero out of a Roman movie." But we do not ask about his character. We do not ask, "How does he live? How does he treat other people? What's his personal life like?" These are very important questions. He can *look* like a saint, but *is* he?

Then we see somebody so ordinary we would not even turn our heads around for a second look. I remember when I met Meher Baba,* with his huge nose and very dark, piercing eyes. He was not beautiful by our standards, yet from what was to me an ugly person I learned the greatest lesson of love. Hundreds of people were lined up to see him, making queues around the house. He embraced everyone who came. He was not impressed or put off by anybody. When people bowed down, he would pick them up and hold them and look at them with an expression of love in his eyes. I watched this for almost three hours. The whole atmosphere in that room was heartwarming. People dropped all their reservations. Then came an old man, toothless, body bent from heavy work, a tattered dhoti, and I could see to my horror bedbugs running up and down the folds of his clothes. I saw Meher Baba give that man the same warm embrace, the same love, and the same compassionate look. In the people around Meher Baba, I saw a wonderful consideration and love.

---

* See Swami Sivananda Radha, *In the Company of the Wise: Remembering my Teachers, Reflecting the Light* (Spokane, USA: Timeless Books, 1991).

Find out what beauty is. You can fall in love with a person's beautiful image. You can fall in love with a beautiful melody. Find out what it is that you are really falling in love with. There is lots of outer beauty. There are lots of beautiful people in this world, lots of very talented people. Fall in love with the beauty of the heart. That's the only beauty there is—that inner Light. Let that inner flame burn, and take care that it keeps burning. Don't let the wind of emotion blow it out and make a lot of smoke. See that the flame burns pure and clear, something that you can really hold up to the Divine and say, "Here it is."

The Immortal Essence

PERSONALITY ASPECTS COME AND GO in our lives. Some we don't have when we are younger; they come as we get older. Some leave when we are in our middle age, and some go when we are even older. The personality aspects are not the immortal part. And everybody knows the body is born and has to die. So what is it that will always "be hereafter," as the Bhagavad Gita says in the Second Discourse?

Lord Krishna makes great efforts to explain that to Arjuna. He says, "Just as in this body the Embodied passes into childhood, youth, old age, so also does it pass into another body. The firm man does not grieve."*

The Eastern teachings do not say *what* is embodied. The translator usually puts the word *soul* in brackets or makes a reference to *atman*. Because no word is used, some people have created a philosophy of no soul, no Self, but a word is needed, even if you use only the word *Self* with a capital *S*. I would probably use the word *essence* because I have adopted this word to explain for myself that which is embodied. When you read the Gita, do not hesitate to use your own words—words that tell you what you mean. But then be careful not to use these words in some other context. (*Energy* is a word which is used in too many con-

---

* Bhagavad Gita, Second Discourse, verse 13.

texts, for example. Most of the time, the word *effort* should be used instead of *energy*.) Essence or Self is difficult to understand, until suddenly one day you *know*, but then you will not be able to explain it. It is a knowing of the heart beyond the meaning of the common words we use in daily life. We do not have words for this knowing. Language has to evolve so that we can express these experiences.

No one can cause the destruction of the essence because the essence is imperishable. Energy is indestructible. Lord Krishna explains this to Arjuna in the Second Discourse by saying that the person who thinks the Self is the slayer or that the Self is slain is mistaken.* Such a person does not know that the essence is immortal. Krishna repeats this and repeats it so that it will sink in and Arjuna will understand.

Very few people want to know their essence. When I think of the many Life Seals®† I have seen where people have drawn pictures of their essence, I am amazed at the pictures they draw. What is usually expressed

---

* Bhagavad Gita, Second Discourse, verse 19.

† Life Seals® is a workshop in which students draw symbols representing various aspects of themselves. Life Seals® is a registered trademark of the Yasodhara Ashram Society.

is an emotion, a concept of life, or an attitude toward life. Really, the best representation of your essence is a tiny dot, because you cannot know what form your essence has.

If the essence is immortal, what is it that can be killed? I can kill the body, but I can't kill the energy that the body is temporarily a vessel for. When we think of accidents or war, we experience pain. Our pain is caused by our emotional investment in the body, by the fear that such things could happen to us. There is also a fear of not having lived life right. All this keeps alive in us our belief in the meaning and the value of the body. Certainly, when somebody has died, we can no longer communicate by hearing through our physical ears. Our eyes can no longer look at that physical form through which that essence, or that Self, was expressed. And that form is what we grieve for, because the attachment was not to the Self of that person. It was to the form. Think how many times you have been attracted to a physical form, to someone who looked beautiful and had charming mannerisms. And think how many times in your life you have been disappointed by such people. We do not want even to think about this, because it's so devastating to recognize how little awareness we have, and how we are overcome again and again, in spite of knowing better, by this attachment which our emotions seem to demand.

In the Second Discourse of the Gita, Krishna says to Arjuna, "This Self is said to be unmanifested, unsinkable, unchangeable. Therefore, knowing this to be such, thou shouldst not grieve."* You should not grieve because your grief is for the shape, the form, the color—for the appearance—and what you have perceived it to be may not be what it really is.

In workshops at the Ashram, we hear many people talk about their spouse in a way that gives us the impression that the spouse must be a terrible monster. And then the spouse comes for a visit, and we find this person warm and lovable.

We create these images in our own minds because what we have isn't the way we want it. We want to control everything. If we can't, we

---

* Bhagavad Gita, Second Discourse, verse 25.

make it into something else. So often what we are grieving for is the loss of this control of our immediate surroundings and other people. Because you are suddenly alone in the house or the apartment, you can no longer say "I want the tires changed" or "Where are my clean clothes?" If you think of it this way, on the daily level of living, it can be easier to understand what is really happening. Sometimes grief doesn't come from a very high motivation.

The adjustment for men who have lost their wives, or for wives who have lost their husbands, is extremely difficult. Why? Just because there is no communication through the senses does that mean we cannot have any communication? That's what you have to find out. I don't mean through poltergeists and mediums. I mean: can you contact your essence? And then can you contact, through your essence, the essence of someone else? You can't if all you knew was just a personality that you found pleasant. It won't work because you have not moved beyond appearance, you are still stuck in sense perception.

Krishna realizes it will take a long time for Arjuna to learn this, even though he has repeated it many times. He tells Arjuna not to grieve almost as a command. Arjuna finds this very disconcerting, because everybody grieves. Isn't that what one is expected to do? Isn't it unfeeling not to grieve? Or is it truly *knowing*?

When there is contact with the essence, there will be no grieving. Here I can, of course, speak only from my own experience. Gurudev Sivananda died officially in July 1963. In May, however, three months earlier, I was quite disturbed at night for almost a week. A friend asked me, "What's the matter with you? You have been in such a bad mood this whole week."

I said, "I'm not in a bad mood, but I'm having some strange experiences that I can't quite explain. I keep hearing 'Sivananda, Sivananda, Sivananda.'"

Then one day I knew that something wasn't quite right, but having been very close to my Guru, I couldn't bear to speculate that perhaps his life had come to an end. But that day, a young woman phoned me and said, "I have been to your satsang, Swami Radha. I don't think you know me. I have never talked to you personally, but I had a dream last night which I don't think is my dream. I think it's a message for you. I dreamt about Swami Sivananda, and he gave me a chocolate brown coat with a golden lining and said, 'Give this to Radha, and tell her I no longer need it.'"

The chocolate brown coat with the golden lining was something I had brought as a present for Gurudev to keep him warm in the winter.

Although the body was still alive until July, I think that the essence had left the body in May. When I was told of his death later, the person who told me tried very hard to bring this sad message to me carefully.

But I said, "Oh, he has died. Well, that's all right, because it's only his body." You see, in all the time after I left India, I had never lost contact with him. And that contact did not take place in my imagination. My imagination helped me to remember how he looked when he was still alive, but there was also that other kind of contact with the essence that we can't really give a name.

When I was with him, I had learned to become very receptive to the flow of one mind to another. The mind has to be receptive, of course, but you don't have to have a physical body for this kind of communication. Sometimes, the physical can even get in the way because it doesn't have a shape or an appearance to your liking.

Theresa Newman, that very saintly German woman who had all the stigmata, was round and overweight. There was no refinement in her face. We think that beauty and perfection on the outside mean that somebody has beauty and perfection on the spiritual path. It is not necessarily so. Appearance is very, very deceptive.

When you do your reflections in the evening, you should think about all these things. You have to allow your mind to get used to doing this kind of reflection. It's a kind of a mental acrobatics by which you can begin to recognize your attachments. Then if one day somebody you are very attached to, someone you think you love, departs from this world, you can understand that through your sense perceptions you were attached to the form, but the essence of that person can never die.

Our perceptions are limited and so we cannot see when this person is going to be reborn, or whether he or she is going to pass into the Light. If you put into the Light somebody who has already passed away, you will get much comfort from doing this. And then one day you will have an inner knowing. It may take two months, six months, two years—the time also depends, of course, on the karmic situation of the person who has passed on—but one day suddenly you will know, "It's okay." Something in you knows that person has made the connection to the Light. The Light is the most subtle image of the essence.

So, what is it that cannot be killed? Because of what I had experienced in Nazi Germany, I asked Gurudev one day, "What happens when the mind of a person is destroyed?"

He said, "Mind? Hmm. Mind is that which can never be destroyed."

The *essence* of mind cannot be destroyed. What is destroyed in the mind is the whole bundle of concepts, rules, and regulations that the mind has created to express itself. We often talk about wanting to express ourselves. We have to be very careful with that, because we can get so hooked into it, and have so many attachments to what we have expressed, that we want recognition and compliments, we want to be told how wonderful our expressions are. Of course, you can elevate those expressions intentionally and consciously by dedicating them to the Most High. Great works of art which were dedicated to the Most High have survived for centuries.

So there's another kind of essence—the essence of mind. That essence is important for you to think about. You have to reflect on this and put it into words that have meaning for you.

At any moment you may have an awareness of your essence. When that happens, stop whatever you are doing. Don't carry on a useless conversation just to be friendly. This moment is very important. It may be a long, long time before that moment, that split second of awareness, comes again. You cannot, and you do not, live to please other people, to make them feel comfortable. That is their responsibility. They have to find their own comfort in this world. That is not your responsibility. We have lots of social laws, and social taboos, and demands, but the demands can only go so far. Then they become a hindrance, they become what the Tibetans call your demons, preventing you from finding and getting in touch with what was there for just a fleeting moment.

When you do have a moment of awareness, you have to think immediately, Where was I when it happened? What was going on before? What came after? You *have* to make the effort to recall that moment if you can, because perhaps if you can put yourself again into the same situation where you had the experience, you may be able to recall it.

I will give you an illustration. It is not precise, but it's the closest I can find. Suppose you were in a room and you wanted to bring something away with you, but you forgot it and now you can't remember what it was. What do you do? You go back into the room, you put yourself back into the situation, and then perhaps you will remember what you were going to bring. But if you just keep on going, and say, "Oh, well, never mind. Perhaps I don't really need it, whatever it was," it's gone. It is your responsibility to get that moment back and to anchor it in your memory so strongly that you will want to have the experience again. It's like any other pleasant experience that you want to have again. It's the memory of the pleasantness that makes you want it again. If you can make the effort and recall that moment when you felt you were in contact with the Divine, you will want that contact again. But if you allow yourself to be sidetracked right away, you will remain in your body and your senses, and that small contact with your essence or inner Light will be lost. It may not come back for years.

Many people have told me of such an experience.

I say, "What happened afterwards?"

They say, "Oh, I had to answer the phone," or, "I had to do the laundry."

Was that important? Those things you have to do all the time, every day. They are not important. They can be done any time.

If you think this is being selfish, then by all means be selfish. In this situation, you have a right to be selfish. Getting in touch with your inner Light, and keeping in touch with it, and knowing something about it—that's the right kind of selfishness.

The Divine Light Invocation

THERE'S A GREAT DIFFERENCE BETWEEN READING about spiritual experiences in books and experiencing them yourself. I didn't realize this in the first few years after my experience with Babaji and the Divine Light Invocation.* I didn't realize that the people who lived with me in those years had no way of understanding or accepting that experience. Then one day the young man who had been with me on that day came to the Ashram. He had immigrated to Canada and had a job as a college teacher in Alberta.

When evening came we went to the prayer room and he said, "I will tell you my experience with Swami Radha in India."

He told it just as he had written it down. Afterwards, when we were walking up from the prayer room, I heard one of the Ashram people saying, "My God, it's true! My God, it's *true!*"

Later some people asked me to publish the story and I did. But for you, today, reading this, it's only a story. You may feel inspired when you read it, but ten years from now just having read it won't have made any difference in your life. You all have to get your own story, your own experience.

If you do, I would like to remind you of one thing: life carries on *after* such experiences. Dealing with your past is an ongoing struggle, a continuing process. It doesn't go away just because you have had a spiritual experience. You have to remember this. Otherwise, you will still be stuck in the same place ten years later. The emotions have to mature through a process of being constantly investigated, constantly examined, so that true feelings can emerge from them. Then you must combine heart and head. It is not necessarily the first and the last chakras that have to be combined. It is the heart chakra and the head. *They* need to be together. But first the emotions must be purified.

---

* The Divine Light Invocation was given to me by Babaji, who occasionally appears to spiritual seekers in India. For full instructions and a history of the Divine Light Invocation, see Swami Sivananda Radha, *The Divine Light Invocation* (Spokane, USA: Timeless Books, 3rd ed., 1990); also *The Divine Light Invocation*, Timeless Books, audio cassette.

It is possible for the head alone to rule you. But it is not possible for the heart to rule alone. If the head is not combined with the heart, then what you think is the heart ruling you is only the emotions. So you have to get hold of your emotions.

In the end, you have to turn yourself into a being of Light and the most powerful tool for doing that is the Divine Light Invocation.

The Light Invocation is really not as simple as it often appears to people. There are many points of concentration, and in focusing on one, you must not lose the others. In other words, to receive that Light, every bit of you—every pore of your skin—has to be concentrated on what you are doing. Most of the time, we are just self-interested, but here is a place where you can use this self-interest as a tool to get you into quite a different perception of yourself. Then one day you will have that experience where the body, besides being just flesh and bone and skin, will be a mass of Light. And that experience is yours. Nobody, absolutely *nobody,* can ever take that away from you.

We often talk about spiritual nourishment. We get inspiration by reading, or coming to satsang, or doing little rituals. But what really gets you to Higher Consciousness is doing whatever you are doing really intensely, being *really* there with every fiber of your being even for just five or ten minutes. That's what gets you there. Some people meditate four, five, six hours, but that is not everybody's way. And what matters is not how long you do it, but how much you put into what you do, because *that* is what you get out.

When I had the experience of the Light Invocation, I did not achieve a state of absolute purity. That would be a very misleading statement. I did not. So, if *I* could experience this, with all the shortcomings that I brought along to India, so can you.

It's really your desire, your longing for the Most High that brings you to the experience. You will not get it from wanting another human being. Any person will let you down sooner or later, because everyone has to go her or his own way, and another person's development probably isn't parallel to yours anyway. So the day comes when people have to part their ways. But if you follow the Divine, the Divine will never part from you.

Maintain the thought that you are really never without the divine presence. Help yourself to remember to be with the Divine all the time. To help you remember, you can link that thought to your breath, because you know you breathe. You can't go for very long at all without breathing. So sit quietly and just *watch* your breath. Let the breath flow into the body, and don't make an effort to breathe. Let the breath flow. Then link it in your mind with prana. That's the Divine within you.

We use a lot of symbolism at the Ashram—many images of many aspects of the Divine. They are just another way to help us to focus. Do you realize, when you look at images of Tara or Saraswati or Siva, that you are in the presence of the Divine? These images are only symbols to remind you of that. You are not paying respect to the symbol but to the very presence, to the very *thing*, that every symbol represents. The image of a Buddha is not just an image of somebody sitting in meditation. The image of the Buddha is a symbol for the state beyond mind.

Images satisfy the very active and ever-changing mind. The mind is like an elephant that sways from side to side as it walks. But even though it sways, you can keep it going in the right direction. The mind sways, too, but you can focus it and get it going in the right direction. Hold on to this. You will always have moments when you forget, but you will very rarely be without that knowing of the Divine presence.

Anything can remind you. Wear your jewelry as a reminder, and change it often, so that the routine is broken. Every time your eye falls on it, think "Om Namah Sivaya" or "Hari Om Tat Sat" or "Om Krishna Guru" or "I am created by Divine Light."

Use all these constant reminders to help you penetrate beyond the intellectual, into the depths of your heart. And then connect the heart and the head. Those things that you understand in the head, root them in the heart. The heart is your treasure. The heart is your temple. Temples and churches are only a reminder of the sacred temple that is in your heart.

Don't wait. Get started and keep going. Get your own experiences. Never mind if sometimes you really have to grit your teeth to keep going, if sometimes your practice is just sheer willpower. That you can't help. But if you stay with it and see yourself through, the Divine will let the sun shine in.

So stay in the Light.

Self-Worth

THE EFFECT OF SELF-WORTH on your spiritual development can become very subtle and easy to miss. It is very important to pay attention to it in your daily reflection, especially if you are wondering why you aren't developing faster, or why you're still so far behind.

It is important to reflect about daily events and see how you would do something differently from how you did it last week. By putting daily events in your diary and reflecting on them, you ensure that you will continue to work. That continuation will ensure your growth. The daily entry in your diary is actually the story of your spiritual development. It reflects the effort that you put in and, accordingly, what you will get in return. If your effort is very lukewarm then nothing much will happen. If you notice in your reflection that you have repeated some mistake, you may think, "Oh, I know all about this," and because you know, you may think you don't need to pay more attention to it. But, you see, when we know things and then act contrary to what we know, that is sin. Sin is not the mistakes we make. Sin is *knowing* what we have to do and not doing it.

When there is low self-worth, the mind and the emotions become greedy. That greediness often has its root in inferiority complexes. The first step in dealing with lack of self-worth and inferiority complexes is to become aware of them. Then you have to work at them, and in the first couple of years of that working there has to be an improvement. Otherwise, your feeling of unworthiness and your inferiority complex just become an excuse for the greediness of the emotions and you say things like "My lack of self-worth makes me do this," or "I did this because of my inferiority complex. I can't help it."

When you acknowledge a problem, deal with it straight and don't use it later on to make clever excuses about why you never make any progress. The mind can become very clever in the practice of spiritual things, so clever that you can still be using these old tales years later as an excuse for not doing what you know very well you have to do. I sometimes meet people I knew ten or fifteen years ago, and it's very sad to see how they are still using these clever maneuvers of the mind. They are still saying, "Well, yeah, it's just because I don't have a sense of self-worth."

I say to them, "But you knew that ten years ago, so why haven't you done anything about it?"

Are you doing something to turn that feeling of worthlessness into something worthwhile? That is *your* responsibility. Nobody can do that for you. We all have these problems. When I say I teach things from my own experience, that is because I have gone through these problems, too. When I learned the Divine Light Invocation from Babaji, I was very surprised. Why me? I didn't think I was good enough to be shown something like that. For a number of years I struggled with acceptance: Why should *I* have been given such a precious practice? Finally, I had to say, "But I'm a sanyasi, so I must be worth something. I will not use that old excuse of unworthiness for not doing my duty clearly."

It was the same when there was a rumor that I was to be initiated at Christmas in 1955 at the Sivananda Ashram. I said, "Oh, my God. I can't take this responsibility. Sivananda really doesn't know what kind of mind I have, and how it can go in circles, and how it can misconstruct and reconstruct and do all sorts of acrobatics just to escape being caught." I went very worried to Swami Venkatesananda, and I said, "I'm not ready. I'm *not* ready! Swamiji, you have to help me. There's no way I can do this! I don't even understand the full implications of it."

Venkatesananda looked at me and he said, "You know, if I were you, *I* wouldn't worry, because after all it's *his* responsibility. If Gurudev thinks you're ready, then submit to his judgment. But then if he *does* initiate you, do the best you can." Anybody can do that. But be sure to ask yourself every evening, "Is what I did today the best I could have done?" Of course, I was not the person to be initiated at Christmas, after all.

I would say to Gurudev, "The other disciples can do so much better. They know all the scriptures. They know all the details. They know this, they know that." Sivananda would look at me and smile.

Suddenly, one day, he said to me, "Haven't you tried enough now? Don't you see what's going on?"

Being unworthy can be also an escape, because suddenly it dawns on you there is a great responsibility in being worthy. If you are really honest, then you have to admit that you want to shove off that responsibility more than you want to be accepted.

As a woman, it is even harder. We have never been accepted even by other women. Women have always turned to men and admired them and adored them. I have seen women by the dozens writing checks out to swamis in spite of what they knew about the swamis' personal lives. It seems to be almost bred into them. So I had a double problem with self-worth: one was the Christian upbringing, and one was that I was a woman. At one point, however, I just had to stop this merry-go-round: "I am not good enough, I am not worthy, I am not good enough, I am not worthy, I am not good enough." I had to acknowledge that I was good enough because the Divine wouldn't have given me the job otherwise.

Sometimes people who have low self-worth will go looking for recognition by emphasizing how difficult their work is, how many problems they have, how much stands in their way. If you are going for the

Olympics, you try each time to surpass your own record, but if you don't make it you can't say, "Well, this time the hurdle was higher," or "I have shrunk, so I couldn't do it." You won't qualify for the Olympics that way. You can take on all the work in the Ashram, but if your attitude of selfless service is not correct, your work is not truly selfless service and you will look for this kind of recognition.

When you look for recognition outside, you don't help your sense of self-worth. Your self-worth comes from knowing, "I did it. It was very difficult, but because I did it, I now know that I can take the next hurdle." If you look for recognition from other people because of your inferiority complex, you may struggle for acceptance with everybody you meet. But even if the whole world accepts you and yet you still cannot stand up, figuratively speaking, before the throne of the Divine, what have you got?

Emperors and presidents of powerful countries have the fear as well as the admiration of the world, but what does it give them in return? Look at what they have. They are not even safe in their own homes. They need a whole battery of bodyguards around.

It is by doing the work that you get the experience and the experience is your victory. The experience is your reward. But if you don't do anything about your problems, there will be no experience, no reward, no victory, nothing. You will have lost a whole life. That is what you're doing to yourself, and that's the price you pay. Be clear about that.

When you struggle for recognition and acceptance, you have to ask also, "Recognition and acceptance by whom?" By somebody who is struggling just as much as yourself? Or perhaps by somebody who is not even trying?

Many years ago, when I was giving a successful series of dance performances, I gave my housekeeper and the janitor a couple of tickets. In many ways they were very lovely people, but they were not culturally educated. The next day when they said to me, "Oh, madame was so wonderful," it was not a great compliment to me because they didn't know what is involved in dancing, what a concert dancer is, and what the important points of dance are.

The important thing is to get the opinion of somebody who knows.

Most of the time you struggle for acceptance by people who are not any further ahead in their spiritual development than you are, and often by people who are much further behind. Why do you want their acceptance? That is a very important question which you must ask yourself again and again.

Think of great musicians who died in poverty. Mozart was one. He didn't have the recognition he deserved in his lifetime. So it is with many great artists. They get recognition in the end, however, because their work becomes eternal. But there are lots of people who were famous in their lifetimes that we have never even heard of, because they reaped all their rewards while they were alive.

Jesus says in the New Testament that if you want your reward on Earth, you will get it, but that will be it. However, if you can forego your reward on Earth, you will reap it in heaven.* So if you have to make that choice, make the right choice. Who else can reward you but the Divine? What is a reward worth from someone who's just as mortal and human and has all the same frailties as yourself?

Write a paper on that for yourself: What is the price you pay for that kind of acceptance? Do you neglect your spiritual practice?

If you spend an evening with a person who gives you that kind of acceptance, you are indulging the personality aspect in you that wants acceptance. You think, "Well, that person was very nice to me so I must be somebody." You may not verbalize that thought clearly in your mind, but your emotions and a part of your mind react to it nevertheless. So verbalize that thought and know it's there.

It's the same if you are fighting for something. Unless you are fighting for the attainment of self-discipline, what are you fighting for? It may be for something that just gives you more trouble, so that you say in the end, "Better I had never put my hands into this."

There is no harm in occasionally saying, "It would be wonderful if I had this or that or the other." But you must not take the competition that we are all trained for in life into your spiritual life—"I must be the

---

* Matthew 6:1, 5.

best speaker, the best dancer, the best hatha yogi or yogini, and the best writer, the best editor, the best of anything." That competition will just stop you from truly becoming what you are meant to become.

The kitchen in particular is a place where people look for recognition. They think, "I don't get any recognition, but if I cook something really extra-special, everybody will come and say, 'Wonderful! Oh, how wonderful! You really put great food on the table'."

There was a young woman at the Ashram who indulged this way, but she failed everywhere else. Finally the food bills got so high, I had to say to her, "You have cost the Ashram several thousand dollars that we really can't afford. And besides, this fancy food is not even good for people's health. You are cooking it only for your own self-gratification." I literally told people in the Ashram not to compliment her, ever. She was a good cook, but she was not cooking on the spiritual plane as selfless service to nourish people who were seeking the Most High.

When you want recognition, look at the facts as they really are. And then wait. When the Divine gives you recognition, what a great joy, because you know it is truly a reward, it is truly something given to you. If the Divine has praise for you, you will get it in time. You don't have to worry about that.

When I returned to Canada, Gurudev never answered any of my letters, and I was very downhearted. I would send off a report every month of everything—how many people came to meetings, what the subject was, the income, the expenses, absolutely everything. I wanted to know if I was doing the right thing, but I finally stopped because I never got any replies. But looking back, I think my motivation was probably only that I wanted to be the best disciple and to have approval for that. When I didn't get any answer, I almost gave up because I thought Gurudev wasn't approving what I did, and my work almost fell apart.

Then one night I had a dream about a little boy who was living in the Ashram with his mother. He came to me in the dream with a whole handful of jewelry. He said, "These are all waiting for you. You will get them one by one." He held a ring out to me, and he said, "That's the first to come."

I looked at this ring, and I was partly surprised, partly overjoyed, but partly shocked. Someone had just given me that ring, with the same design of a Crusader's cross.*

You will get the signs when you need them, and it is important to remember that. All that effort to get recognition from the people around you should go into self-discipline. If you conquer some bad habit, you are free of it, and there is your reward.

To overcome feelings of low self-worth, you need to confront spiritual greed and inferiority very strongly, and the sooner and the more intensely you confront them, the better and the sooner you will be helping yourself. Do not let feelings of inferiority grow into a complex. The other antidote for lack of self-worth and emotional greed is to allow yourself to grow into a sense of gratitude. Don't concentrate on what you have to complain about, what's not one hundred percent according to your hopes and expectations. Look at what you already have. Concentrate on that. It doesn't mean you cannot vent your complaints occasionally. That's better than sweeping them under the carpet, but don't make a big issue of them.

Also, be careful where you vent your complaints. Talking a lot about complaints isn't very inspirational. Other people need to learn to become grateful, too, and see the many good things that they have: most have their health, they aren't starving, they're not living on the street. They often just have some psychological quirks in their life that need to be straightened out a little bit. These people don't need to hear your complaints.

And don't let your complaints kill your sense of gratitude. Acknowledge immediately after you have voiced a complaint, *immediately*, how much you also have reason to be grateful for.

Gurudev said to me about a young fellow that I took along to India on my second visit, "He's not grateful for what he has. Why should I give him more?" That left a very deep impression on me.

---

* For working with dreams, see Swami Sivananda Radha, *Realities of the Dreaming Mind* (Spokane, USA: Timeless Books, 1994).

If you are not grateful for what you already have, don't ask for more. And don't complain, because nothing in life will ever go exactly as you want it. Why? Your imagination plays tricks on you. It embellishes things, and then you think they should be the way you imagine them. But life has some cruel facts that are contrary to your imaginings. Instead, when you do the Divine Light Invocation, use the power of imagination to visualize yourself filled with Light, clearly and intensely. Then sometime you will have the experience of your body as a mass of spiritual Light as the reward of your efforts. And I emphasize this—*your* efforts.

Your effort is very important. If you don't make a good effort, you won't get anything and then you will think the Divine is starving you, never giving you anything. But you have to look at how lukewarm and halfhearted your effort is. If somebody worked for you in a lukewarm way, you would say, "Well, that person is not doing well at all. Some of the work is almost thrown at me like a bone to a dog. Why should I be concerned about that individual?" So, be aware of your effort. Make it strong.

It is your daily practice that keeps your awareness alive and will eventually expand it. But when you are not doing your practice, what can grow? If you don't water a plant, it will die. Your spiritual inner existence, your inner being, has to be carefully nourished and watered, too. Let it grow.

You may dream sometime that you have a baby. Men dream about this, too, even though they don't give birth. This means that your spiritual baby has been born or is in the process of birth. You have to nourish it. You have to protect that inner spiritual being, particularly if it's still very weak, very immature, and has no voice of its own yet. It can't slap your face and say, "Come on, wake up. What are you doing?" If you are not nourishing your spiritual being, you are really starving yourself. And one day you will wonder what you have been doing all these years of your life. This is true whether you live in a city or in an ashram. Of course, it's worse if you have lived in an ashram and have not nourished your spiritual being.

There are a number of people who left the Ashram, saying, "Well, there was really nothing to develop."

I asked them, "What did you think would happen?"

And they said, "Well, I thought you could make me a saint."

I can't make anybody a saint. It's very childish and naive to think that, it's even stupid. And to say that after having lived at the Ashram for many years shows that they never did any serious thinking, or any serious listening.

So make your own efforts and nourish your spiritual baby.

If you feel unworthy of divine grace, you can let a natural feeling of gratitude grow. Hold that feeling of unworthiness right in front of you, not to judge yourself as worthy or not worthy, but to say, "In spite of everything, I am committed to gratitude." If you hold on to this, gratitude also demands a great deal of humility.

Intuition and the Unconscious

ON ACCOUNT OF THE BODY you forget your divine being, but Krishna will remind you. And when he does, you ought to anchor that in your own mind. You can't always have someone following you around to remind you.

The next time you go to a drugstore, go to the shampoo section. Decide beforehand which shampoo you want to look for. Then see if you can see just that bottle; see if you can ignore everything else around it. I am sure you have all had this experience. You look for something and you can see everything but that one thing. The thing you are looking for is right in front of you but you can't see it.

In the same way, you can look at what's going on in your mind, what is hidden from you (actually it's only partially hidden from you). You may find there is something in the foreground that you have not been seeing. Then you can look at it and find out why it came forward. It may be because there is something pressing that is overpowering everything else in your mind.

For instance, a man came to the Ashram once to do The Straight Walk®* workshop. I gave him a space in the kitchen to do the walking part. While he was walking and trying to observe what was going on in his mind, he stopped suddenly and said he would have to leave because he had to check something out—he didn't say what. In this moment of quietness, suddenly a thought arrived within him that everything was not in order at home. He didn't come back until early the next day. Sure enough, something was wrong. He had told his wife he would be gone for three days. She had used the opportunity to meet with his manager in a very intimate situation, not in the house but in the office, and that's where he went. The unconscious had told him something about his marriage that needed to be cleared up—his own transgressions, as well as his wife's.

Some years ago, there was an old wooden bridge on the road to Castlegar and the airport. It was old but it was said to be safe. However, on a particular day, one man decided to park his car and walk over the bridge. He had just reached the other side when the next car went down with a portion of the bridge. The man said he didn't know what had made him park his car and walk across the bridge.

The unconscious knows a lot more about the events around you and it will tell you, if you pay more attention to your unconscious than you do to your desires. The unconscious can say a lot then, but you have to push your desires out of the way. Mostly, when a situation comes up, what you understand is what you can see. You cannot get the other kind of knowledge out of the unconscious. Maybe it's right there, but you can't see it, so you can't understand anything beyond what you are seeing.

---

* The Straight Walk® workshop is an adaptation of a Tibetan technique for investigating the contents of the mind. The Straight Walk® is a registered trademark of the Yasodhara Ashram Society.

Intuition is not quite the same as the unconscious. There are some very fine distinctions between them. The distinctions relate to evolution which is a much bigger subject. We usually think that when a group of people evolves, all the members evolve together in a certain orderly fashion. That's really not true. Evolution happens by leaps and bounds which may occur after a long time of no forward movement.* In the same way—suddenly—you know something. There has been no gradual approach to the knowing. Suddenly you understand. You have known whatever it was all the time, but suddenly you understand it in depth. The knowledge did not come suddenly—it's just suddenly in your awareness.†

The unconscious is a confusing term because we have different definitions for it. The technical definition, for example, means "not conscious." By that definition, it's a vast, impersonal thing. However, I often use the word unconscious to mean my soul. So it's a "catchall" term in many ways.

There is also the subconscious, and Western psychology talks about the superconscious, as well as the conscious and the unconscious. Other languages have more divisions of meaning for this word. When we try to answer the question, "Is intuition unconscious?" we find that present-day language is pretty limited. You can say intuition is unconscious, but the moment you know, it's no longer unconscious.

Intuition is often defined as a process that is unconscious and becomes conscious to you for only one moment. But it is different from a conscious, logical thinking process, and so in that sense, it is somewhat unconscious.

It's almost as though there are different levels of intuition, depending on the importance of the situation. For instance, you can recollect experiences where you have said, "Oh, I should phone so-and-so," and you go to the telephone, and the connection is already made. The person you were going to call has called you.

---

* For a discussion of the evolution of consciousness, see Swami Sivananda Radha, *From the Mating Dance to the Cosmic Dance* (Spokane, USA: Timeless Books, 1992), chapter 1.

† I think evolution happens that way also with language.

If we could understand a little more about what has transpired here, we would have a greater sense of security in trusting the unconscious above our logical thinking. Sometimes when I am trying to see what I should do about a particular situation, I feel I zigzag back and forth. Sometimes I think I am trusting the unconscious, and then I'm not. Then I rely more on thinking things out, then I drop that. But in the end, I find it easier if I go through the process of figuring it all out, and then let it go. I don't possess it, in other words, and it doesn't own me. I just let it float away and see what comes.

It seems almost that I do the figuring out by sheer memory because this kind of figuring happens so many times in life. Often when I become aware of that, I say, "What a waste of time. Why not just stop thinking and do something else, and let it happen?" I'm sure it is just a different degree and more subtle form of self-importance that makes me think, "I can do it that way", or "I should be doing it this way," or, "If I do it this way, that's the best way." Self-importance takes many, very subtle ways, even if you have managed to pull away from the very blunt kind of self-importance.

But you still have to do this thing I call "doing your homework." You have to work things out as far as you can. When you feel you've gone as far as you can go, and you know you can't get the answers that way, let it go. Then the answers will come. But the homework must be done first.

It is possible to talk about doing the homework. There is a vocabulary for that. But there are things about the unconscious that cannot be voiced because there is no vocabulary. There are a lot of things I have experienced that I can't put into words.

There's a beautiful story about Lord Buddha that you all know but perhaps you have never given it any thought from this point of view. He had received enlightenment, and it was a wonderful state to be in. But he was not going to tell anybody because he had labored so hard to obtain it, and most people wouldn't understand anyhow. And then a voice said—and what voice could that be except the voice from his inner being—"There are some. There are some."

Western psychology would probably say that the duality in him came to the foreground because when you get something, the need to share what you have, to pass that on some way or other, seems to be almost human nature. But I think that voice is where all our spiritual texts come from. It is what is often called "God's word." And it is meant to be shared, otherwise it would be a kind of selfishness that is so explicit it becomes actually indescribable.

If you want to change your concept about yourself to something more positive, it would really pay you to write down all the times you have received answers or messages. Put them into your diary. Watch for particular dreams, and also daily events. If you retrace your steps through the day and realize that you have forgotten something important, what does that tell you? In interactions among human beings, you may pick up some ordinary thing that tells you some disaster is coming. I find in the drawings people do in Life Seals® or Music and Consciousness* that the unconscious always speaks. When people have gone through several Life Seals®, and they think, "Ah, now I know what that symbol means," the unconscious puts it somewhere else.

There is also a prejudgment of dreams that is often a grave mistake. Sometimes I would write a dream down and say, "Oh, my gosh! No, I don't even want to look at that, it's so horrible." But then when it comes into my hands a couple of weeks later, I think, "No, it's really great that it happened. I was so busy during that time something had to crash against me to get through to me." Dreams like that say to me, "I can't reach you unless I really crash into you."

I remember, for instance, often dreaming I was driving my little car, and there was always a huge truck behind me. I would think, "*What*? What in me is chasing me?" Then one day I recognized the driver, and then I knew the dream was trying to break through to me about this person who was troubling me.

All dreams should be looked at on all levels, including the spiritual level, because I think dreams often have more than one level. You should classify your dreams, and this will help show you what they mean. Sit

---

* Life Seals® and Music and Consciousness are workshops given at Yasodhara Ashram and at its affiliated centers, the Radha Houses.

quietly over them and sort them out—the people, the animals, the events, the same symbols coming over and over.* You may see that you are getting some slight indication about something. If you pay a lot of attention to it, and give it recognition (you can say, "Thank you for warning me"), you may develop a very useful tool. First, you have to put it together, and then you have to give it recognition. Then the meaning can become very, very clear.

Mind and Ego

IF YOU HAVE GREAT ADMIRATION FOR A BRILLIANT MIND, for great intelligence, the powers of your mind will raise their ugly heads until the belief in a transcendent ego has been destroyed. The ego says, "Ah! I, or he, or she, but mainly *I*, have a brilliant mind. Everybody tells me how intelligent I am, what a wonderful mind I have." And that's where you get stuck, because intelligence is one of the powers of the mind. What you want are the divine insights and those come only through surrender.

Let your intelligence take action. Your God-given intelligence is one of the biggest jewels that you have, so take great care of it. Don't bury it under the carpet. Intelligence has helped you to survive in life up to this point. You have been able to perform your various duties because of it, but do not overvalue it. Do not make yourself entirely dependent on it. That dependency will cost you a high price.

I have met too many people who have just a tremendous supply of words. There were many people like this at Sivananda Ashram. One day, when I was on the veranda of Gurudev's kutir, he took me to the door and pointed to a group of people standing by the river, and he said, "See those people down there? Ten years ago they were standing right there, debating about meanings of words. They are still there, hairsplitting ideas.

---

* For instructions on how to work with your dreams, see Radha, *Realities of the Dreaming Mind.*

They haven't moved an inch in sincerity or in the depth of their spirituality. They haven't any more compassion than they had ten years ago. All they do is engage in debates."

Later, back in North America, I was invited to be on stage with a group of professors, but when they found out I didn't have a degree, they asked me to sit on a chair off to the side. I didn't mind. I had found out it was the same chair they had asked Papa Ramdas to take because they thought he didn't have a degree. He had an engineering degree, but he didn't tell them.

I haven't met anybody who has made any real progress exclusively by great endeavor of the intellect, such as knowing all the scriptural texts. Intellectual fireworks will not get you there. My Tibetan Guru said, "A keen intellect is necessary, but arrogance and pride of intellect will keep anyone from Higher Consciousness."

Debates can occasionally sharpen your understanding, but they will not get you to Higher Consciousness. The temptation to debate is often great when people get together to talk about spiritual subjects, but it comes down to this: What can you put into *action* in your life that will indeed make you more compassionate? You can't be compassionate without understanding. Unless you have understanding, you are just sentimental, not truly knowing where and how to help. And without understanding, you will not get transcending insights which are truly yours and which give you more knowledge on the spiritual level. These are what can take you to that act of surrender where the ego-mind* won't come in and interfere. Debating about words cannot do this.

Many of the very abstract ideas and concepts are better left alone for a long time, unless you use them just as signposts to find your way around. But reaching the goal of ultimate freedom cannot be done through abstract ideas.

I find it is safer and easier to think of the inner Light, because even

---

* I don't usually use the term *ego-mind*. I call it "body-mind," because you can experience the body-mind. Something carries on your digestion, your blood circulation, and so on, so the body has a mental capacity. But then there is consciousness which is another part of mind. That part becomes a kind of gateway to a consciousness that makes the mind expand.

our concept of "soul" is distorted. Our concept of Higher Self gets shattered by different viewpoints and the perceptions of different schools. But there has to be *something*, because even the Tibetans, who deny the existence of soul, say there is something that takes rebirth. What is it?

You can use the word *essence*, but essence is a word like *power*. You can't really put your teeth into it, and particularly not if you are a concrete thinker. But the idea of *Light* is elusive enough not to interfere with the kind of transcendent insight that cannot be put into words.

To think in terms of higher and lower consciousness, higher and lower levels, is unavoidable for communication purposes. If you are not where you once were any longer, then you have moved. But where have you moved to? You may think you have moved forward but there really is no forward and backward. If you think of moving forward and backward, you will get yourself lost in a maze of ideas that have little value in getting you where you want to go. People often want to look for a universal concept of space but that will not get them to Higher Consciousness either. You should not think too concretely about these things. To explain this, I can use an example from Indian dancing. You can think

of moving your hand through space in a dance. If you move it the wrong way, then you need descriptions expressing precisely what movements are required. This is a very concrete situation. But you cannot think about levels of consciousness or about moving on the spiritual path in this concrete way.

Ego is another word that presents problems. In the West we have a very different concept of ego from the East. I wonder if Indian yogis have ever really grasped what we mean by ego, or selfishness, or egocentricity. We think of the ego as the force that makes a person act, that makes one acquire things. In the East, the view is that ego is strongly linked to emotions. Emotions are certainly to the largest degree the expression of the ego. If reincarnation is accepted, as it is in the East, then the accumulation of emotions from one lifetime to another also has to be accepted. Memories are triggered by these accumulated emotions.

There is also a school of thought which spells ego with a capital *E* and calls it a binding force holding all the personality aspects together. We have to loosen them up one by one. The personality aspects are like a bundle of sticks which are held together by a rope that I call "ego."

But it does not help us to go into these differences of meaning. We do not need to talk about very fine differences of perception or understanding of ideas. That understanding does not get us where we want to be. You do not find ultimate freedom by shifting the concept. Ultimate freedom is the application of your understanding, the application of your own transcending insights to your daily life. Insights and intuition will help you get there, and I think we are quite clear now that insights and intuition are not characteristic of ego.

Each one of your personality aspects has its own particular type of ego. That personality aspect—whatever it is symbolic for—that wants to fight, that wants to win, that wants to have the upper hand in your life, that wants to have the fame and be in the limelight, surely *that* cannot be of any value in taking you higher. If we mean transcending vanity and pride when we talk about transcending the ego, certainly we have to transcend that. We can't take that ego along. If we want to communicate, we have to be careful how we use words which represent concepts. However, don't be hung up on debates about what they mean.

Look instead at your obstacles. The deadening powers standing in your way can even be your own beloved and your relatives. You think they are your obligation. You think your first commitment is to them. No. The Divine comes first, and everything else after that. If you have to take care of children or of someone who is sick, or if like myself you have assumed some responsibility for a group of people, the Divine still has to come first, and then the Divine will tell you what's best to be done. The more you leave the mind out, the better it is. That is true for everybody.

If you can sit and let go of your own ideas about how a problem should be solved, you can say, "Here is the problem. I can solve it this way or this way or that way, but I don't know if any of these three ways is correct." Then let this just hang in midair. Don't cling to your anticipations. If you can do this, the insight which transcends the ordinary body-mind will light up and let you know, and you will wonder, "Now, where did that come from?" You will know quite well that you didn't find the answer or the solution yourself. And yet it came. You can practice this by assuming the responsibility for an action or a duty or solution. Use your intellect to find one or two or three or four different ways to deal with it, and then say, "There, that's what I see myself capable of. But if none of them is right, then show me what is. Or if one of them is good enough, then show me which one." Practice surrender—everywhere.

To reach the ultimate goal of freedom you have to destroy the deadening power of ego—this idea that "*I* am doing everything." *I* can't even make my fingernail grow, or my hair. There is something else involved. When that is realized, then we can see our limitations without feeling distressed and saying, "I am powerless." We are not powerless. Look at the powers we already have. Surrender is one power. Gratitude is another enormous power. Acquire these powers, cultivate them, and use all of them wisely.

The method you use is very individual. In the end, you experience everything through the mind. But the mind is like concentric circles. Which of the circles are you in at any particular moment? The path is the process. *Your* process and *your* own way, because it's the *only* way for you. However, although there is an *only* way for you as an individual, there is *not* an only way for all the members of a family or a group or a country. *Each person* has his or her only way. To find your only way is your purpose. When you have found it, the idea: "I am on the path," will drop away. But let things drop away naturally, rather than saying, "Well, I should now be at this level, or having that experience," or whatever.

If you talk about spiritual levels and then follow a worldly path, that shows that the mind is weak. You have to open up new avenues, look at things differently. You have to break away from mechanicalness, from routinely acting, routinely *reacting,* and from routine thinking. These are very deadening powers because they take the life out of your actions.

The purification of the mind is a very difficult thing to establish. I asked all the Gurus I met about this because I thought my own mind was the worst of anybody's. The answer I got was never harm anyone and always share what you have. Gurudev Sivananda would ask a person, "Do you have a house?" If the person answered yes, he would say, "Let other people use it. Have satsang in your house." It was the same with a car. He would say, "If you see a woman carrying a heavy load, give her a ride. Then you can have the car." Or food: "If you have good food, share it with others."

In dealing with the personality aspects, the mind chooses what you will hear, or feel, or touch, or do. Then it interprets the sense perceptions. This means you live in the mind, so the mind must be pure. But it takes a long time to build purity of mind, and if there is an overblown ego in the mind, it can destroy anything you build up in meditation.

Impure mind is keeping things exclusively to yourself, not being willing to share, having great attachments, holding on tightly. It is this exclusive *me, me, me* that is absolutely the wrong attitude. This is one of the very wonderful, very basic ideas that I have received over the years. Of course, that doesn't mean you have to allow someone into your house who breaks all your things. You have a responsibility toward what is yours. However, most of the time broken things can be replaced, but broken people are harder to fix, so never harm anyone.

It's my prayer that you have many spiritual, divine insights by transcending your mind. Start now.

Human Mothers

MANY PEOPLE ARE DEALING with their problems by trying to put the fault all on to their mothers. This is not realistic. From the Kundalini system we know that on a very human level there are people who are sattvic, those who are rajasic, and those who are tamasic. If we first look at our own personal qualities, we may be able to get a glimpse of the qualities of our mothers: whether they were tamasic or rajasic or sattvic as human beings, and what their qualities were as teachers and nurturers.

In some areas they may have been very rajasic, but as teachers they may have been very tamasic, because they didn't have much to give. If they had not been given much themselves then they would not have much to share with their children. But even if our mothers had very good qualities as teachers and as nurturers (which are the mother's main roles in the child's life), and if they really were sattvic—of the highest and purest quality—there are other powers that could have interfered. Some of these powers are biological. Sometimes, a woman doesn't really know what it means to be a mother, even though her intentions may be good. Her own needs may be creating strong filters that block out her sattvic quality. The sattvic quality may be there, but she has not the skills, or perhaps the awareness, to uncover it. Like many people, she may have a treasure in her own back yard, but she doesn't know it is there. Various emotions can also filter the sattvic powers which she may have.

When we have recognized those interferences, then we can ask the question: How can any woman who is a mother, or wants to be a mother, achieve that wonderful, pure, human love? What does the love of a mother really mean? If you then think of your own mother, you can ask yourself what aspects of her love you can recognize, through your own filters and distortions, as showing the purity of her love for you.

Love has to be examined in conjunction with biological urges and personal needs. We have to look at what happens to love when our emotions interfere, or our mother's emotions interfere. We have to investigate how, from all this confusion, love can eventually emerge. We know that basic good intentions are not enough, so we have to ask how those good intentions can be activated so that they can manifest.

We have to realize that everything has its seeds. If we compare human beings to flowers, then in the life of your mother, in her unfoldment, the seeds that emerged from her flowering are, on the biological level, other bodies—babies. This has little to do with love or nurturing, or with intentions. The strength of the powerful urges for the biological continuation of human life is much underestimated. The mind and emotions make up stories and fantasies to put pink ribbons on these basic biological urges.

If you ever have the chance, ask your mother, "What were you thinking when you got married? What did you think after the marriage ceremony? When you were on your honeymoon, what was going on in your mind and your feelings?"

Your mother may say, "Oh, I wanted children, but not right away." Perhaps she wanted first to get to know this human being she had attached her life to by becoming a wife. Perhaps she had great uncertainty about what her life would be with this person. We barely know ourselves, so how can we know someone else?

At the time of marriage, there is a big question mark in a woman's mind. Many women have said to me that when they went to put their signature on the marriage document, they suddenly thought, "Maybe I shouldn't do this." Some have admitted (men and women alike) that if they had followed this inclination, they would have avoided many mistakes. Others have told me that they had the same thought and later wondered where it had come from, because the marriage turned out to be wonderful. So emotions cannot be trusted completely. We can't say, "My intuition is always right." This takes more preparation, more meditation, more ability to tune in with yourself.

When the body produces other bodies through its seed, it also produces other lives—many years of lives. A woman certainly doesn't put babies into the world in the hope they will die in a few days or a few weeks, after she has enjoyed giving birth. But she still has little awareness that she has contributed to a new lifetime for a being. She does not reflect, "I know nothing of what this life will be, and with all my good intentions, I will have little influence on that life." In fact, her influence will not be more than fifty percent. That little being brings its own ways into the world.

We may not accept ideas of the East about reincarnation, but ask any mother who has had three or four children and she will tell you that every pregnancy was different. Sometimes she could barely sleep, the little creature moved around in her so much. With another pregnancy, she may have worried whether the baby was still alive because it was so quiet. Even with the same father, the same mother, the same building tools, there is a difference in the makeup, in the temperament of the child. Obviously, this new little being already has its own ways that it is bringing into this world. The other fifty percent of the child's makeup is the responsibility of the parents, of which the mother's part has the greater weight, because she spends more time with the child. She has already spent nine months with this little being before she gave birth to it.

A woman may also experience great fear at the prospect of becoming a mother. Suddenly the weight of the responsibility may settle on her. She may say, "Oh, my God, no. I don't think I can do this," because of her feelings of personal inadequacy, her lack of self-worth, or an overestimation of the immensity of a new life. All this can cripple a woman right from the beginning and stop her from being the mother that perhaps another part of her would very much like to be. Emotions are very powerful. They are often underestimated.

Whenever I have had the opportunity to talk to a young couple, I have said to the husband (and to the wife's family), "Never mind the idiosyncrasies she will display during the pregnancy. If you want a healthy, well-balanced, happy child, you have to have a healthy, happy mother. Bear with all the idiosyncrasies. They are just of a biological nature. It will pay you very well in the end."

We do not prepare young women to be mothers. This is a grave mistake. We learn to handle all these technological gadgets that come in new models every year, but we do not learn how to handle babies. There is also a continuing chain of cause and effect which plays a large part in what kind of mother a woman becomes. Your own mother is the product of your grandmother; she is the product of the kind of mothering she received. What kind of mother she was to you is influenced by that, for good or bad.

I will give you an example of something that can interfere with what kind of mother a woman becomes. What woman hasn't worried that after pregnancy she would not look young and beautiful any more? I have scarcely ever heard of any man being attracted to a woman because she has a beautiful character, a beautiful soul. He marries her, or he's attracted to her, for her outer beauty. This is a very sad state of affairs for the woman because she can never live up to his ideal of outer beauty. And she can never reach a level of awareness in herself because all she knows is to put every effort into a beautiful appearance. She knows that what she is on the inside really doesn't matter to her husband. He doesn't care. That may be the tragedy of your own mother. Do not forget that.

Also, you may not have any idea how your father treated your mother before you were conceived or in the first four or five years of your life. You might say, "My mother was terrible." She might have been, but was she always this way? Would your father have married a terrible woman? No, he would not, but he may have created an illusion about what he wanted her to *be,* and perhaps her struggle to be that illusion made her terrible.

It's hard for a woman to tell her husband honestly what she feels when he has shown her that only her appearance is important to him. If he says, "Don't cry. I don't want to see that lovely face with tears. You look ugly," she will be afraid to show any pain or even to be sick. He loves and worships only her beauty. Honesty between a husband and wife can be established only by mutual consent, by the understanding that mutual honesty is the only thing that will make a husband and wife true friends.

It would be good to reconsider what you may think are justified complaints about your mother (and sometimes, also, your wife). There may be something behind that complaint—that I would not deny—but try to see also the human being that your mother has been.

When we talk about the problems we are having with people, we simplify too much. We say, "Well, why don't they *be* different?" Can they? Can *you* be different? It is by going through this whole process and seeing the complexity of every human life that you will perhaps gain an understanding, at least on the intellectual level, of your own mother's fears, emotions, and degree of awareness.

Self-Development

THE TRADITIONAL SPIRITUAL TEACHINGS I received in India did not bother about psychological problems and difficulties. The tradition is just to put everything into spiritual practice. Circumstances and inclination made it possible for me to do a lot of practice. But I found that the practice by itself would have to be so rigorous to eradicate all the psychological problems that I felt the combination of the two was necessary. That combination is what I have introduced at the Ashram. We look at our psychological problems and imperfections, and then in combination with spiritual practice, we try to overcome our difficulties. I call this cooperating with our own spiritual evolution.

My experience is that this combination is necessary in dealing with illness, too. I became acquainted once with a psychiatrist who wanted to bring people out of the mental hospital and back into the world. He had worked for a long time with a couple of ministers and priests, but prayers alone did not seem to do it because people will even try to make God responsible for their shortcomings and bad deeds. They will say, "That's the way you created me, so you take the responsibility for the way I am." You cannot say that. You have to take your own responsibility.

For most people, both spiritual practices and psychological self-investigation are necessary. Prayer alone is not enough.

I read Milarepa's life* and the dreams he used, and the *Hundred Thousand Songs of Milarepa*† very carefully. His advice to members of his family was very down-to-earth: "Look first at your attachment. You see, you are doing this and that and the other. And that is where all your energy and your attention are going. *But* if you can leave this behind, and move up here. . . ." However, unless you know first where you *are*, you can't move. You don't even know you should move, because you have little awareness of the capacity of the mind to create illusions.

---

* W. Y. Evans-Wentz (ed.), *Tibet's Great Yogi Milarepa* (London: Oxford University Press, 2nd ed., 1951).

† Garma C.C. Chang, *The Hundred Thousand Songs of Milarepa* (Boston: Shambhala Publications Inc., 1962), vols. 1 and 2.

You cannot trust the mind. You have to question it always, and ask constantly, "How do I know?" Many things affect the mind. We are formed not only by our family and teachers or by our friends and neighbors, nature itself also has an impact. If people live where the temperature is a hundred and ten degrees day in and day out, and they become wet with sweat just from walking across the room, they will be very different from people who live in mountains in great cold and lack of comfort, where they cannot even take a bath all year. Even in our part of the world,* if there is very low pressure for just one day, there is a physical effect which can change your mood all of a sudden. Then, when it passes, you may almost feel as if a heavy weight has been lifted from you.

These factors are often overlooked or not given sufficient attention, but they contribute to how we feel. Unless we know about them, we may make ourselves feel unnecessarily guilty because we are not cheerful and energetic. Accept whatever is there. Just don't get stuck in it. Be reminded that nothing lasts. Everything changes. Sometimes things change rather fast, faster than we can adjust to. It is important to see that, too, and accept it.

The personality aspects have their reflection in the mind, so they need to be dismantled. I find it is helpful to look at my list of personality aspects and take the one that causes the most trouble and say, "I am going to choke this until it is dead." How can you do this? By trying to infuse that aspect with the spiritual, because wherever the Light goes in, darkness has to go out. Then ego and all the negative things are bound to change because you incite everything to make that change possible. That is important. Then you can tackle another personality aspect, and another, and however many there are. This is much less difficult than to say, "All of my mind has to change," because you live through the mind, you function through the mind. The identification with the mind is much more difficult to change. That has been my observation in all the years I have been helping people with these things. But you *can* conquer one personality aspect, and this gives you the courage to conquer another

---

* Yasodhara Ashram is located at Kootenay Bay in a mountain valley in southeastern British Columbia, Canada.

one, and another one, and another, and then finally you have the feeling: "I am coming to that essence that I am."

Childhood experience also affects the mind. How much does our childhood experience really scar us? We are all very busy looking at that. We say, "Well, in my childhood such-and-such happened and that is why I have these problems." This is true, and yet there is evidence that although some children in a family are scarred by the family's experiences, others who go through the same experiences are not. Why is that? There must be a different type of essence in the different individuals, in the different children.

By that I mean we are the total of our karmic situation. If there has been a lot of accumulation of good karma, then perhaps it's much harder to scar such an individual. This means that in our present life we have the opportunity to collect good karma by just doing a lot of good things and overcoming our selfishness and our need for comfort, and by going *beyond* comfort and *beyond* personal needs, and not clamoring constantly to have them filled. It's *selfless service* that gives us the best karma— it's consideration for other individuals. I have often said, "You can't love everybody, but you can be considerate to everybody." There is no question about that.

You can't always do what you feel like doing. Most of the time your feelings will put you to shame, so if you think you have to express all of them, you will feel ashamed often. It's better to acknowledge these feelings quickly, but not to indulge in them. Turn again to spiritual practice and prayer, and change your focus to the Divine. The greater the effort needed to shift the focus, the more necessary it is to make that shift.

I found recently some writing I did years ago when I began to wonder about my childhood and the dramatic circumstances of it. I remember quite a bit of what affected me. Of course, the tendency is for all of us to say, "Oh, great. Here's the explanation for why I'm not any better yet."

Then I had a dream. In the dream somebody said, "I think you should go over there and look at this little girl. Her mother didn't want her." This was followed by a number of the details of my own childhood experience. In the dream, the aspect that is Radha went over to look at the little girl, the aspect that is Sylvia, and said, "But she has no scars." It was the spiritual practice that had removed the scars. If you feel that you have been hurt very much and that you carry deep scars, nothing will smooth those scars except your gazing at the Divine.

By *practice* I don't necessarily mean saying a thousand prayers or a thousand Mantras. I mean practice getting out of the way you indulge yourself and cater to your comforts. Turn this completely around. That is only possible if you say, "Yes, it is *this* bad. Where else can I turn? Where else will there be help? There isn't anybody. There certainly isn't another human being who can do anything to help." The help then comes from a very different source. Turn to that source and become aware of the radiating power of knowledge, and become eligible for the manifestation of that grace.

When I came back from India, I was swamped by psychologists who asked me, "What was your childhood like? What did you do? Where were your parents?" I told them a little bit about my background, and their conclusion was: "How come you haven't any criminal tendencies? That's usually what happens in a case like yours. You should hate society. You should be wanting to take revenge, trying to make up for all the bad things that were done to you."

I can only think perhaps I did some good or decent things in some past life which gave me the insight to go beyond my childhood experience. I had what I call some spiritual capital. You can put a lot of capital into your spiritual bank account, and when you need it, you can draw on the interest that has accumulated. But accumulating the interest is your responsibility. It won't be done for you.*

When we think about cooperating with our own evolution, we have to think about how much we all want power. We all want to control. Well, begin with controlling your destiny. That's the step to begin with. How much can you control yourself? You may control a whole army, but that doesn't mean anything if you can't control yourself. You can see that in politics. Presidents of countries have a lot of power and they try

---

* See the section in this book on "Spiritual Capital," page 143.

to exercise enormous control. But if there is no control of self, all the power that can be exercised somewhere else doesn't mean a thing. It leads to your own undoing. You either fall from your high position, or you get sick, or you have some other destiny that brings you down.

In Germany, first the aristocracy had the power. Then in their love for power they were so blind that they couldn't see their own undoing and it was all taken away from them. Then the Nazis came, and they were blinded by power and lost everything. And then came new governments—one in the east and another in the west. All this is just the shifting of power. Nobody benefits from it, and it is often very destructive.

The real power is in the Divine within. To attain to this power, one has to surrender self-will, because self-will, like self-love, is very destructive.

Taking revenge for whatever we think was done to us won't help either. During the Nuremburg trials,* the names of Nazis who had been arrested were given every night over the radio, and people who had grievances against this or that particular Nazi were asked to come forward. I could have come forward, but I didn't. It wasn't out of the goodness of my heart. It was just that my common sense told me, "If we don't stop taking revenge, where will it end?"

People often think, "For so many years of my life, people have taken advantage of me." They feel they should have revenge. In the Old Testament, God says, "Vengeance is mine."† What others do is their problem, as long as you do the right thing and free yourself. Let go of your grievance. You won't miss it.

But you should also consider that perhaps you are being taken advantage of because for many years, in this life or a past one, you took a great deal of advantage of others. Being taken advantage of will end when your karmic bookkeeping is balanced.

The negative lasts, and is very powerful, but the positive—bless-

---

* After World War II ended, several months of war crimes trials were held in the German city of Nuremburg under the auspices of Britain, France, the United States, and Russia. Thousands of Nazis of all ranks were tried and convicted of crimes against civilians and prisoners of war.

† Deuteronomy 32:35.

ings and inspirations—will also last if we just put our confidence in that. I once spent some time in the garden of Theresa of Avila. It's a small garden with very formal, stylized flower beds, but it still holds the calm and the peace made by all the years of prayer that had been done there. Divine inspiration can last a long, long time. Theresa of Avila lived in the sixteenth century, yet that inspiration is still available.

The choice of whether you will take to spiritual life only, or whether you will also look into self-development is an individual choice. But from what I saw of those long sessions of prayer for healing with the psychiatrist and priest at the mental hospital, and all the reading I have done on Lourdes where thousands of people have gone, yet very few have had lasting cures, my observation is that we can have a shortcut on our spiritual path by using both spiritual practice and self-development.

If you bring gratitude to this work, it will be a great help. Gurudev used to say, "Let it be known that gratitude is one of the strongest powers and the finest emotion that a human being is capable of." How you cultivate gratitude is again very individual. You can begin by being grateful for what you have, right now, right where you are. For example, you are not living in medieval times where houses were cold and clammy when it rained, or there was not enough wood and everybody had to be in the same room to keep warm. We have tremendous advantages. Let's not waste this life and become lazy and take things for granted. Rather, let us cultivate that finest feeling, gratitude.

The Guru

THE GURU IS YOUR CONSCIENCE, your spiritual surgeon. I used to travel a lot on behalf of the Ashram, giving talks and workshops. When I came home from these trips, there would be nobody to welcome me. People would just disappear. I had become a symbol of conscience to them, and they did not want to see me.

The Bhagavad Gita says that help comes from the Guru. The Guru points out to the disciple the path of liberation and shows how to move from ignorance into knowledge of the Divine in all and the Divine within. In doing this, the Guru makes you look at your behavior—no hiding, no excuses. Gurudev Sivananda, my Guru, had been a medical doctor and often used medical examples to illustrate his lessons. One day he pointed to his hand and said, "If there is a boil here that keeps on festering and festering, you can put some ointment on it, but if treating the surface doesn't help, you will have to cut the boil with a knife to get the pus out. *Then* the healing can take place. Would you rather somebody lost the whole hand or the whole arm, just because you are afraid you won't be liked and accepted?" So the Guru may appear harsh and even judgmental, but that may be the treatment you need to clean away something that is festering in your mind.

Mothers understand this very well. The instinctual mother love that wants to protect indiscriminately does not help children to face life and its difficulties. A mother who really loves her children will *prepare* them for life, not protect them from it.

The people I have initiated have accepted me as their spiritual mother, and I have to do the same kind of things an ordinary mother does. If I want to prepare people for another life or for a higher state of consciousness, I cannot be concerned that they won't like me if I have to criticize them to make them pay attention to the things they need to do. I don't gain anything by criticizing and I take a chance every time I do it that they will not like me. But if I worry about that, I am serving only myself and my own needs.

If I think I have to survive in someone else's opinion of what a spiritual leader should be, or what Divine Mother should be, then I had better beware. That would mean I was fooling myself about having finished my battle with my need to be accepted. The test is whether I can look at you here, one by one, and say, "It really wouldn't matter whether, on the next heartbeat, anyone here in the room accepted me or not."

The Guru holds a high office and no one can hold that office who has not the courage to stand up and say what needs to be said. Hushing things up or excusing people's faults, for fear of not being liked, makes a person absolutely unfit to take the responsibility of high office. There is one consolation in that: you at least know where you stand with your spiritual mother, Guru, or teacher.

I have often come down very hard on people and wondered later how I could have said anything so harsh. It has often taken me weeks or months to realize that my words did not come from my conscious, intellectual mind. I did this once in India. I was so upset about it that I went to Gurudev Sivananda and told him the harsh words I had said to a Western visitor.

"Now," I said, "all my spiritual practice is lost. I should not even have had such a thought!"

He asked, "When did you think this thought?"

I said, "I didn't. It just popped out!"

And he said, "Aha! You want to be the messenger of the Divine only for the pleasant things. You want to decide when to be the divine messenger, and when not. But pleasant messages are very few. You will wait a very long time for them."

He stopped there and walked away.

I said to myself, "Hmm. Yes. It's like performing an operation. I cannot say, 'I can't cut into this body because I don't want to hurt this person,' or, 'I can't give this medicine because it tastes so bitter.' I cannot let someone die. If I can help a person to avoid having another twenty lives—or maybe one hundred and twenty—then I must do so, whatever it takes."

Many people think that by imitating their Guru they can *become* the Guru. This is not so. You have to become a being entirely on your own. The Guru can help you by saying, "This is the way I did it. This is what helped me. This is what I have seen work with other people." But the Guru cannot reform you. You will always be basically what you are. If you have blue eyes, you have blue eyes. They cannot be made brown or gray. But the Guru can help you to put God's Light into your eyes. The Guru can coax you and do everything possible to help you to *want* to have God's Light in your eyes, but you have to *do* it yourself. There is nothing the Guru can do if there is not a true, honest desire for the Most High, for companionship with the Divine.

Mantra initiation is a form of spiritual marriage and whenever a Guru incarnates, all the initiates have to come along, like it or not. Swami Sivananda said when he took life again, all those who had been with him before had to come along, too. This was very hard for me to accept. I wouldn't say it was not possible, but I wondered how he could possibly know, how *anybody* could know.

Years later, I had a dream that I felt was inspired by Gurudev Sivananda. I was in a heaven with a lot of dignitaries at a big conference. A voice said, "We still need more help. Who will go?" I felt the voice in the dream was directed to me, so I said, "Well, nobody knows for how long. Nobody knows what the world is." But I felt that I had to respond to this call, so I said I would go.

When I met Anandamayi Ma, I asked her, "Is it true that one is called again and again to go back and work? Does this mean it never ends? Even if you leave this plane and you go wherever you go, do you keep on working?" I saw the serious faces on her disciples. It seemed to me they were thinking, "If we tell her this now, she may be totally discouraged." But I'm ninety-nine percent convinced now that even when you give up your body, you work in different ways somewhere else. So do your job well here. Get all your tools in good order, otherwise it will be tough.

You can't have a Guru on your own terms, but you can't have your life on your own terms, either. Don't waste your time Guru-shopping or playing games. Surrender means that you can't have things on your own terms.

All Gurus are demanding, and usually only a small group of people will accept that. They are the inner circle. Then there are those who can't take such heavy demands, so they are in the next circle, and so on. Some people exist just on the periphery. However, with a true teacher there shouldn't be any favorites. Everybody should and will have the chance to make their way into the closer circles if they want to, but they have to make the effort and they have to have the desire to be there. With all the temptations of the world, that can be hard. As dear old Papa Ramdas used to say, "Ram, I am weak. I can't hold on to you. You hold on to me." Make that a daily thought.

Spiritual Mother

It is not only women who can be spiritual mothers. My own spiritual mother was Gurudev Sivananda. But if we want to understand what a spiritual mother is, first we have to look at the human aspect of a mother. There are women who are mothers simply by giving birth to children. There are some who take care of children, and they are mothers in an indirect way.

What would be the ideal mother? From a child's point of view an ideal mother might mean candy, chocolate, late nights, and movies! I think the ideal human mother's first obligation is to prepare children to face life, to stand up in life, to be able to handle the various situations life presents. This may often mean discipline and restriction, but not without love, not without explaining and helping the young person or the child to understand—and never with that arrogance that many grown-up people have toward children. Children are little people, and if they are treated with dignity, they respond in dignity. This has been my experience.

But very few of us have had the ideal human mother. As children, we had lots of problems because our mothers had *their* problems. Children are very impressionable, so as adults we often have much difficulty because the effects of our childhood relationship with our mother have not been conquered. These effects are very lasting.

It was when I was thinking about the problem I had with my mother, and wondering if it was resolved that I had the dream of the little girl who had not been scarred by having a mother who didn't love her. Then I knew for sure. Dreams can be a wonderful source of knowledge. Take them seriously. Get your guidance from your own inner Light. We become stronger when we recognize our milestones and know we have done the right thing.

If I had a lot of tail-feathers hanging on from my nonexistent relationship with my mother, this would be very bad for the work I am trying to do. My Guru's order to me was, "Be a spiritual mother to all." That would be difficult to do if I still had loose ends left from my problems with my mother.

Because my mother was not really a mother to me, and because I have not had children, I do not have that experience to use in being a spiritual mother. I can only be a spiritual mother the way I think it should be done.

To help people as a spiritual mother, I had to ask, "What would it mean on the purely human level to be not the perfect mother, but the best mother that I can be?" Adults don't need to be mothered the way children do, so how else can you be a mother? One thing a mother must do is let her children be free. She doesn't have to monitor every step, but still she must be careful that there is no early development of habits or patterns which later on are difficult to overcome. In fact, if these habits or patterns develop, they will need to be destroyed if a person is to be naturally creative.

You can be a spiritual mother only by becoming the handmaiden of Divine Mother. This means finding out what Divine Mother means to you. Of course, she is all your ideas of perfection and beauty and love, and many other wonderful things. All these manifest in Divine Mother, so pleasing Divine Mother is not a bad thing.

Gurudev Sivananda was my own spiritual mother, but I was not with him for very long. I had to learn on my own for many years. Indira Devi has said, "There are Gurus who give you a Mantra and send you down the road. You are on your own. Then there are Gurus who treat you like an outpatient. And there are Gurus who take you right in."

Gurus, like Anandamayi Ma and Indira Devi, take you in, help in the birth of the spiritual child, and carry on to nourish it until it can walk on its own, until it is prepared to combine the realities of daily living with spiritual life. They show you how to look at the powers of wealth and money and sex and possessions, so that you will learn not to give power to things which will not give any benefit, blessings, or grace in return.

Being a spiritual mother is for us women our duty. Don't think just of the children you put into the world. Be a spiritual mother to anybody that you can help. That is a very sacred duty for any woman. But first, before you truly can do this, realize the divinity within yourself.

But even with no Guru at all, if you make yourself—man or woman—a handmaiden of Divine Mother, then her grace comes to you. This grace functions on a different level, an in-between level, in a sort of twilight of life, a twilight of the spirit. It only comes, from my observation, with complete surrender to the Divine. I have said, "Well, here it is. The spiritual children are here now. What should be done? And there are some others over there. What should be done there? And there are more somewhere else. We can't get them all here, so what do you want to do? Open the doors."

And that is what happens. I often have my own convictions about what should be done, but I sit back and wait. I ask, "Are they correct?" You have to ask this, because you go through life with a lot of convictions. Most of them you have to throw out. They are more a hindrance than a help.

I remember waiting once for more than a year for an answer about

whether I was taking the right course in being a spiritual mother. Then two people from the Ashram went to India, and when they came back, one of them said, "I'm glad that we have you for our Guru, because the women Gurus nourish their spiritual babies, and we need this. The men are quite different. Most of them, once you have initiation, just shovel you out. But you take care of your spiritual babies. I am very glad, because I don't think I would have made it this far, otherwise."

It was another wonderful confirmation for me. I had seen in India that disciples were often very much on their own. I didn't want to do this to people because I know how difficult it is.

Certainly we grow in strength by making decisions and taking responsibility. But when you are dealing with people's lives, when you know you can influence them, you want to be sure that you are doing the right thing. You aren't asking for visions; you just want to know that you are doing the right thing. I feel that if you work in an interaction with Divine Mother it is much easier to do the right thing, because you can say, "It's your job. You created the world. I am just here waiting. Here are my hands, here is my voice. Use them. You do it." This is surrender.

If you want to ease your burden, never let a day go by without your reflection. In one day, you hear all kinds of things about what you should do, and you are left thinking you should do this or you should do that or you should do some other thing. At the end of the day in your reflection, take a little time to ask, "Have I done what *needs* to be done, not what I decided to do or set out to do, or what I thought I should do, but what really *needs* to be done?" If you haven't, then go and do it. If you can't do it, ask for help and you will get it.

There is a story told about Sarada Devi that after Ramakrishna died, all his disciples left, and there was Sarada Devi all by herself. She wondered why she was alone, because she had cooked for them, she had comforted them. One day she went to the roof of her house and she asked Divine Mother, "Where have all the children gone? They need a home and I am here." It didn't take very long. In a few weeks, a few months. Ramakrishna's disciples, the ones who had listened most carefully to his very wise words, came back one by one. She was overjoyed. Eventually, the numbers doubled and tripled, and she said, "He's sending them on to me like a line of ants." She was very pleased.

Sarada Devi was simple, but quite practical. She gave the disciples what they needed on the human level, also. She took care of needs that are not fulfilled and satisfied by all the philosophy and the big words—the Absolutes, and the Voids, and what-have-you. If you have not attained an understanding where these words have meaning to you, it's not wrong to acknowledge your needs and make them known.

Think of yourself as a human being, as a divine being, and as an extension of Divine Mother. Think of being her handmaiden. Give yourself to her and say, "I am here. Now take me. Or pick me up, if that is necessary." If you want to be picked up, I assure you, she will do it.

Sacrifice and Essence

THE ESSENCE OF A PERSON, or the essence of an action, or the essence of all that one is, that is God. That is the spark of the Most High within all of us. You cannot *become* that. To find that essence, you must leave aside all identification. When all identification has been set aside, nothing but essence is left. We cannot visualize essence, but we can use other things to represent it, such as images of Divine Mother or other deities. The image often used in the East is a tiny dot, because essence has no form.

When you sacrifice everything that you have identified with, and all that you think, then you have sacrificed your whole life. Dedicating your whole life to the Divine is the real sacrifice, and the degree of your sacrifice is determined by how much you can let go of the many things you wish to do, that are dear to you, that you hope for.

Even if you think you are giving up everything, you are really giving up only attachments which have brought you nothing but hardships, tears, disappointments, and disillusion. If you don't give them up by your own efforts and give them up willingly, then traumas and dramas come into your life and circumstances force you to give them up. How different it is if you come to the Divine by your own decision and say, "Here they are. I give them to you."

When I became a sanyasi, people said to me, "Why would you throw away a life that has been so effective and useful, that has been such a good influence on people?" This was a great obstacle which I had to face over and over. People would say, "See what you can do?" and "Isn't that enough?" It was true that I had done a lot, but there was still too much involvement of my personality aspects. Then one day, I realized, "I am not really giving up anything. I am throwing off my burden."

If your sacrifice is absolute, if you have sacrificed all your feelings, your attachments, your emotions, your identification, and all that you think, your whole life becomes a life not *for* God, but *in* God. Then your actions are not really your own, because each action has an essence and you can't own that essence. It's there or it isn't.

We can't all start at the same point in the practice of sacrifice, because as individuals we are all different—although as far as the essence is concerned, we are not different. Where you start depends on your personality aspects, your attitude, your actions, and the motivation of your actions. Your sacrifice may have to be quite simple in the beginning. You can start by just looking at your attachments, your possessiveness, and your desires. Perhaps you will be able to begin with the sacrifice of what you possess—money, objects.

For the literal-thinking person in India in ancient times, there was a lot of animal sacrifice, and perhaps in some hill tribes there may have been human sacrifice as well. In fact, the one human sacrifice which is very well known is the burning of the wife in the funeral flames of the husband. This was done so he would have a place in heaven, because it was believed that only she could take him there.

We talk about sacrificing food or flowers, or burning candles, but that kind of sacrifice is not very valuable because we didn't make the food, we didn't make the flowers grow, and we did not make the wax or the oil we burn. We have to take all that from somewhere outside ourselves. We have to be aware that we are offering these things to the Most High because we really haven't anything else. Nothing is ours. We have to take it from somewhere.

What are your sacrifices, then? Real sacrifice, for the true seeker who is beyond literal thinking, is the sacrifice of selfishness. This makes you free to function, to be truly human, to be truly liberated from the confinement, constriction and the straightjacket of selfishness. Selfishness on the rampage tyrannizes. Nothing good comes from that in any part of your life. It just is not a blessing. No light emanates from your heart or from your eyes. You are in a darkness, imprisoned by this terrible, evil force. So when you sacrifice selfishness, wherever you have it in your personality makeup, you really set yourself free, and you set in motion the process of becoming truly human.

How can you sacrifice? Begin with all the things that you love, that you want to acquire or attain to—social position, career or profession, wealth, marriage to your dream lover. The real sacrifice is that which you are most attached to—the little self, the personality aspects, your desire for special food, whatever you are attached to.

That is what you have to give up. These are the real sacrifices, because they are the desires of the lower nature in you. Look at them for what they are. Money you can always earn again. Food needs only to be nourishing; it doesn't have to be fancy. The marriage to a dream lover can take a terrible turn. Your company can go bankrupt leaving you with no job. And yet you think your security is in these things.

As your understanding of sacrifice grows, you will find there is much to be sacrificed in your life. You can sacrifice your comfort. If you do this, you will be free of the desire for comfort and you will be able to do anything you want.

You can sacrifice your personality aspects. If all personality aspects are sacrificed, they melt away. If this kind of sacrifice agrees with your temperament, it is one way of getting to the Most High. I would call it a process of awareness, and some processes of awareness are more difficult for some people than for others.

There is also sacrifice in Karma Yoga. The Gita says that we have the right to work, but we have not the right to the fruits of the work.* So there is a sacrifice in that.

Tapas is sacrifice, also. You may offer your chanting or your meditation for the benefit of someone else. That is sacrifice. People who are very focused on Hatha Yoga can offer the asanas as their sacrifice. Prayer dance can be offered because it is an expression of devotion. You can also use activities such as prostrations, particularly if you leave everything that you put down with the prostration. If you pick it up again, you haven't made a sacrifice; you have made a gesture. When you sacrifice to the Most High by putting down whatever ego is present at that moment (at least, that you are aware of), leave it. And then keep reminding yourself that you left it. The Buddhists do one hundred thousand prostrations as a reminder that we have more than one hundred thousand things to sacrifice. But with every prostration there must be the accompanying thought of putting down the personality aspects or whatever it is you are sacrificing. If that is not there, you may do eighty-nine thousand prostrations in vain. Prostrations can be a gesture, or they can be a sacrifice. That decision always belongs to the individual. Everything you do can be a sacrifice to honor the Most High if you just offer everything you put into what you do.

This brings us finally to the sacrifice of the mind which is an expression of self-will and, of course, to your thoughts and opinions. You have to sacrifice your opinions. Very often the questions brought to me are just statements of someone's opinions. It is difficult to deal constantly with someone who is opinionated, because opinion means nothing. Many

---

* Bhagavad Gita, Second Discourse, verse 27.

of your opinions are not correct anyway, so do not hesitate to sacrifice them.

You have to sacrifice, also, thoughts which are stimulated by the currents of your emotions, particularly if you want to stop thinking in certain ways that reinforce your emotions. Then your personal energy, your physical energy, is in the work, and then it goes into the service of those who seek the Most High.

You will also have to sacrifice your intellect. Theoretically, you may know this. People can become expert debaters and have brilliant minds, but they are unfortunately usually more clever than wise. You may know, in theory, that the intellect can take you only so far. But to remember and be aware of that at all times is a tremendous sacrifice that you can make.

You will have to sacrifice wisdom, too, that which you think you know and understand. Intellectually, you may be able to say, "Well, I know that I don't know anything," but you have to touch the very essence of that thought.

You will also have to sacrifice those little stepping stones you get along the way—those things that give an indication you are going in the right direction. When they all disappear, this is a difficult renunciation because we always want to have confirmation we are doing the right thing.

Eventually (and this may startle you), you will have to sacrifice even your devotion. But you cannot do this until all your emotions are absorbed in devotion to the Most High.

All these sacrifices are processes in coming to the full awareness of your essence. Essence, which is also sometimes called Self, is beyond all actions. Self, or essence, is actionless. It's not the essence that acts.

So there are different processes in sacrifice, and you will have to put them together as you need them, as you see what your obstacles are. There is no particular order that you have to follow in doing this.

When everything has been offered as a sacrifice to the Most High, if a person is absorbed in doing all activities in the service of the Most High, then all these things are not really action. *That* is the essence of action—that is the divine spark. In the East, they would say at this point,

"You are Brahman. That is Brahman." In our culture we do not say "You are God" or "You are the Goddess" because that is not how we say things. But you can think that in your heart without voicing it.

And those moments—when you know that you are Brahman or God—those are your most sacred moments. Hold on to them. Collect them. You can't hang on to them completely, but you can let them enlarge, the way many little candles, when you light them one after the other, make more light.

Using the Divine Light Invocation

I am created by Divine Light
I am sustained by Divine Light
I am protected by Divine Light
I am surrounded by Divine Light
I am ever growing into Divine Light

It's not so easy to get rid of all the desires that we have, but we can perhaps take *one* desire and let that rise over all the others. Make that one desire *I am ever growing into Divine Light.* The Divine Light Invocation is the best way to transform desires.*

After I had finished two years of long Mantra practices, I recognized that I had many desires. There were many things I wanted to know, many interests I wanted to follow, many things I wanted to understand, to experience, and to accomplish. Then one day I asked myself, "And after I have done all this, then what? If I died right now, where would I go?"

Very soon after this, a young woman visited me from Montreal, bringing a package from a man I knew there. He had sent me some information about my astrological chart. It said that I would have only three and a half years to live. I did not necessarily believe the prediction, but it all came together at the right time to give me an idea: "What would I do if I were going to die in three and a half years? Well, it's better than three and a half months!"

I decided to strengthen my practice of the Divine Light Invocation and to begin practicing it two hours a day for the next two years. Then maybe I would know enough to teach it to other people. Then the thought came to me: "I can have all the desires in the world, but if I remind myself over and over and over, and each time I do the Light Invocation, 'I want to grow into Light,' I don't think I really have to worry that I will be overrun by desires on an emotional level." We all have our emotions. I have mine. You have yours. But what we do with them, that's a different story.

When you practice the Divine Light Invocation, be emphatic: *I am ever growing into Divine Light.* Let that be your foremost desire. Even if you live another fifty years, a hundred years, who cares? The mind is such a villain. The more time you have, the more it takes to impress that desire on the mind, because there are already so many other desires in

---

* For information about the Divine Light Invocation and full instructions for the practice, see Radha, *The Divine Light Invocation* and *The Divine Light Invocation* audio cassette.

there. They have made grooves in the mind and you have to clean some of those grooves out to get anything else in.

You can do the same with people you love, people for whom you want the very best. Put them into the Light, and then in a prayerful attitude, say, "It's my desire that you may grow into Light with every day." That's a spiritual gift of great value, great magnificence. There is nothing better you can give.

When you do the Divine Light Invocation, you have to be able to visualize yourself being filled with Light. Visualize your body as a glass vessel being filled with Light. That's one way of doing it. There are other ways, and you have to find your own. If you see that your visualization is slipping, always start again from the beginning.

When you do the Divine Light Invocation for someone else, you do not have to spend a lot of time visualizing the person, as long as the name flashes through your mind once. Focus on the Light, and then invoke all your finer feelings. In this way you refine emotions, and you give the practice the intensity necessary to bring about the result. Take your time and visualize your own body being filled with Light. You can't just go through the body movements without the visualization. However, the movements also are important. There is more concentration, no question, when you tense the muscles and hold your breath.

Without the visualization, you would have to do the Divine Light Invocation a hundred times a day to get the same results. You can practice many things with visualization. I couldn't practice my dancing during the war. There were just no places for that. So I had to close my eyes and see myself doing the dance in my mind—a whole program of eighteen dances. My husband who was a musician would sit and play music in his mind because even after the war it was a long time before he could locate an instrument.

The Divine Light Invocation was a real God-given blessing which I was taught by Babaji. My mind can go in ten directions at once. It was only by practicing the Divine Light Invocation that I really got my mind under control so I could use it for spiritual practice, or for concentrating on the Most High, or for just being *there*, without it being filled with thousands of other thoughts and preoccupations.

Practicing Surrender

SURRENDER IS ABSOLUTELY NECESSARY if you are to have success on the spiritual path. But surrender has to be done with awareness and discrimination. Otherwise it may be just apathy or indifference. Surrendering doesn't mean you don't have to make plans. You do. You must make the best plans you can, and then turn the whole thing over to the Divine. I call this doing my homework—I do my best to look at the situation, then I make one or two or three plans, and then I wait to see what the Divine has to say about all this.

You can begin to learn how to surrender by practicing. I began to practice before I ever went to India to meet my Guru. I was told about surrender by some Indians in Montreal who invited me to dance for them to celebrate their independence from Britain. I asked them what it means to have a Guru, and what the next step is once you have found him or her. I was told that I would be well-advised to prepare myself first of all by writing down all my shortcomings—and be clear about them, admit them quite freely. The next thing needed was obedience. That worried me greatly because, never having had brothers and sisters, I never had to give in the way most people do.

At that time, I was giving classes in Montreal on dancing, creative movement, and photography to make extra money for my trip to India. I had one young dance student who had learned some simple folk dances and I decided to ask her to teach them to me. She was nineteen.

She said, "Oh, Mrs. Hellman. You wouldn't be interested. They are only folk dances."

I said, "That doesn't matter. I would like to learn them."

In the lessons she gave me I observed myself and my reactions. She was a young girl, nineteen, and I was forty-four, a middle-aged woman and a professional dancer. I thought, "If I can surrender to how she teaches me—if I can handle this—then I don't need to worry about surrender once I meet my Guru."

It was quite an ordeal because she showed a very different nature then—a different tone of voice, a different vocabulary. She even called me stupid. I could see how the Divine used her to bring it home to me that surrender can really be very difficult. But even after that, I had *no* idea what Gurudev Sivananda was going to ask of me.

In surrendering, obedience is an absolute must. If you don't practice obedience, you will never follow instructions correctly. If you do a practice incorrectly, saying, "Oh, this is more comfortable, I like it this way better," you will never have the result of the practice. Often people say, "I have done this for five years and I haven't got anywhere." When I ask them to show me what they are doing, I can always see that they have made changes to the instructions.

To learn surrender you have to look for opportunities to practice. I found opportunities in my travel. Wherever I went—and I have stayed in many houses, in many places—I never made any special requests. Until I had my first bout with arthritis, I accepted whatever was offered. If somebody gave me a bed, it was great. If it was a nice bed, that was fine. If it was a lumpy bed—and I have slept in many lumpy beds—I never said, "That was not a good bed," or "I won't go there any more because I will get a lumpy bed." You accept what is. If it's good, say thank you. If it's not that good, still say thank you, because you had a roof over your head, you had a place to sleep. One person will give you a chest of drawers, another will just let you live out of your suitcase. Whatever comes, you adjust—wherever you are.

Use any such travels to surrender to what is. Don't say, "I don't like this table. Can I take it out?" Don't change the room around because you like it better a different way, even if you are going to be there for a month. In other words, subdue all thoughts that you have about making immediate changes. That's very important. The only exception is a change that serves your spiritual practice. Then *ask* if you can make the change you want. Or learn to adjust your practice to whatever the circumstances are.

Practice your surrender in the small things so that you slowly get used to doing it. If you can make a big leap and go to the biggest, the most difficult surrender, so much the better. Then the other small things will easily fall into place.

But do not practice self-inflicted pain to learn surrender. Just accept whatever circumstances come.

To practice surrender, I would sometimes promise the Divine that for a particular length of time I would do anything a certain person wanted me to do. Then for a time before beginning the practice, I would put that person into the Light. I have prepared people this way for a week before beginning, and sometimes up to three weeks if they were really difficult. I always made it clear in my preparation period that I would not go against my conscience, but anything else I would go along with.

One time, when I was doing all the housekeeping at the Ashram, I was practicing this surrender with a fellow who had a workbench in the basement where he sawed wood. We had forced air heating with big ducts. He reached up and rubbed his hand over one, and he said, "Look at that. You call that clean?" Well, it had never occurred to me that it was my duty to clean his workshop, but I had said I would do anything, so I cleaned it.

At one time that promise to surrender to someone cost me two thousand dollars. I had to decide whether to follow my decision to surrender or save the money. I said, "This is probably a very special test. How far will I go? Will that include money, too?" So I let the two thousand dollars go out of the window. That was a tremendous amount of money in those days, when I was getting only fifty dollars for a lecture. I had to give many lectures before I got that amount together again.

In doing this practice, you don't sacrifice your ideals, you don't go against your conscience. But you sacrifice whatever else you have to sacrifice, and one day the time will come when most of your surrender is no longer a sacrifice.

I became aware, also, that unless I surrender my habitual thinking, the habitual quick response in my mind—in other words, my own mental activity—I can't really hear what anybody is telling me. In any human relationship (not only in marriage), if you want to hear somebody, you have to surrender at that moment and really listen to that person. If you practice that, thinking each time, "That was another little opportunity to be better able to listen to the still, small voice within, to listen to the Divine," then surrender becomes second nature and you don't have to make a conscious effort. When surrender has become part of your nature, you will no longer have to say to yourself, for example, "At five o'clock Jane will come to talk to me and I had better surrender so I will hear what she says."

At times, if something comes out of the blue or somebody drops in unexpectedly while I am busy, I may not hear what is being said. As soon as I become aware of that, I say, "Repeat that, please. What was it?" At that moment, then, I drop everything else. Now this means I can forget a hundred and fifty other things, but this is what must be done.

Sometimes my place is like an airport with all the people coming and going. But I have made it that way on purpose because surrender means not saying, "I open the doors from three to five only, and if you don't make it, that's too bad." You have to surrender to the Divine twenty-four hours a day. You cannot do it part time.

How do you do a spiritual practice if you keep all your doors open and somebody walks right in? Well, you have to learn to incorporate that person, that conversation, into the practice of surrender, even if you had intended to do something entirely different. And don't get irritable, don't get impatient—particularly if the interruption isn't all that important and the work you were involved in is important.

This practice teaches you to surrender, to be quick in adjusting your concentration, to be able to go back to where you were quickly, and it deepens your acceptance of what is.

When that is well established, then you can say, "Okay, between seven and nine—that's my time." But still be willing to surrender to circumstances and adjust your time. If you don't, impatience comes in the door. You will begin thinking, "Oh, I can *never* finish anything. There are *all* these disturbances. There are *all* these interruptions." That impatience reflects later on in other areas of your spiritual practices and your daily life.

For me, all these things were particularly difficult, not having grown up in a large family and having no brothers and sisters. To me, people meant problems, and who wants problems? However, I made up my mind I would do it, never mind what it was, and there's no question that I had my hard times. But victory comes only if you allow it to happen.

Judgment

WHEN YOU LIVE in the world of competition, judgment comes up constantly. Judgment means that you pass a sentence on somebody or something: good, bad, unacceptable, interesting, boring. But you can look at judgment a little differently. If you see something—let's call it an "imperfection"—in someone, you can use the "imperfection" as a point of reference for where *you* are, and how *you* have developed. You can say, "I don't have to do what this person is doing. If I pay attention, I can avoid being like that or making that mistake." Instead of passing judgment on somebody, use what you see in that person as a point of reference or recognition. In other words, learn from the mistakes of others. After so many years of living, you cannot avoid recognizing behavior that doesn't fit into the standards you have set for yourself, or the general standards of social life, or religious or yogic life. But you don't have to judge. There is a very fine distinction between recognizing that somebody doesn't meet certain standards, and judging them because they don't. Make that distinction and don't talk yourself into judgment.

Judgment makes life extremely difficult. Things happen, and it's really impossible to say why they happen in this way or that way. It would be foolish to pronounce any kind of judgment. We don't know what decision a soul makes about coming into life. I knew a woman who was in a wheelchair. She was seventeen when she was hit by a car and had her spine injured. She later married a man who had wanted to be a priest, but realized that he wasn't born for it. He decided that his service to the Divine would be to marry this woman and take care of her. All his friends discouraged him, but he made this promise to God: "I couldn't keep my promise to be a priest, but I will be the best possible husband and friend to this woman."

When they heard that I was going to India, he wanted me to take her, too. So I wrote to Gurudev and told him. He sent me books and said, "You give these books to her, and explain everything to her. Tell her not to come. Everything will be all right."

I gave her the books and I told her a little bit about Gurudev. Six months later, when I came back from India, I went to her place. A lot of people were going up to her apartment, and I heard them saying, "How wonderful! Isn't she a marvelous example? Here we are in perfect health, and there is this lovely young woman in a wheelchair with so much *healing power.*"

Most people judge—and, of course, I did too. We say, "I can't help anybody if I'm not healthy myself." We forget examples like this. Needless to say, this marriage lasted.

This is a wonderful example of how divine love and grace can work in somebody's life. She had surrendered: "I can't be well, but I would like to serve. What can I do?" Gurudev Sivananda wrote about selfless service in all his books, and in the letters he wrote to me he asked me to tell her about that, and so she didn't ask for health—she asked only to be of service in some way.

Health gives us a certain responsibility, but if we don't have it, perhaps it's because we agreed when we took birth to give evidence to something else. This is the meaning of the story of the blind man who was healed by Jesus.

Jesus was asked, "Why is this man blind? Is he such a sinner?"

Jesus said, "No."

They said, "Oh! Then is it because his parents have sinned?"

He said, "No."

They said, "Then why is he blind?"

And Jesus said, "So that the works of God should be made manifest in him."*

We have to get away from oversimplification. We cannot say that things happen for this reason or that reason, and therefore something else is so. It's not that simple. Divine Law doesn't function quite that way. It's much more complicated.

If you had seen a dancer on stage that everybody praised, and lots of people (men, particularly) sent flowers and chocolates to, would you have thought that dancer might one day be a swami? You would have

---

* John 9:1-3.

bet anything you owned against that happening. So would I. I would have considered myself absolutely unfit, and if you had asked any of my family, they would have said, "She? You must be dreaming!"

When I heard there were four people to be initiated by Swami Sivananda at Christmas in '55, and some people guessed that I was to be one of them, I didn't think for one split second that I was. I considered myself absolutely unfit. But who's to say? Let me remind you that two prostitutes, one in Jesus' life and one in the Buddha's life, became foremost disciples and devotees. So let's put all our judgments aside.

People who live at the Ashram are not conformists. If they were, they wouldn't have to defend what they are doing from criticism by their families. But when people have been living in an ashram for a long time, they can begin to think everybody else should conform. That is wrong thinking. It's not possible for everyone to live in one way. Everybody is an individual, and each one has to be given time to develop in his or her own way. Mothers sometimes tell me, "This child here, when she was two years old, she was already dry. That one there took six months longer. The other one started to talk a year later. That one didn't want to walk." Why all this comparison? Setting children up, tiny little tots, against each other is very damaging. I have had to do a lot of digging in people's pasts to help them get over those insults.

Let's not do that any more, now that we have wakened up and understand more. Let's not make comparisons and judgments with our children, our friends, our co-workers, our gurubhais, our spiritual friends, or whomever. Let's drop that and let people be where they are, because we don't know. Divine Mother alone knows. And it's her business to look after all that.

We can only say, "Use me as an instrument for Light to help others strengthen their faith and have the courage to keep going." If you do this, you are Divine Mother's handmaiden.

Be a good one.

Divine Mother's Handmaiden

You HAVE TO BE STRONG to be Divine Mother's handmaiden. You have to be willing to be the messenger of the Divine, *regardless* of what the message is. If you say, "I want to be the messenger only for the good and inspirational messages," you are not fit for the high office of divine messenger at all. You have to be willing to take risks. Being a divine messenger can be risky because the human mind can be very unreliable. Your message may be misunderstood, misinterpreted, or received with anger, and you may be reported, even arrested. You may throw yourself open to somebody who wants to take revenge. People who spoke out against Hitler in Germany during the Nazi years were often reported and arrested, and many were killed.

If you don't want to be strong, stay in the background. Just become a little nicer, a little easier to get along with, and leave it at that. But you will have to make up your mind *some* day where you want to go, because the purpose of life is to prepare yourself for Cosmic Consciousness.

When you are a handmaiden of the Divine (and the word *handmaiden* applies to men and women, equally), you may risk great danger. Anybody who has ever taken a course in lifesaving knows how the drowning person struggles. If you are not skillful, you may drown, too. If you are not spiritually skillful, you cannot discriminate clearly between sympathy and true compassion. Then you are in danger of sympathizing by helping the person to cover up his or her faults, trying to offer comfort.

Let us explore that a bit. Suppose a married man or a married woman is having a secret love affair and then asks a friend to help keep the secret. The friend becomes sentimental and says, "Yes, I understand. I will help you cover up. You can use me as an excuse." Many years ago, while I was still living in Germany, I went through this situation myself. Women friends would come to my place at midnight from meeting a lover, and stay the rest of the night with me. They would say to me, "If my husband phones before I get to your place, just tell him I went out to buy some cigarettes."

Then one day I realized there was something very wrong with this. I didn't want to be part of such deceptions. At the same time, I didn't want to tell the husbands what the wives were doing. I was on a teeter-totter, saying to myself, "I don't like what they are doing and I don't like my part in it. But, oh, maybe it's not all that bad. It's really *their* affair, not mine." Yes, no, maybe. These are all excuses. We think this way when our ideals are wishy-washy because we have not clarified the principles by which we live. It's equally bad to minimize another person's wrong action. You are not helping that person to meet himself or herself on the gut level.

None of this helps you, either. You don't get stronger, and the people you wanted to help may now really drown, because you were too concerned with being liked. If you can overcome the need to be accepted by others, then you know that you can become truly the instrument of the Divine. If you want to be counted as Divine Mother's handmaiden, get it out of your head that anything else counts, or that anybody else's opinion counts. If you know that your surrender to the Divine is complete, nothing else matters.

Sometimes you may think that you cannot act or speak at all because you have done similar things yourself, and you feel that the same judgment or statement applies to you, too. We have all made mistakes. The important thing is not to continue making the same mistakes, and then to help others stop making them. Nobody is perfect. We must all help each other from our own experience.

Being Divine Mother's handmaiden may also open you to despair. You will seldom be able to say, "I had a great day! I have been Divine Mother's handmaiden." More often in a day you will have to pass on an unpleasant truth, or perhaps in your struggle to help somebody you find that person biting the very hand that is trying to help.

A situation where you cannot help someone can really bring you to despair. Many times at the Ashram I have despaired over not being able to help a person. I used to get in the car sometimes and drive to a little cafe on the highway. I would sit at the table, drinking coffee and thinking, "What ever am I doing? What am I supposed to do? There is nothing I can do."

It is not easy if your commitment has been tested by the Divine and you have tried to meet the test, but have not been able to achieve anything. I recently had a letter from somebody who said, "I am the same. I still cannot deal with my problems." This person has lost fifteen or twenty years of life. When this happens, my first thought is, "Have I failed that person somewhere? What more can I do?" In this case, I had really gone far out of my way, counselling, writing letters, sending tapes, and doing hypnosis, so the individual was at least able to finish an education and now has a career to fall back on. But I cried when I got that letter.

At times like that, there seems to be no inspiration and you may feel almost cut off from the Divine. If you let your mind run wild at such a time, it can come up with dozens of horrifying thoughts that only make you feel worse. Despair is something that you will *have* to accept. If you have chosen to become Divine Mother's handmaiden, you must go on even through the times when you think it is useless because you are not accomplishing anything. You have assumed a certain responsibility in becoming Divine Mother's handmaiden and you cannot give that up.

Getting Along with Others

IF YOU WANT to see the Divine in everybody, you can't say, "No, I don't want to have anything to do with this or that person." Start off accepting everybody in the way in which you yourself would want to be accepted. That would mean everybody else would have to surrender to the way you are as an individual. In that same proportion, you have to be able to surrender to whoever approaches you. This way you'll learn your lesson pretty fast. You may get quite a bit of strong opposition, or somebody may cut you off, or look at you as if to say, "You are dismissed!" But you have to accept that and surrender to it. Think about where you may have done the same thing, though maybe not to the same person. If you really want to pursue surrender, the Divine will give you these comebacks often—and quickly, sometimes within a week. If you ask, the same day!

Don't avoid the sources of your awareness. That is very important. Rather, accept the challenges and seek them out. The person who is challenging you with anger or injustice is only an instrument of the Divine, because you need the lesson. If you handle the challenge well, you won't have to learn that lesson again. That's your reward. But if you want additional reward, then you will have to face this challenge again, because you did not act selflessly. To know and understand that needs thinking in depth.

Don't say, "Oh, I won't talk to so-and-so, I won't sit at the same table because of the terrible things he said to me yesterday." That means only that you are still nourishing your wounded sensitivity, your ego. Direct your sensitivity to receiving the messages you are being given, not to comforting the ego. If you don't like being criticized, find out as much as you can about yourself and then don't give any cause for criticism. That's the best way, because you have to practice a lot of awareness to succeed at it.

There is no question that eventually you will have to come around to the person who is sharply critical of you, even if it takes you a year or two to recognize that *somebody* had to be the one to give you that message, or to make you take this action, or to bring a certain thing to your attention. We had a fellow living at the Ashram once who was just incredibly difficult. To him I never sat right, I never walked right, he challenged my practice, he called me naive. At satsang he would say I wasn't holding the tone right, or my rhythm was not perfect. Anything. Everything. Sometimes I was so upset I would drive off and park somewhere and think, "What shall I do? How can I not defend myself?" It was important not to defend myself. We are all easy on ourselves, always justifying what we do or think, but the lesson is not to justify. I had come far enough to have recognized that.

Then one day I heard a minister give a sermon on the story of Judas. He said, "Without Judas, the crucifixion wouldn't make sense. There had to be somebody to play the part of Judas."

I thought, "Of course, there has to be somebody in my life playing that critical role." But still sometimes I didn't know what to make of all the criticism from this fellow. It took me two years to realize that these challenges had made me think ten miles deeper than I would have without them. Once I recognized this I had no more problems with that person. I could understand that he was playing in my life the same part that Judas had played in Jesus' life.

These things are bound to happen because they are tests of your faith, your sincerity. Do you really mean business? Or do you just want to play around? How serious are you? How much do you really want the Divine?

When difficult people come to you, don't say, "Oh, I don't like him or her. He is always like this or like that." Accept the challenge. This is a test. Do you want the Divine? Do you make the effort to see the Divine in everybody, even in the person who opposes you most and makes the greatest difficulties? The opposition is there because you cannot yet see the Divine. The problem is always with yourself. It's never the other person. Sure, there are certain people who are more difficult than others. There is no doubt about it. And we all tend to stay with those we find agreeable. But that's easy. Anybody can do that.

If somebody comes to you and says, "Oh, you are so wonderful. All those things you said—they really helped me," and so on, surrender that. Let it pass. If you don't let it pass then the same day or a couple of days later, somebody will tell you some horrible gossip in which you have been torn to bits and pieces. The Divine does all these things to keep you in balance, so you won't get attached to this or that. Instead, be attached only to your chosen aspect of the Divine, and stay focused with that. Shift all your attachments there.

You have to learn to accept the good and the bad, just as you do with the weather. Can you change the weather? The weather is a marvelous lesson. You can complain about how cold it is, how rainy it is, how it's this, that, and the other. But you can't change it. So it's better that you fit yourself into the weather and take as little notice of it as possible: "Well, it's raining today. So what? It has to rain. Otherwise nothing grows."

Think of people like flowers. Roses are beautiful but they have thorns. You have to be very careful before you touch thistles, but even weeds are healing plants. There really isn't anything or anyone absolutely bad or negative, and nobody benefits from your effort to understand that, except you. It helps to remember that each one of us is not an island, and that we have our seasons, and our ups and downs. Life is not just a straight line. It's a wave. Sometimes you are on top of the wave, sometimes you have to go to the bottom, and then you have to make sure you have enough momentum to come up again on the other side.

If your problems are sky-high and you are really being driven into a corner by someone, and you are wondering how much you should defend yourself, here is a beautiful little story to think about.

A saint came to a village, and he stayed there for a while. The villagers were very happy to have his presence. When he was about to leave, they said to him, "You must do us one favor. On the outskirts of the village, there lives a cobra. If anyone comes too close, the cobra attacks and bites, and her bite is poisonous, so people die." They told him how many people had died of this cobra's bites.

As the old saint was leaving, he found the cobra, and he said, "What are these terrible things I hear about you? Why would you attack people? When I return, I don't want to hear any more about this."

Time passed and the saint returned. The villagers told him, "It has really helped. The cobra doesn't attack anybody any more."

So the old saint went to find the cobra to praise her for listening and obeying. He found her wounded and in pools of blood. He said, "What has happened to you?"

The cobra said, "You see? When I was striking at people, they respected me. But now that you have said I cannot return their actions in kind, they take sticks and beat me, and the children throw stones."

The old saint said, "I said you should not kill. But I didn't say you could not hiss."

Human nature is such that we always want to defend ourselves somehow, so we have to deal with that desire and learn not to be so defensive, but eventually you can speak up, you can hiss. But not strike.

The sooner you begin to practice surrender and the more serious you are, the better. Don't think that you have plenty of time. Even if you have twenty years, you cannot know that for certain, and it will take ten years just to hit the bottom of your solar plexus. When your time is up, you have to surrender all your desires, all your hopes, all the wishes that you still have, all the things that you haven't done, and that you thought you might like to do. It doesn't make any difference how old or how young you are.

May you be given the strength to surrender to the Light.

Becoming an Aspirant

SPIRITUAL ASPIRANTS have many expectations and assumptions which must be counteracted on entering spiritual life. First of all, you must clarify—if you haven't already done so—what your expectations are, and you must keep clarifying them. I suggest that people examine their expectations of spiritual life as often as once a year. Reflect on them for however many days or weeks are necessary. Ask yourself: "How reasonable are my expectations? Are they within the reach of what I am bringing to my spiritual life?" You may have a lot of things to clear away before you can have expectations about seeing the Light, or having insights or spiritual experiences. You do not get something for nothing. Even your body is not your own. It was built from the body of your mother.

It is difficult to do spiritual practice without assuming that at some time you will get something in return. You should not suppress such assumptions or expectations, but you should not be unrealistic about them. To have realistic expectations, you need some idea of the karma you have accumulated in this life up to the time you started on your spiritual path. You need to know also if there is any good reason to assume that some of it has been cleared away. When a large portion has been cleared—a little more than half—then perhaps the Divine will give you some signals that tell you to keep going.

Many people make assumptions about where they are or where

somebody else is on the spiritual path. Such assumptions are not good. Assumptions are very easy to come by for everyone and there is no special exception for me. I cannot assume a person is here, or there. I have to find out where each individual is. The only assumption you can make is that the way to the Most High is open and available to you at all times. But you cannot assume you are already there.

Some expectations or assumptions are good to have. For example, it can be helpful to assume that you can and will clear your karma. But then you must put great intensity into the effort to do so. You must also keep your reflections going, because your efforts and your reflections have to go hand in hand. You have to acknowledge what you are and what you are doing. You have to acknowledge your mistakes (at least to yourself), and then you have to correct them. If you do all this, you can have some hope that the Divine will say, "I am here. I am standing behind you. I am walking at your side."

You have to understand that the power of choice is yours. You have to understand, also, that there is tremendous power in choice, whether you make the right choice or the wrong choice, so be careful.

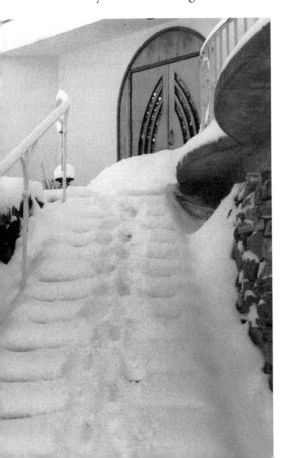

Many aspirants have the naive belief that all will be well on the spiritual path if they just do the work they are told to do, even if they don't really want to do it. That attitude is not sufficient. Your service to the Divine has to come from the heart. You have to give it your all and it has to be selfless. That is often not easy. The pearl of Higher Consciousness is a pearl of great price. Do not ever assume that you can have it for nothing, or for very little effort, when you are overloaded with karma caused by vanity, pride, selfishness, or self-importance.

Look at all your personality aspects, count them, and examine them.

You may find you have a great many that need to be eradicated with the help of your practice before you can have any expectations about Higher Consciousness.

One of these aspects may be criticalness. Find out where your criticalness is. Find out what you do with it, and where you join criticalness to judgment. You must overcome criticalness, because you cannot have the pearl of Higher Consciousness unless there is great sincerity in your directed self-will to forgive. There is no forgiveness for you if you won't forgive others. In the New Testament, Jesus said people have to forgive seventy times seven. That is a lot of forgiveness, but you can't want forgiveness for yourself and still be highly critical of everybody else.

Spiritual life cannot be lived in naivete. You have to grow up. If there is a little boy in the man, or a little girl in the woman, who throws tantrums, that immature part has to grow up. There are no exceptions; everyone has something of that nature within. Try to become aware of that aspect, and be ruthless when it throws tantrums. A large part of this immature aspect is the ego, which wants to have its own way. Destroy that ego. Destroy vanity. Destroy pride.

How do you destroy ego? Don't fight it. If you fight it, matters will only become worse. What you *can* do is subdue it. You can command it: "Out! Don't you dare interfere!" Say that to all the things that go on in the mind. Then immediately either switch to the Mantra or focus on the inner Light. Later you can give time to this aspect in yourself as you would to a child who throws a tantrum. Ask it, "What do you have to say?"

I used to do that with the children when I lived with a family. When the little boy screamed, I would say, "I can't understand what you are saying." When he stopped screaming to take a breath, I would say, "Talk normally, now. Tell me what you want."

Finally he would say, "I want a cookie."

Then I would say, "Now I can hear you. You can have your cookie after you have had your dinner. Here's the cookie, but you eat it after dinner."

That part of you which throws tantrums must not be allowed to make demands or to command your actions. You can say to it, "Yes, here's your cookie, *but* you eat it after dinner." Make sure you carry this out. That immature aspect in yourself will do everything it can to manipulate you, just like a person having a tantrum. Don't be moved by its tears. In this way, you can finally get rid of those interfering personality aspects and then you will begin to focus on that inner Light that is your true being. Make the choice to give power to that spiritual aspect which brings you to the spiritual path. Then that spiritual being, your Higher Self, will have control over the part which tries to throw tantrums.

You can do the same thing with other personality aspects. When a particular one comes to the foreground, ask yourself, "If this were a person, how would I deal with him or her? What would I say to this person?" If you try to comfort and cuddle or soft-pedal that aspect in yourself, you are refusing to deal with that which wants to destroy your spiritual life.

Sincerity is essential to success on the spiritual path. Acting spiritual isn't enough. I once knew a minister who for twenty-five or thirty years had given a sermon every Sunday in which he said wonderful things. His congregation always told him how much they enjoyed his sermons, how inspiring they were. One day he had a very bad heart attack. He was told that he had escaped death by a hair. That made him think, and he came to the understanding that *he* was not inspired. He didn't believe what he was saying in those wonderful sermons. He bathed in his success as a good speaker every Sunday in church, and that was as far as it went. It was tragic for him to realize that all those years were lost.

You cannot merely act spiritual. It is not good enough just to give a performance. However, there are moments in life where you may not be able to escape doing that, because you can't just say, "Look, don't bother me. Today I can't be real. I would only be putting on an act." For the sake of the person who comes to you for help, you may have to put on an act. But afterwards put that individual into the Light, and say, "I had nothing to give. All I could do was put on an act for that person's sake. The Light has to add the blessings because I had nothing else to give."

I have often had to confront this. There have been many times when I have wanted to give someone my time and attention and some comfort, but it wasn't a true giving. I was just thinking, "When will this be over? I have something else to do." This is a very human reaction, and you have to accept your human side. When you become aware that this has happened, turn to the Light and say, "May the Light do what I was incapable of doing." Be honest with the Divine, and put the person in the Light. In that way, you admit your shortcoming. This will prevent you from getting caught in putting on an act, as that minister did.

You can also put the other person in the Light whenever you give advice. You cannot always know if your advice is the right thing. You may be quite sure that you did your best, but *did* you? We often know very little about ourselves in the moment, so ask for the blessing of the Light.

To break resistance by the ego forces, a dramatic event may be needed. The personality forces of the ego block off any insight that may truly come from the Divine. The dramatic event, however, *forces* the doors open. Live or die, spiritually speaking.

Take into your heart that which comes to you through dramatic incidents, because the intellect, with all its capabilities, has its limit. You may have heard the saying: When you meet the Buddha on the highway, kill him. That's because what you are meeting is only your intellectual concept of the Buddha. However, with the Divine Light Invocation you don't need to kill the image of the Buddha or Divine Mother or whatever image of the Divine you prefer. You can put the image into the Light, and in due time you will see the image dissolve into Light—this I promise you. It will disappear in an incredibly beautiful star of light. You will never forget it.

When it is over and you're through being overawed, you may think you have lost the experience and that you no longer have any feelings. But this is not what has happened. You have just moved out of your greedy emotional responses and now you have true feelings.

When you are in a state of egocentricity, you are in a state of ignorance. Intellectually you may know everything you need to know, yet that immature part in you insists on not understanding, on being innocent, on not knowing. That false innocence has to be eradicated. Otherwise, you are trying to climb the ladder of yoga without making one move upward. You are only gathering a lot of stones around you, each one symbolic of your intellectual concepts. No true action is occurring.

Make your spiritual practice come from the heart. Create your own little ritual for residing in the cave of your heart. Put something precious there. Put the flowers of your devotion there. Turn your aspirations symbolically into flowers. Worship there. Kindle the Light. Express your feelings in a most positive way. Let your feelings turn into a longing for the Divine. Don't let your intellect get the better of you. The intellect is like a thief in the night. When it sees it has been discovered and has no place to hide, then it can go on a rampage. It's like an angry elephant that will trample everything under its feet.

If you leave the spiritual path, it is *very* hard to start again. Even if you were doing only a formal practice, not one from the heart, it's difficult to start again. Some people maintain that you can never start again. That is not true, but it is ten times as difficult.

The choice you make is your responsibility. But you *have* the power of choice. Write that somewhere in your daily diary where you can see it when you open the book, perhaps at the top of every page, so you won't forget. If you let that inner Light, your true inner spiritual being, make the choice, you will never make much of a mistake. Perhaps you won't be very effective or skillful, but you won't go wrong if you put the power there. But if you give the power to the ego, it's a lost battle, and nobody can help you.

All the talking and thinking in the world will do nothing. The only solution is to turn a hundred and eighty degrees to the Divine. Talking and thinking can achieve only one thing: you may talk or think so much that you have nothing more to say, and you may realize suddenly that you are just going in circles. If you stop talking or thinking, you may get what I call a divine insight.

A surgeon I knew once told me about an operation he had to do. He said there was not enough tissue to do this operation and he didn't know what to do. "I thought of this possibility or that possibility. I thought of everything," he said. "Finally I just couldn't think anymore, so I went to the cafeteria for a cup of coffee and I had to admit I could not think of anything to do. And then—insight came!" I have since heard similar stories from other doctors. In a sense, talking and thinking can exhaust you, tire you out, and when you are tired enough, suddenly a flash comes. Instead of talking and thinking, take things into your heart.

If you make a promise to the Divine, be *ruthless, force* yourself to fulfill that promise. Use all your willpower, all your stubbornness, if you can't do it any other way. The repercussions of not fulfilling a promise to the Divine could be very serious. Because you have broken your word, your promises might never be believed again. This could be for many lifetimes. I wouldn't take any chance like that. I wouldn't even try to find out what would happen.

You know how you feel if somebody promises something of im-

portance to you and lets you down. Realize that with an unfulfilled promise to the Divine, you let the Divine down, and that creates huge karma. It's hard to estimate how many lifetimes that might cost you. If becoming a sanyasi can be a blessing for twenty-one generations before the birth of the sanyasi, and twenty-one generations afterwards, can you imagine what it would mean to break that promise?

Gurudev used to tell the story of the merchant who promised the Guru a carpet, but the carpet never arrived. After some time, the Guru sent a disciple to remind the merchant.

The merchant said, "Oh, thank you, thank you for reminding me. I shall give you a carpet twice as big and twice as thick."

The disciple was angry because now he had a heavier load to carry home.

He said, "Funny, the Guru tells us we should be renunciates, and here he is sending me after a carpet."

When he arrived back, he threw the carpet on the ground, and said, "There's your carpet!"

The Guru said to him, "What's your problem?"

The disciple said, "Well, you teach us renunciation, but here you are running after this carpet."

The Guru said, "The merchant had broken a promise. Would you rather see him develop some very bad karma?"

Each time you let somebody down by breaking a promise, you create a greater distance between you and that person. Finally that person won't pay any attention to your promises any more, because there is an expectation they won't be kept. Then the distance between you becomes very great. If you break a promise to the Divine, you will create distance between you and the Divine and that distance will be much more serious. Can you bridge that distance ever again in this life, if you even come to the understanding of it? You can, but it takes ten times the effort.

To make a promise to a Guru who has dedicated his or her entire life to the service of the Divine is the same as breaking a promise to God. I wouldn't even dream of doing anything like that. My curiosity doesn't go far enough to want to know what would happen then.

Every time we give in to our negative characteristics, our negative aspects, we sacrifice the spiritual. If you sacrifice your spiritual life for the gratification of pride and ego, that is a very poor choice. Even the possession of the greatest intellect cannot rescue you. But there is something anchored in the depths of the human mind that says, "You must atone." So if you hear that voice and you realize you have made a wrong choice, hurry, hurry back. If it means crawling back like a worm to the place of the holiest, do it.

Sacrifice ego, pride, and vanity. Don't sacrifice the spiritual Light, for then you will live in darkness. Keep the Light burning. Protect the sacred flame in your heart.

Sacrifice with Discrimination

THE BHAGAVAD GITA SPEAKS OF SACRIFICE to the gods, but which gods? The Gita says that often it's just the gods of our attachments that we worship.

What is it specifically that you are attached to, and that you worship in an almost godlike manner? Some people worship the god of wealth. They want lots of money, lots of financial security. Others worship the god of beauty. They want only good-looking people around. Others worship love. Still others worship sex. Some worship acceptance by other people.

People may say to someone on the yogic path, "Well, all that worship you people do, that's really beneath my dignity." But they worship movie stars, rock singers, and hockey players, all people who have attained a specific kind of success. Many a woman is worshipped only for her sex appeal. This worship arises from the competition between men. One says, "I can afford her. You can't. She's too expensive for you." All these things need to be looked at very clearly.

You may also worship your own self-gratification, your own vanity, self-indulgence, and self-importance. These are also gods. The Tibetans call them demons and dragons.

If you are worshipping your own personal attachments, you are worshipping the wrong gods. If you are worshipping the wrong gods, you don't have any understanding of what is worthy of being worshipped.

When we worship these gods, what is it that we sacrifice? Arjuna is told the gods must be offered sacrifice.* In order to worship your gods of attachment, you sacrifice the Most High in yourself. You sacrifice the best in yourself. How many people sacrifice the best in themselves for personal security, when security can be found only with the Most High?

There are some people who make sacrifices in order to pursue a very rigid program. The rigidity is what they are attached to. A rigid program should be pursued only to establish discipline, because through discipline we can overcome our selfish characteristics. In other words,

---

* Bhagavad Gita, Eighteenth Discourse, verse 5.

we can slay the false gods that we worship. Rigidity should not be practiced as an offering to the Divine. The Divine doesn't need that.

We can also practice austerity for the wrong motive. "See how much you need, but *I* can sleep on a board, and in the snow, and on the roof." Or, "I need only one blanket, one set of clothes. See how great, how austere, I am?" Austerity has to be practiced simply to know how deep-rooted our desires are, how much we want, and how much time and energy we give to the fulfillment of these desires. But if you can be satisfied with what you have, without making a big show of it, then all the energy that goes into scheming and the fulfilling of desires is available for spiritual practice.

If you have ego involved in your sacrifices, you will be making sacrifices to gratify your pride and to compete with others. In India, there have been people who have held up one of their arms for weeks and months until it finally withered away. Where is the sacrifice in that? There were people who came to Sivananda Ashram on silence and wouldn't talk. One was a wonderfully talented veena player. He would not talk, but he would chant. He would not give you a single answer. He would just strike a few chords of a raga on the veena. This might have been a very accurate answer from his point of view, because he knew some four or five hundred ragas, but other people did not have this knowledge.

People can sacrifice the voice just so they can claim that for so many years they have not spoken a single word to anybody. This is again saying, "See how great I am?" A young woman, who was a disciple of another Guru, came to Sivananda Ashram. She had by this time practiced three or four years of silence.

Gurudev said, "Say the Lord's name."

She wouldn't.

Every day when she came to the office or to satsang, he said to her, "Say the Lord's name."

Finally she broke down in tears because she was in such conflict.

He said, "Observing mauna—silence—means not chattering with people. It never means that you should sacrifice your God-given voice."

From then on she chanted every night in satsang, but she kept her vow of mauna.

Sometimes very fine discrimination is needed. Mauna doesn't mean not using your voice at all. It refers to your need to communicate. We make such a big deal in North America about self-expression: "Everything I feel must be expressed. What I think must be expressed. What I like must be expressed." You can become so absorbed with yourself, there is no time even for developing and cultivating spiritual feelings, spiritual words, chanting. Krishna says in the Fourth Discourse of the Bhagavad Gita that some people sacrifice, or offer, the senses. Knowing that sense perception is not reliable anyhow, give it back to the Divine. You can offer your sense of hearing when you discover that you are listening to your own voice and are enchanted with hearing yourself talk. Offer that. When you chant a Mantra, offer that. Then at least you can break the habit of being entranced with the sound of your voice. Our self-importance has become such a weed that we can barely cultivate a spiritual flower in our mental garden. There is a great need for the higher mind to be in control.

But the practice of yoga will not keep you kindled always. The practices alone are not enough. You have to study and acquire knowledge of their true meaning and purpose. The young woman did not know the true meaning of mauna. Lacking this knowledge, she had given up the human voice entirely and did not speak at all. However, she may have been having lots of mental conversations caused by the psychological pressure of not talking. Chanting Mantra, then, gave her a means of expression to return all her feelings to the Divine. Nobody else can help you with your emotions. Other people have enough to do with handling their own. But emotions that cannot be handled shouldn't be swept under the carpet. Put them into the Mantra and give them back to the Divine. By giving them back, you are asking the Divine for help to deal with them.

You have to have the right attitude before you make sacrifices, or they are not offerings at all. Several people have had great plans about what they wanted to do for the Ashram. Some said they would make money with a rock group. First they would finance the rock group, and then the profits would go into building the Ashram's guest lodge. Other people were going to make money on the stock market and turn those profits over to the building of the Temple. Nothing ever came of these plans.

This is a lazy way out. You make apparent promises to make yourself feel good, knowing very well that if the money doesn't come (and it's always "hundreds of thousands of dollars") you can say, "It's just too bad. I couldn't help it. You see?" But the money that went into the stock market or that went to finance the rock group would have been perfectly sufficient. I could have built two temples with that.

What, then, can we offer? In the beginning, what we give is a sacrifice as we mean it in the West. We mean giving up something we did not want to give up. This is very different from the way the term sacrifice is used in the East where it means an offering. The Bhagavad Gita says, "Whosoever wants to be liberated from the miseries of this world must understand the real nature of renunciation. Acts of sacrifice, gifts, austerities, should not be abandoned, but should be performed. Sacrifice, gifts, and also austerities, are the purifiers of the wise."* The Gita gives many, many approaches to sacrifice so that we can learn to focus on the Divine, and only on the Divine, by whatever name. If you read the Fourth Discourse of the Gita, you will find many more ideas.

But we can use the Western meaning, too, as a reminder to our self-will and emotions that they cannot have their own way, that they will have to give up all the things they want. When you begin to practice sacrifice, you will see that the emotions don't want to go along, and a few of your personality aspects will constantly rebel. They don't want to give up what they have.

It's not the Divine who needs sacrifice. It is you. You have to strip yourself of your desires, of the impact of your senses. The Eighteenth Discourse of the Gita, which deals with renunciation, was the one that I worked with mostly in my meditation and my reflection. I received a copy when I was in India in 1956. It has pretty much fallen apart, but that tells you it has been used. It has not sat on the shelf. Read your own copy of the Gita, and use your own thoughts to help you think more deeply.

---

* Bhagavad Gita, Eighteenth Discourse, verse 5, and commentary to verse 4.

If you want to offer your life, do not do so because you have a martyr complex. If you are acting on a martyr complex, you are not giving anything. It is only a compulsive action of the ego to glorify itself: "See how much I have done?" If you play that game with the Divine, you are a loser right then and there. That becomes sin. So be very careful.

If you want to sacrifice, do your service in honor of the Most High. And be very clear on that. Remind yourself that is what you want to do. Write it in your diary every now and then. Reflect on your diary and find out whether you really did your service in honor of the Most High. Then you will have no regrets. Then it doesn't make any difference whether someone says your work was wonderful. You only have to know whether it was a true offering.

If you reflect daily and deal with all these things on a deeper level, not just skimming the surface, one day you will find yourself in meditation. There will be no struggle to keep your mind still because the garbage which has kept the Divine out will have been cleared away by your efforts.

Sacrificing Attachment

HUMAN BEINGS HAVE A DUTY to dispel ignorance by learning, by studying, by thinking in depth, by investigating, and by doing spiritual practice and keeping a daily diary. By reviewing your diary you can find out whether your ignorance is being removed and you are growing in wisdom. If your daily journal shows that, then you know you have been following a path with a solid foundation, one you would do well to continue following throughout your life.

Ignorance is one side of a coin and egoism is the other. They go hand in hand. Ignorance can be overcome by learning. But egoism is overcome only by offering what you have, that to which you are most strongly attached. This can be your spouse, your children, your job, your intellect. Whatever it is, that is what has to be offered to the Divine. You are only a caretaker for these, anyway. They have been given to you as temporary assignments. The real work is done by your Divine Committee. And it's not so easy to tune into that unless you really want to and put a great deal of effort into it.

There are so many things we can be attached to. We can be attached to smoking, and we can be attached to not smoking. We can be attached to the idea of sanyas, and we can be attached to the idea of remaining just where we are.

We can be so attached to things that really they possess us. Back in Germany I had a lot of very valuable antiques. I had to take great care of them. They had to be cleaned with special little brushes that could get into the fine carvings without scratching them. I didn't realize then that my antiques possessed me. It was only after I lost them that I could see how free I was without them.

We can be attached to people, too. A wife, for example, can be like a piece of property which is possessed, guarded, protected, and kept within limits, so nobody else can have it. Life shows us what attachment does when we want to put someone into a straightjacket. Trust, love, and affection do not grow if we try to possess and limit another person. An undue attachment should be replaced by true concern.

Concern is something quite different. It is not limiting. You can be concerned for all and everyone who needs your concern. True concern can also lead to a non-possessive love. To be non-attached does not mean to be separated. It means to be aware of where the attachment is, how strong it is, and how you can rise above it. You can love without possessing the other person, and you can possess things without an attachment to them.

If you can walk away from fame and self-importance, then you can be pretty sure that your attachment is small or nonexistent. My Guru said that the fault or the defect of karma is not certainly in the karma itself, but in the expectation of the fruit and the attachment.

Yoga teachers often have deep attachment to their work. They have to ask themselves, "Can I let it go? Can I do something else?" Time away from their teaching is often necessary. It's like taking a sabbatical to do research—they need to take a sabbatical to do some more work on themselves.

After wearing the orange robe for seven years, I thought it was time to take the robe off, so that in my own mind I would not be linked to the teachings through the robe. I should be able to do the work with the same conviction, without the robe as a protection for myself or as something that marked me as being different from other people.

At another time I asked myself, "Can I walk out of the Ashram?" I had lots of emotional investment there and years of work. But if you offer all that investment and work, and consider yourself—man or woman—to be just a handmaiden of Divine Mother, there is very little chance you will attach yourself to the results.

Sometimes we have to learn to renounce our deep desires the hard way. We get knocked on the head to make us wake up and think. We get catapulted out of comfort and attachment to make us think. But if you cooperate with the course of your own evolution by doing your daily reflection to find out where your attachments are, you won't need to get hard knocks. Instead of being sad, disappointed, and hurt, it is better to accept the challenge to give up your attachments. Look at each challenge and say, "Well, here's my opportunity now. Can I do it? I think I can." Do it. Do not hesitate to sacrifice anything you are holding on to in the mistaken belief that it is what keeps you secure.

Getting rid of attachments is really no sacrifice. It is what sets you free. Give with joy whatever must be sacrificed, because when you can function from your heart rather than your mind, you have a place in the heart of the Divine.

Swami Radha in the early days in the Beach Prayer Room

Greed

For the first sixteen years, I did most of the cooking at the Ashram. I learned a great deal by doing that. I learned how people project their self-criticism, their dissatisfaction with their own development, into food and eating. Very often people who are overweight are projecting their unhappiness into their food. If something isn't going their way, they go to the fridge and say, "I will treat myself. Nobody likes me. Nobody treats me well. I will give myself a treat," and so they eat a whole cake, a whole pudding, a whole container of ice cream. This is a projection of dissatisfaction in oneself. I learned that by observation.

In the early days, when the Ashram was in Vancouver and we had very little money, I made a pudding with cream of wheat and milk. I served some strawberries with it, and that was our dinner. It was not an expensive meal, but someone criticized me for spending an unreasonable amount of money on the strawberries. Someone else raved at me because he thought the meal was too rich. "How can you do this! The people here are trying to practice brahmacharya, and here you are feeding them all this rich stuff."

I said, "Brahmacharya starts in the mind, not in the stomach."

Another time, there was a woman who had followed Ouspensky's teachings. Ouspensky was a very strict disciplinarian, and this woman was very strict about the amount of food she ate and very critical of what she thought was excess in others. She thought what I was serving was an absolutely unnecessary luxury. But discipline is not achieved by giving people more or less to eat. Discipline is shown in how much you eat, or in whether you eat slowly or just shovel it all down. Discipline is in your choice to eat good food, not just cater to the taste.

And some people are very picky. They stand over the food and they say, "What's this? Hmm. I'll try a little of this, some of that." If they were this picky about what is going on in their lives, great! But it's so much easier to project it into food.

I also learned a lot about greediness in my years in the kitchen. I saw people who just loaded their plates and dribbled food all along the floor, with no concern for whether there would be enough for everybody. The mentality of stuffing oneself with no regard for anybody else is quite remarkable. People did this even in the days when we had very little money. So when people who work in the kitchen say to me, "I'm only in the kitchen," I tell them, "You will learn more about people in the kitchen than you can learn anywhere else. I could write ten books from my experience of being *only* in the kitchen, and I could create at least two workshops on just the psychology of eating and choosing your food."

Some very difficult people have come to the Ashram. One was a person who really shoveled everything down. There was also a couple who were very indulgent, loading up their plates, and then in the end throwing half of it in the garbage. They wasted a lot of food. But they talked in big words about how much more spiritual they were because they were one hundred percent vegetarians. They wouldn't eat an egg, they wouldn't even drink milk.

Finally, in a meeting with the residents of the Ashram, I said, "How will we get it across that one has to eat with reverence for the food, because whatever we eat had life, too?"

Then I thought, and I said, "We have to have somebody serve the food to make sure everybody gets something. Then if there's anything left, these people can have a second and sometimes even a third helping."

It isn't only the expense. It sometimes takes two people three hours just to wash the lettuce when it comes from the garden. People work very hard to get the vegetables clean because we don't have big machinery like fast food restaurants. Here lettuce has to be washed one leaf after another by hand. Then it goes into the garbage can, with a big hullabaloo: "I'm vegetarian!"

You have to have reverence for life everywhere. Just because you can't hear the nuts and seeds that you grind with your teeth screaming at you, it doesn't mean that you aren't killing life. Every time you eat, you kill a form of life. If you can say thank you to the plant for giving you its life and nourishing your body, and if you are nourishing your body because you want to serve the Most High and find God-Realization, then you are justifying your life and how you stay alive. But otherwise, there's no point.

When you want your body to be healthy for the worship of the

Most High, you spiritualize your food and then you don't need a lot of it. Spiritualize everything. When there is too much clatter and talk at meals, your mind is not on the life that is on your plate to nourish your body. Certainly some food can go to the compost heap, but there is *no* excuse to throw good food away.

Gratitude begins right there. Every day that you wake up, be grateful that you are alive because there is no guarantee that you will wake up tomorrow. You take it for granted. You don't even think about it. But there is nothing that anybody can take for granted.

At the Sivananda Ashram in Rishikesh, there were people who went on long, long fasts. One of them was critical. Nothing pleased him. Sivananda asked him, "How many days did you fast?"

The man said, "Nine days."

Gurudev said, "Wonderful. How many more days do you want to fast?"

"Oh, maybe another ten days."

"Wonderful," Sivananda said, "But you should fast the mind instead. Then you wouldn't say such bad things."

He was very often much to the point.

Renunciation

PURIFICATION LIES IN THE ACT of renunciation, in giving up your desires. In renunciation, you purify your mind and your emotions, you remove greed and attachments. When all that is gone, you are ready to receive what the Divine has to give.

When I was in India at Sivananda Ashram, Gurudev gave me this advice: "In the beginning, renounce what is easy to renounce. It's easy to give something away to somebody who admires it."

I had a gold locket on a chain which was very much admired by a European woman who was there. She would ask me to open it and show her the pictures in it.

Gurudev said, "Why don't you give it to her?"

I pondered this for about a week. It was something that had been in my family a long time. Did I have the right to give it away?

Finally I decided, "Well, if they wanted to keep it in the family, they should not have given it to me!" So I gave it to her. I could see by the way she wore it and handled it—always patting it—that she was very happy with it.

I met this woman again many years later. She still had the locket, and she asked if I wanted it back. I said no, because it had been given in a spirit of renunciation. It was my very first act of renunciation.

When you start to renounce, that's the best way to do it—if somebody admires something, give it away. Something else will come.

Renunciation of things is very easy. It may not always feel that way to you, but it is, because things can always be acquired again. It's just a matter of time and effort.

To renounce your cherished beliefs, something that you hold dear, something by which you have survived, that's much more difficult. But at some time, you will have to do this. You will have to renounce even those things you have used for survival on the spiritual path.

You have to listen with the heart, not with the mind. You can follow the Divine will only if that surrender is there. And it isn't easy. You may be asked to surrender your deepest desires. Perhaps you would like to have just a slice of the bread of life—I'm not talking about cake, just plain bread of life—but you may be asked to give all that up even though you may have barely tasted life. I gave up my career, but looking back today I don't consider that a loss in any way.

Don't think about what you have sacrificed, because if it was true sacrifice it will come back a hundred times. All the things that I have given away—my jewelry just to mention one thing—have come back. Don't have any fear that you will lose. You are given much more than you ever give. And the things that you have given are only big in your eyes as long as you are ignorant. At some time in your life, you will look back and feel that what you gave was not really all that much, not such a big deal. It was the degree of your attachment that made it look like a big deal, and that attachment didn't give you any blessings in return. Attachment never does. Shift your attachment to the spiritual. Shift your attachment to an aspect of the Divine. That's where your blessings are.

You cannot give to the Divine, and then say, "I didn't understand what I was saying." Marpa said to Milarepa, "You gave me your life. You can't take it back now."* Don't say it if you don't understand it. But if you say it in spite of yourself, you can be sure it didn't come from the monkey mind. It came from some other, deeper source in yourself where the Divine was speaking and pushing it to the surface.

Many of you have not had to renounce much in this lifetime. The Gita explains this by saying that at some time the positive karma we have accumulated will be available to support us in another life. It is very important for those of you who have not suffered terribly in this lifetime to remember this. Let it be a warning. Do willingly, and surrender willingly whatever your hidden desires are (human hearts have a lot of desires), and then take it from there. Don't play with your destiny. Don't waste this opportunity just because this life seems so easy. You never know when you'll get another opportunity.

Also, you cannot know what test you may have to face. If you are not aware every moment, the test may come and you may fail without realizing it. And whom do you fail? You fail the Divine, and then you must make double and triple the effort to regain the opportunity you gave away.

When you begin renunciation, don't make too many conditions. Don't say, "First this should happen, then that should happen, and then I might consider it, and then I will weigh it again. I want to be absolutely certain that I am doing the right thing." Look at other aspects of life, such as choosing a profession. How do you know it's the right thing? How do you know you will do the job for the rest of your life? Or getting married. How do you know you will not grow apart? Or having a family. Where is the security in getting pregnant? Do you know that your baby will be healthy? You have no guarantees anywhere. Excuses and conditions are just your way of delaying action. And all those delays will require you to put in twice or three times as much effort as you would have had to do at the beginning.

Look at your excuses in the right light, and then see what you have to do. And when you have done it, don't take it back. Once you have

---

* Evans-Wentz (ed.), *Tibet's Great Yogi Milarepa*, chapter 5.

given yourself, you cannot take it back. You may think you are not strong enough. How do you know? Sometimes you just need to wait a little longer until you grow stronger and pray a little harder to get that strength. You are ready any time you really give your heart.

When I went to India, I had to quit my job in Montreal. My boss called me into his office and said, "Mrs. Hellman, by the time you come back you will be forty-five. I can't re-employ you."

I said to him, "I remember you told me that you are the treasurer of your church, but can you be sure as long as you have even a hundred dollars in your bank account, and as long as you have a job, can you be sure that you *really* want God?"

He looked at me for some time, and then he said, "I understand."

Beach Prayer Room. The adjoining cabin was one of Swami Radha's early residences.

Commitment

PRACTICALLY SPEAKING there is no life that does not include commitment in one way or another, though we may sometimes violate or even break our commitments, such as those to honesty, or kindness, or dependability. And we often don't really know what we are committed to. A man once said to me, "Now you have to understand one thing—when I die, nobody will be able to say I have not been honest." He was committed to that statement, not to honesty.

Commitment begins at birth. As babies we have already committed ourselves to life. The moment we are born, we cry to make sure our parents take care of us. As we proceed through life, we undertake constant commitments. One of them is to keep our bodies healthy. Though you may not think of it as commitment when you look for healthy food instead of junk food, you are showing a commitment to the idea of health.

Friendship is a commitment to our friends. We may sometimes feel so committed to our friends that we do not want to leave a city or country in which a friend resides. As children we often have strong feelings about letting friends down.

Another commitment we make is to learn, to evolve. Some of the commitments to learn are made for us. For example, our parents send us to school to become educated, to learn a trade, to learn to stand on our own two feet. These commitments are the duty of parents who want to see their children survive in a world of competition, controversies, and constant rapidly changing circumstances.

Many people have a commitment to loyalty. Loyalty is a word that has to be included in any investigation of commitment, because without knowing what you want to be loyal to, your commitment will be very shaky. You must clarify your ideals about relationships, about your way of life, and about the purpose of your life, so that you know what you are committing yourself to.

As you take commitment further, you will find there are many different ideas to which your mind is committed. You hold convictions because you are committed to the ideas that led to them.

Even our hopes represent a commitment. Parents have hopes for their children's future. They may commit every ounce of their energy and money to make those hopes manifest, because they are committed to the survival of their offspring. Survival is not just physical survival. The idea of survival may include psychological, spiritual, economic, and social matters.

As you look at some of the things you hope for, however, you may find that your commitment to them is ambiguous. Perhaps you want to belong to an elite group. The members of an elite group put power, time, and energy behind what their group represents.

Perhaps you want to belong to the group but you don't want to put the power, time, and energy into it.

The most common elite group are the wealthy. People who have amassed money are committed to this kind of success, and they give it all their time, efforts, and energy. Friends and family who may want some of that time and energy receive nothing. They are treated instead like objects—put on a shelf when there is no time, and then taken down when there is a need for a little distraction. And what are they like, those successful men at the top in business, in politics, in science? They have single-pointedness of mind. They are completely dedicated to the ruthless pursuit of the goal to which they are one hundred percent committed. They will wipe out of their way everything that hinders their pursuit.

When you enter a relationship, whether it's between friends or between husband and wife, you are only fifty percent committed because you want to see what you'll get before you give any more than that. Then you give a little more, hoping you'll get more. People always want more than they are willing to give. In my Guru's words, you want to receive a cup of coffee and give back only a glass of water.

The questions that must be asked in any relationship are: "What are these two people committed to? What is this relationship based on?" Each is committed to what he or she wants, and those wants must be investigated. A ruthless search may show that the desire for the relationship is based on self-gratification or an impossible dream. We can wear many disguises, and it is difficult to be honest—to meet ourselves at the gut level—but we must look ruthlessly at that gut level to see where our commitment truly is. Of course, there are many gradations. Nobody is *only* selfish or *only* dreaming. But it is important to know where you are on the scale between true commitment and dreaming, or between commitment and selfishness, because your commitment is influenced by where you are on that scale.

Commitment belongs not just in daily life and relationships, but in spiritual life, too. Here, again, we have to go to the gut level. What is your motivation for wanting to lead a spiritual life? What is your hope, your dream? What are your expectations? And what place does commitment have here?

When I look at what goes on in many spiritual groups, what I see is the commitment to a hope that some of the leader's great powers will rub off on the followers. There is also a commitment to the idea of an elite: "At least *I* am not like everybody else. *I* belong to a higher kind of elite, one that is above money." However, there is often very little commitment to the opportunity for development being offered by the teacher.

There have been people who have left the Ashram because they were convinced that they could worship, meditate, and pray anywhere. They had a dream that if they renounced a little bit for a little while at the Ashram, they would reap huge rewards. This is a great mistake that even many quite serious and otherwise well-trained spiritual people make. Indira Devi said that when she had given up family, money, and security, and then expected the Divine to reward her, she little realized that she had only just launched her tiny boat on a large and turbulent spiritual ocean.

Many people have come to the Ashram for the wrong reasons and in many cases that is obvious right from the beginning. All I can do is put them into the Light,* and hope and pray that the true reasons will rub off a little, and that they will finally discover, accept, and nourish those true reasons. Satsang, meetings, classes, and courses at the Ashram are all directed to helping people do that. They pose the questions: Who is going to wake up? Why are you here? I have often let people stay at the Ashram, even if they were not totally committed, in the hope that they would wake up one day, that they might develop at least a little bit of

---

* See Radha, *The Divine Light Invocation.*

selflessness in doing the work here, so that they could pay off some of their karma. But wherever you are, the more selfless your work can be, the better.

We will never be one hundred percent clear about a commitment. That is a naive belief. But we must still attempt to carry it out. I have gone through this myself, saying, "How could Gurudev Sivananda ask so much of me? He should have known that I wouldn't be able to handle it. I know nothing about running an ashram." While this was quite true, it still didn't give me the right just to throw up my commitment and run away.

Criticism does not give you the right to abandon a commitment either. In the early years of the Ashram, I heard much criticism about myself, and I said, "Shall I pack and go? If this is what they think of me, then there is no point in my being here." Sometimes I felt horrified by all the people crowding in on me. I would jump into the car and drive to a park and sit there, saying: "How do I solve all these problems? Why didn't Gurudev know I wasn't cut out for this?" But I never dropped my commitment.

I had to realize that I am not here for anybody else's sake, and that's what you have to know about yourself. You are not here in your life for someone else. I wasn't there for those critical people. If I had gone somewhere else, there would have been *other* people just as critical. I was there because, with all my inadequacy and human frailty, my commitment to the Divine was complete. I was not letting other people dictate to me or persuade me to be a traitor to the Divine.

Never think you are too low, too bad, too weak, or incapable of committing yourself to the Divine. This is just a trick of the monkey mind. The Divine doesn't care about the kind of perfection that we demand in other people. Most of our ideas about perfection come from our upbringing. They are just our preferences about what sort of things we like, what kind of people we get along with better. These have *nothing* to do with spiritual perfection. Never seek perfection for recognition. Seek it only in the service of the Most High.

We all enter situations where something irks us, and for a couple of days we may have all sorts of mental conversation about it. If you can put these insignificant things aside without being disturbed in your peace, your sense of harmony, and your sleep, you will have taken a great step toward conquering yourself. Many of the things which bother us are very insignificant. We give them a big importance from our sense of perfection, but most of the time our idea of perfection is insignificant. It really doesn't matter.

Look at your life sometime from a cosmic view: here is this whole cosmos and there, somewhere, are you. What do these things really matter? Your needs for exaggeration and self-importance are insignificant. You have to learn to step away from yourself and see that, because where will you be if every grain of sand becomes a big issue? And really the events of daily life are only insignificant grains of sand.

All our thoughts, our dreams, our speculations, our opinions, our convictions, and our beliefs really don't amount to much, except in the area of Higher Consciousness. It is your commitment to the Divine that is the important thing. *That* is what gives you your place in the cosmos.

The commitment to your own development cannot be replaced by a commitment to another person, and it cannot be imposed on you by someone else. You have to exercise your own free will about commitment, and then put your will behind that commitment.

You will always have highs and lows in life, and you will have them in your spiritual life. Don't think you will always be riding the crest of the wave. When you do that, spiritual life is easy. But when you are down in a valley and you think the big wave is coming down to crush you, that's when you have to stand up and look at your commitment and remind yourself. Put yourself into the Light. Bring Light into your life and into your dark corners of selfishness and self-importance. What you are committing yourself to is eternal life. The choice to do that is yours.

Good Intentions

WE TAKE FOR GRANTED that we will wake up tomorrow and the day after tomorrow, and a month from now, and six months from now; and we don't question ourselves to get an understanding of that which we take for granted. That is a fact that needs to be investigated.

In order to decide what you want to do with the time that lies before you, you have to find out what you have done with the time you have already had. If you set out to accomplish something, did you do it? If not, that should go right to the top of your list.

We can plan the future only on the basis of the past because the present moment is too short for us to grasp unless we really still the mind—really think about it. We live much of the time in a foggy existence where we are not clear about the purpose of what we are doing. We *think* we know. Many people think they already know the purpose of their own life, and so they think they can put this question to others. But how often do they truly remember what the purpose of their life is? We live in constant forgetfulness.

Good intentions to learn this thing and do that thing and think about some other thing are not enough. It's like setting up a new law—unless you enforce that law, you don't get anywhere. In spiritual life, you have to set up and enforce Divine Law in yourself, so that you become both the lawgiver and the law-enforcer. If you don't enforce that Divine Law, nothing changes. You can have many laws on the books, but if they are not enforced, life goes on as if they did not exist. Nothing happens.

With human law, we get away with a lot of things. But with Divine Law, there is no way you can get away with anything. The evidence of this is not just in the Eastern teaching; the evidence is also in the Christian teachings. Jesus said to forgive everybody seventy times seven, because we remember so well those things we don't want to forgive, and we hang on so tightly to them.* Our good intentions to be forgiving come to nothing because we do not think things through—we don't try

---

* Matthew 18:22.

to understand. You cannot forgive without understanding the forces behind the actions you find unforgivable. Yet, you want to have all the understanding possible for the things you do, especially the ones you don't take fully conscious responsibility for.

I have initiated many people who had great enthusiasm because they were thinking, "Wonderful, wonderful. Now I don't have to do anything anymore. I can sit back and things will be done for me." That is not so. In fact, sometimes karma can speed up very fast after an initiation, much faster than under normal circumstances. If you don't have the right attitude, the right relationship and the trust, you should not toy around even in your mind with ideas of initiation. Clarify. Put yourself in my shoes. Whom would you initiate? What would be the conditions under which *you* would initiate somebody and how much of the responsibility that goes with it are you willing to carry? Anyone who has already been initiated should think about that also.

We can be very generous with gifts, with things, with money, but we can be very picky when it comes to finding little bits of criticism of the Guru. If you are in that frame of mind, you had better drop the whole idea of asking for initiation. It will do you only harm. We all have our struggles, we have the best intentions of being the best disciple in the world; but, again, if we don't reinforce that, nothing comes of it. Nothing happens. You have to understand that. You can have very good seeds, but if you put them in poor ground they will not even take root and no shoots will ever come up because they are not nourished. If you put your spiritual seed in poor ground, it is exposed to all sorts of things like competition and envy: I'm bigger, you have been initiated longer, I'm first. These things do not belong in your spiritual life.

What happens to all our good intentions? We must carry them through and not stop short. When you start some work, you finish it because you want to see the finished product. If you go to university, you want to get a degree, and even if you don't pass every course, you carry through until you do. Then if you want to go on further, you may have to find a different university which is more specialized and meets your needs better, but you still carry through.

On the spiritual path, things are pretty much the same. You have to find where your needs are met. And you have to find out what kind of needs you want met. Needs for emotional satisfaction? No. Because as long as we are busy scheming all sorts of gratification and plans to satisfy these emotions, we are focused absolutely on the wrong thing. Your experiences in daily life show you that when you are really focused on something, you can reach a good deep level of concentration that will get you to the result you want, whether you are writing a letter, fixing a car, or figuring out accounts. It is the same if you want to achieve Higher Consciousness and greater awareness. Even if the idea of this is somewhat murky or cloudy in your mind, you must be really focused on that achievement.

You cannot run away forever from the purpose of your existence, because this slows down your own evolution and extends it tremendously. Lots of people have good intentions about being on the spiritual path. They talk about it and tell about all the wonderful things they do, but unless they have changed in those aspects of their characters that are undesirable, inharmonious, or destructive, all the talk is only self-gratification. Nothing is going to happen.

I remember Gurudev saying one day about somebody, "Well, it might take another two thousand years."

I said, "What do you mean, two thousand years? Do you just want to shock him into doing something?"

He said, "There is no guarantee that we will be reborn in a few weeks or months. And if we think we can bring only the best with us and leave all the negative things behind, the chance to have a favorable life for the achievement of Higher Consciousness may not come back for two thousand years."

Many religions speak of hell. Hell can be life on earth. You can make your life harmonious or you can exercise your self-will and bully everybody. And there are some people who say, "I want to put it all together, to make myself whole. I want to bring peace." That prayer alone, even if you say it at five o'clock in the morning, is not sufficient to make changes if you don't try every day of your life to make that peace with another person. You have to make the effort that says you are finished with some of the old events in your life. These events have given a certain richness of experience to your life, not necessarily always pleasant. Yet even the negative experiences are blessings in disguise—something you have to see, to know about it, and to learn from.

Make a list of your intentions, but remember—the list only brings them clearly before you. This list is like all the papers that many of you have done over the years in Kundalini class—if changes don't come from your insights, the paper or the list is worth nothing. Such a list can even be inverted ego: "See how great I am. I can admit my worst faults." But if you are not prepared to do anything about them, what good is the list?

I have emphasized over the years that we must carry out at least one practice, and that is the reflection on what has taken place in the day. If you've lost your temper again, you can decide that tomorrow will be a different day, tomorrow you will have more control. Or if you throw everything down and become very negative, you can still say, "Gee, I missed today, but I'm not going to miss tomorrow." Things will improve and then some day you will be able say, "Well, I nearly slipped, but I have become a little bit more aware."

The evolution of consciousness does not depend on all the good things you do. You can give everything away, but if you are then very proud that you did it, that pride nullifies your actions. The good intention of renouncing, of being generous, is not sufficient if it doesn't go with a certain depth of feeling. Evolution of consciousness comes only when you use the challenges that daily life brings you in the circumstances in which you find yourself, and when you do something in a positive manner to meet those challenges. Then you will be able to conquer yourself and come to a point where you can say, "This man or this woman has made my life so difficult with all sorts of rejections and unjust criticism, but now finally I can go to this person and say, 'Thank you'." The divine messenger is not just the person who gives you a lovely gift, but also the one who tells you very truthfully where you are. You need to know that, and the person who tells you was chosen to do this by what I call your Divine Committee.

Sometimes people think they cannot take the criticism and they want to leave the Ashram. My Guru said to someone who wanted to leave, "Okay, if you want to go, go, but realize God gives you a hand only once in a lifetime. There's no coming back a second time." That has to be remembered. The ego and the world with all its manifestation, all its maya, are very, very powerful. I formed a little prayer about maya once: "Maya, maya, Om Namah Sivaya!" Let Siva destroy the maya because sometimes we don't even see what it is or what's about to happen.

So think about your intentions—good intentions, bad intentions. What are you doing about them?

What have you accomplished in the past year? What is left undone? Take just two or three things that you want to deal with. If you take too big a mouthful, you may have trouble swallowing it all down. Look at the intentions that are not yet implemented. How can you go about implementing them? Can you use some good insights from the past? What is helpful?

Look also at the intentions you have fulfilled. You should never just look at the negative side. See also what you have accomplished, and where your good intentions gave you enough impetus to put things into action, and then reinforce that.

Spiritual Capital

IF YOU HAVE BEEN PURSUING yoga for some time, you can be assured that you made a start on this in some past life. Then perhaps you made mistakes, or weren't serious enough, or didn't make deep enough inquiries about the purpose of life or about what kind of person you wanted to be. So your experience of yoga went into the recesses of your consciousness until such time as there was enough positive karma accumulated for you to have real benefit from it. Some people slip into spiritual life and seem to be able to do it easily because spiritual capital has already been accumulated in many other lifetimes.

In today's language, I would explain it this way: if you save money and put it into your bank account, only when you have sufficient money saved can you live on the interest. In this life you are putting spiritual capital into your karmic bank account. Even if you cannot make the final step, you are at least accumulating spiritual capital that will become available at some other time.

People who work at the Ashram often think they are doing the work for the Ashram or for Swami Radha. They are mistaken. They are really working for themselves. Selfless service, whether you do it at the Ashram or somewhere else, is your opportunity to create spiritual capital so that you will have it available at another time. But you really have to count your pennies—be very careful what you do—because things can accumulate in many ways in the karmic situation.

Some may start very young, and some have to wait a few years. I was forty-four when I started, so there is hope at any age. However, it is wise not to say, "Oh, I have more lives. I will do it next time, or after this happens, or after that, or tomorrow." It's the same as in daily life. If there's something that you don't want to do today, and you put it off until tomorrow, tomorrow will never come, and it will never be done. There is no work, no success, no amount of money as important as your spiritual capital, because in the end nothing else will carry you, nothing else will nourish you, never mind what worldly successes you may achieve.

How can you accumulate spiritual capital? It's not by just being a do-gooder. This is not sufficient. You have to bring changes into your thinking, into your attitude, into your interaction with others. If intense daily work and prolonged times of spiritual practice would do it, all the people who have spent years and years in monasteries would probably be saints.

The accumulation of spiritual capital doesn't happen just because, let's say, you chant for five hours a day, even if you do it for five years. That's quite an undertaking, but unless you are *with* it, truly with it, it's no different from washing dishes three times a day for five years. You don't achieve a perception of purity or cleanliness from washing dishes unless you are fully involved in washing. It's the same with spiritual practice. The making of the spiritual capital lies in the involvement of yourself in what you are doing, in being *with* it, giving yourself to it.

If you chant Mantra for five hours, you must think about it. You may not be able to do this in words—you may find language too limited. But you must think about what the Mantra really means and how you can perceive that. You may ask, "What is the sound I'm creating? Where does it vibrate? What happens to the sound? Where does it go? Can I go there? Will it die out? Will it travel around?"

Why is this important? Because by this line of thinking, you open yourself up to a perception of sources from which knowledge radiates, sources that you cannot otherwise contact.

You may have already experienced this now and again. You say, "I don't know where it came from, but suddenly I knew." You cannot re-trace your steps to discover how you knew unless you make a very great effort in a kind of surrender to that greater force. Then little by little it seems that the curtain gets drawn aside. You may not have a name or a word for it, but you recognize it and you know through your heart as much as through your mind that there is another source from which that knowledge radiates.

What is the source? One way we can understand it is this. There are a number of great spiritual geniuses who have left their physical bodies, for example: Papa Ramdas, Anandamayi Ma, and Gurudev Sivananda. So there is a vortex of consciousness of these three people. You can at-tract this vortex of energy, if, but only if, you make yourself a magnet for it. A magnet will not attract just anything. You are not attracted to just anything or anybody. When you are attracted, it's to someone who has some of what you have in yourself. You may walk into a restaurant in a strange city and the first person you talk to is somebody who practices yoga. If you are a musician, you will find yourself meeting other musi-cians in completely strange cities.

If this is true on a daily level, it's easy to understand that if you are something more than a musician or a yoga person, if you really are so intense that you become a magnet, then you will attract this vortex of spiritual energy.

This is Higher Consciousness, where there is no interaction on a purely physical level. Nobody says, "Yes," or "No," or "Correct." There is no hearing and speaking, but that doesn't mean there is no communi-cation. Knowledge that you haven't achieved at this point in your life can radiate to you from this vortex of energy. But you have to open yourself up, and then you have to make the knowledge your own. Even though it may be freely given, you have still to make it your own by thinking about it, by ingesting it, and by chewing it through in your reflection time.

Your time of reflection is extremely important. If you have a desire to spend a lot of time figuring things out, that is very helpful, because these mental acrobatics are a necessary preparation for the mind, as well as for the emotions. Then if you come into the position of receiving knowledge from such sources, you will not be frightened or so overwhelmed that you say, "Oh, it's useless. I will never be able to reach this or do this."

If you make yourself available to those sources of knowledge, then when you read about such things, you won't

say, "Well, that's strange. That could never apply to me. What would *I* do with it?" You will know, rather, that you have to think about such knowledge, that you have to make your own decisions to do the best you can with it, and to stay on the yogic path. Do as Papa Ramdas did when he had difficulties on the yogic path. Say to the aspect of the Divine you feel closest to, "Hang on to me. I can't hang on to you." When you continue to say that—"Hang on to me"—you can be sure that if the desire is there, it will be fulfilled.

It's very hard being in a human body. You go through periods of difficulties, particularly if you come to the spiritual path in the later stages of life, after experiencing career, family, children, and all the other things that control most people's lives. When that is what you have been used to for a long time, it takes extra-special effort to put cares aside and say, "No. The Divine comes first. From now on, from today, the Divine comes first, and then comes everything else."

When that decision has been made, the Divine comes first and you

act on that. You don't *say* it, you *do* it. Once you have done that, the Divine truly does come first. Then if something comes up from your old life, you will say, "No. I thought I had a duty here, or an obligation there, but I don't any longer." But then, you can't say, "It breaks my heart that I have to turn away from that duty or obligation." The Divine takes better care of things and people than you ever could. That is something that you will understand only when you have made this attempt.

I tell people, "You can ease your heart by putting the Divine first, and then you can ask Divine Mother, 'Please take care of my parents, take care of my children.' Ask the Divine to take care of whatever you think your obligation is." I don't take care of everybody in the Ashram on my own. That would be impossible. I would be so overwhelmed I would say, "No, I can't do this," and I would run away. But I know that other sources are available to me and I can say to Divine Mother, "These are my hands. These are my legs. This is my head, my ears, my eyes, my mouth. I am your instrument." I have to put my own mind and my own concept aside, but I don't have to carry the burden of the responsibility because really I can't. I may have a feeling of obligation that I should do something for this person, and something else for that person, but am I right? If you are open, the Divine can always give you a sign. You can always say, "I feel in a dilemma. What should I do? Where is my duty?" As Arjuna asked in the First Discourse of the Gita, "What is my duty?"

You can ask, "May I have a dream?" But don't think the dream will come the next day, the next night, or even next week. Your mind is so packed with concepts that the Divine really has difficulty getting through. I sometimes had to wait three or four months, particularly in situations where I didn't feel sure that I was doing the right thing, because my understanding hadn't expanded sufficiently, my own courage hadn't grown enough, and my faith wasn't deep enough. It took weeks and months sometimes, and then suddenly the answer would come. I had made up my mind to rely on something in the Christian teachings where Jesus said, "If you ask for bread, you won't be given stone."* You have to ask to be shown what is truly your duty and not just a desire of your self-importance, or a desire arising from ambition, or some way of using someone for your own ends. The answer will be given to you if you just sit there. If you have to wait long periods of time, you can be sure that you have a lot of concepts stacked away in your head and it takes even the Divine time to throw them all out and get through. It's like a steady drop of spiritual water making a dent in stone, trying to make a hole eventually.

Those concepts are there because you needed them for survival at one time. You just have to accept that and know that they were the only way you knew to survive in the world or in your own eyes. You do many things not because you are terribly bad, but because that's the only way you know to survive.

Now, when you open yourself up to those other sources of knowledge, you become a magnet to them and much of your worry about survival will go. You will be shown something, something will come your way that will answer the big questions: What should you do? Where should you go? What is your direction? Do not ever doubt the rightness of the directions you are given.

Many people have come to the Ashram. Some live here, some want to live here, and some have lived here for long periods of time. It is their positive yogic karma, accumulated at some point, that has brought them here. Now it is up to them to say "Thank you" with a deep feeling of gratitude, and make the best possible use of the opportunity.

Start now to accumulate more of that spiritual capital, because none of us can be sure how many more days of life we will have. Is there enough time to make it to the top—to complete surrender to Higher Conscious-

---

* Matthew 7:9.

ness? You must go as far as you can, and make sure that your own self-importance is not standing in the way. Look at all your concepts. See if you can intentionally throw some out. Put an effort into deepening your faith and accept that faith has to be tested.

Sometimes the karmic situation isn't obvious. Sometimes you don't know what promise you made in a past life, or for what purpose your soul decided to come into this life. If there is a conflict between the life that you are living and the one you should be living, your inner conflict will grow and grow and grow. Then the Divine will say, "That's enough now. I have given you a lot of rope. You have tried all the things that everybody else is doing. That's finished now." And then something dramatic or painful may come into your life to make you change.

Sometimes we just don't understand, we are too ignorant. When I was young in Germany, I had no help with understanding my nature or the nature of things, so I followed all the social customs: a girl gets married, a girl should become a mother. But the Divine took away one thing after another, in a sense relieving me of decisions that I would probably have had to make later on. But I see so many people where this no longer applies, who have been set free, and who then just try to find something similar and start the whole thing all over again.

You may lose that spiritual capital you have accumulated. Be extremely careful. Don't squander it. Take a lot of time and think. Can you find out, can you remember why you took birth? Can you remember what propelled you here into this life? Pursue it.

I often say, "We are not all here together by accident—we are here together by divine appointment." I think about that when people are difficult. Some people have given me a terrible time, but I couldn't just say "Go," because the Divine has often taken great trouble to bring people together. All of us belong to a spiritual family of which Divine Mother is the head. Surrender to that, because there is little power that we have on our own. Our power may sometimes look enormous, but it isn't much.

We depend on that greater power, so make yourself a magnet for it. Start accumulating your spiritual capital.

Faith

Gurudev Sivananda used to say, "Give the Divine a chance to prove itself to you. It has put you into this life in the first place and it will also maintain you." That takes faith. Where does such faith come from?

Faith is not something that comes once and then you have it forever. You have to nourish your faith. You are responsible for it. Faith is like a flame. Sometimes it burns down to an ember, but you must keep the ember alive. You have to make an effort. You are responsible, as the women were who took care of the sacred fire in ancient days. They were responsible to see that it didn't go out, because it was not easy for them to make fire. Fire became something very sacred—the symbol of the Light in a very tangible sense.

Keep the fire of your faith going. Remember that it is not a gift you can take for granted. It's a gift the first time, but from then on, you have to take care of it.

I am not speaking about *blind* faith. We all have blind faith in the beginning. When you take lessons from somebody in playing the harmonium, you have to have faith that this person knows how to play. But as you learn, you can determine whether you have a good teacher or not. It is the same with the teachings. As you grow, your ability to assess the quality of the teachings will increase. So blind faith you have only at the very, very beginning. You can never really have it after that.

Faith can be cultivated and increased by practicing devotion, because devotion gives purification. Devotion is a selfless act. It cultivates the emotions toward sincerity, true giving, and selflessness. So when you pray, give all that you can give, give the best that is in you, give your finest feelings.

Gaining self-mastery and control is another way of intensifying faith. It is a clearing and cleaning process, by which we come to another state of clarity in our own minds, as we move from ignorance into the Light of understanding. The workshops given at the Ashram speed up the process so that you can clear away what would otherwise take lifetimes to discover.

But what if you do not have faith in what scriptures and Gurus say? Then you have to look at yourself. Where does faith appear in your life? Many people say, "How can I have faith? I don't even have faith in myself." Do you have faith? You may have more than you think. For example, are you writing your will tonight because you don't have faith that you will wake up in the morning? Don't you eat vegetables because you have faith that they will do you good, that they are not poison? It is just that you have not given faith your attention. You have more faith than you think. Find out.

If you undertake a new job, and you say, "Can I really do this? Well, at least I can try," that's a step toward faith. If you keep taking steps, you're bound to get there. Steps mean movement. Movement means not standing and stagnating. Movement will encourage you, and each time you succeed, you will also feel elevated.

Your greatest enemy is self-doubt. It stands in your way of having faith in yourself. If I had let my doubts and fear overrun what my heart told me to do, I would never have been able to establish an ashram. I remember sitting on the rocks by the Ganges after my Guru had told me to return to Canada and found an ashram—without taking a job. I thought of the New Testament where Jesus said that the birds had a nest, the fox had a hole, but he had no place to go.* I felt precisely that way, but I knew I had to try.

If you doubt that you can do a job, keep saying to yourself, "I know I have doubts, but I will try again and again, and by pulling myself up by my own boot straps, I will get there." You can overcome self-doubt.

The worst kind of doubt is that which undermines your faith in spiritual life. That doubt comes from the ego which just doesn't want to move. This lazy beast says, "Well, I have a roof over my head. I have something to eat, and it's warm. Why should I do anything? Life is so difficult. Wouldn't it be foolish to add more difficulties?" All I can say to this is you have to meet the challenges life has to offer. Do you want to go through another ten lifetimes, each one just another painful struggle, and perhaps in circumstances much less comfortable than this one?

---

* Matthew 8:20.

Sometimes our faith is strong, and at other times we are on a teeter-totter, questioning the same thing over and over again. But if you pray, particularly to Divine Mother, this will help you to strengthen your faith. At some time you will have to accept the challenge to walk through life in darkness, not knowing really where you are going, hoping it's the right direction, toward the Divine. Increase self-mastery, increase self-control, increase your faith, increase your desire to gain in wisdom, because that makes for liberation and sets you free. And always remember that the divine spark, the essence, is imperishable.

Here is a prayer to Divine Mother that has helped me many times. For a period of three or four years, I made it a point to say this Mantra twenty-five times a day, in spite of all my other Mantras and practices. It makes an impact.

> Oh, Divine Mother,
>   May all my speech and idle talk
>   be Mantra,
>   All actions of my hands
>   be mudra,
>   All eating and drinking
>   be the offering of oblations unto thee,
>   All lying down,
>   prostrations before thee.
>   May all pleasures
>   be as dedicating my entire self unto thee.
>   May everything I do
>   be taken as thy worship.

Separation from the Divine

Away back in eons of time we separated from the Divine and since then have gone through all the various manifestations of the various worlds, having lost the identity of our divine nature. Coming back full cycle to where we took off originally happens very slowly. However, we have come this far, so we have made some effort. We have gained consciousness, we have gained awareness, we are able to discriminate and have the power of reason, so all this should give us some idea of how to go about it from here.

There's a story of Siva and Parvati in which all their children except Ganesh have gone to see the world, to see this beautiful creation.

Parvati says to Ganesh, "Why don't you go, too?"

He replies, "Why should I? Where can I see more than I can see here at the point of creation?"

Then he walks around Siva and Parvati three times and kneels before them, and Parvati in her great delight gives him the beautiful pearl mala she is wearing.

Even if you don't see your separation from the Divine in such a cosmic sweep, you still have the awareness that at some point you became separated from the Divine, and now you must put every possible effort into getting back. How important is it to you that you get back to the Divine? That is the question that you—only you—can answer.

It is necessary that you look into your connection with the Divine and find out for yourself what you think caused the separation. You already know within yourself what caused it. I can sit here and say, "It was your ego, your pride, your vanity," but those are just words. They have no meaning unless you really investigate which of your negative characteristics are most powerful and may have gotten you into hot water. By using the opposite of them, you can come out again. If your problem is vanity and pride, the opposite is humility. Accept humility whenever it comes along. Don't revolt and cry, "I've been badly treated!" It is by the opposite characteristics that you can make it. In the same way, if your trouble is a kind of ambitious dominance, then selfless service in all cases is the antidote for that. Sometimes your trouble may be a combination of things, which means you will have to use a combination of opposites to help you to overcome them.

I don't need to give you a lot of examples. You can figure this out for yourself quite easily. When you have figured these things out yourself, you have more confidence in your self-investigation. But then you must do something about what you have discovered. Through this experience and experimentation you can find out how to separate your aspects, your thoughts, whatever needs to be separated, so that you have only the best remaining.

There are divine forces in yourself trying to work underneath to get you back to the right place. You must let them work so that they can be effective, and eventually there will be a movement that will become a steady reminder. When we are separated from a loved one, perhaps somebody who has died, we grieve. We can hardly forget that person for a moment. Our mind is almost completely captured. Separation suddenly brings that person so definitely to our attention that there seems to be more power in separation than there is in togetherness. The memory that we have been one with the Divine can be like this. It is so powerful underneath that it surfaces every now and then, usually when we feel we are in trouble or having big problems.

Why do we seek the Divine? If there had not been any separation, we wouldn't want to go back there. We would say, "Well, I don't really know about this unknown quantity of energy and I can't be bothered with it." But the connection we had with the Divine at one point made us aware of our own divinity and so we want to go back. At some time all of us have heard Krishna's flute. We were entranced and we want to hear it again.

There are many lovely stories to inspire us in our search to be reunited with the Most High. For example, there is a story about a bird that said, "I will not eat anything any more. I will live only on moonbeams, so that I can become so light I can go back where I came from." The poet, Kabir, wrote a poem in which he asked a swan, "Where did you come from, and where are you going?"*

---

* Rabindranath Tagore, trans., *Songs of Kabir* (NY: Samuel Weiser, 1977), p. 55.

Where did *you* come from and where are *you* going? That again is a question that only you can answer.

In your thinking about your life, where you're going, and what you're doing, there is always a mixture of fact and fantasy. That is so even if you are a sanyasi. Fact and fantasy. You have to separate the facts very carefully from your fantasy. The fantasies can be very lovely and inspiring, but it's a great mistake if your mind takes them to be factual.

Also, your consciousness needs to be separated from your general mind. By "mind," I mean the monkey mind. If you live by the monkey mind, you cannot achieve much. The monkey mind will just take you for a ride, giving you nothing but disappointment and pain, and perhaps anger about its betrayal. You have to find out, too, how many levels of your consciousness you are aware of, and how you understand mind within consciousness, or consciousness within mind. What do these words mean? If you fantasize about them, you can really get into a trap. Without the separation of fact and fantasy, there's no clarity about your path, whatever path you have mapped out for yourself. Sure, there is no direct line anywhere, and sometimes you have to go in a roundabout way, and sometimes you have to go slowly, sometimes a little faster. Nevertheless, you have to know *where* you are going. That is the deciding factor of your life. It is of such importance that I really cannot emphasize it enough.

If you really want to know where you are going and how to get there, you need determination and self-control.

Separation forces you to focus much more intensely on whatever it is that you are separated from. If you want to present a dance performance, and you're doing pretty well but you're not really ready yet, this will be on your mind and you will take every spare ten or fifteen minutes you can find to practice a pose or a few steps, or to go through the dance in your mind. Then when the time comes, you will be ready. But if you just let it slide, you will not be ready. When you focus on something that isn't complete, your focus intensifies. If you focus on the effort necessary to achieve something, you will be able to bring that effort to success.

However, be careful, because doubts come if you flirt too much with success and the world. You may say, "Oh, no, I don't do that," but you are doing it. If you weren't, your renunciation, your giving, would be much more complete, much more to the point.

Much poetry has been written in various countries and various languages about love and separation. Being in love with an aspect of the Divine, however, is perhaps more painful than ordinary human love once you have become acutely aware of the separation. Then you wonder when you will have that sense of divine presence again, and you wonder if you will ever again feel elevated beyond your ordinary life. Then you begin to wonder if you can do something to bring this about. The answer is no. You can't. In one of the Krishna stories, the gopis sing a song to Krishna, trying to get him to come back by singing louder and louder. They think if only they can sing loud enough, he must come. But that is not so.* The Divine takes its time and comes for you when you are *ready*. So get yourself ready. Occasionally, you may think, "I should really find out about my divine nature and get connected again." But it doesn't work that way. The real feeling comes only when there is a longing for the Divine, and that comes only when you have accepted wholeheartedly one particular aspect of the Divine. When you have done that, it is as if you are saying, "I'm not *any* devotee, I'm *your* devotee. I will sit here and wait." In doing this, you almost put an obligation on the Divine, and that's perfectly all right. You can be very intense about this longing.

---

* Swami Sivananda Saraswati, *Krishna, His Lilas and Teachings* (India: The Divine Life Society, 1981).

I have seen more happen on a devotional level than on a highly intellectual level. Intellectual people want to piece it all together and think about it. When I met Dilip Kumar Roy, he said, "Swami Radha, if you want to talk about intellectual things, I have nothing to say. I'm not talking any more. I spent so many years of my life talking. Now, I'm only interested in devotion." It was devotion that was taking him where he wanted to go, not his brilliant mind. He had been in contact with many world-famous people, but it was not until he put that all aside and just gave his heart that he was ready. So you might keep that in mind. Separate the monkey mind from the intellect and let your true inner mind come to the fore, and that will offer itself.

Siva and Sakti are sometimes shown as one—half man, half woman. There is also a Radha-Krishna film in which Radha and Krishna change places with each other. This says they are the same, they are one. It is for the sake of the devotees—so the devotees can understand—that they become two. Both are really one. How will you become one? That depends on what you have to offer—whether you can put your intelligence aside and offer your heart. If you can, you will have quite different results. To re-establish your oneness with the Divine, to end your separation from the Divine, it has to be your heart. Life will then take on a very different atmosphere.

All your work, if it is truly selfless, will put you in good standing with the Divine. Even if you have been doing this for only a short period of time, you can look back and see what you have achieved even in so short a time. You can reflect about what you have given and how much of it has been truly selfless, and that can be your thread to re-establish your oneness with the Divine.

You can't ever say the search is done, that you have already found what you need and there's no more need to search. You have to keep removing all the things that impede you and keep moving ahead toward that union with the Divine. Be strong and persist. Endurance is a challenge in itself, and one that is worth meeting. Persistence will make you a winner.

Stealing from the Divine

LORD KRISHNA is the biggest of all thieves, but he uses no force to take anything from you, because Lord Krishna is a very skilled stealer. He takes away from you what you are most attached to. Before you realize it, you've lost it. It has no more meaning for you anymore. You perceive its emptiness, and you wonder why you had so much attachment to it.

It is your attachment that Krishna steals. Sometimes you may wonder how, without any particular work or struggle on your part, things fell by the wayside. It is because, in a moment when you weren't paying attention, Krishna took them. But he gave you something else in return. You have to watch for this. He never takes anything from you without giving you something else.

What Krishna takes from people most often is self-centeredness, and very often he also takes self-deception. It's so easy to deceive yourself, to think, "I understand everything, I know everything." But your actions fall short of what you profess to know, because you have deceived yourself that you are somewhere that you are not. Krishna makes sure that you will discover that. He will steal your self-deception in a moment when you aren't paying attention, when your attractions to things or people are so intense, when you are so absorbed, that you don't realize that he is taking something away. In the end, if he cannot steal it, he will tear it away.

Krishna's stealing is all tied up with his love for his creation. We are all Krishna's gopis. We may be women, we may be men; it makes no difference. It is because of this indescribable divine love that he takes away from us those things with which we hurt ourselves most.

He's very clever. He comes in many disguises. Sometimes he appears as a simple cowherd, sometimes as a secret lover, sometimes as a real Casanova or a Don Juan. He's well known as the dancer—he can dance with you and intoxicate you—or as the divine flute player. We put so much effort into muting the alluring sounds of that flute, into deafening our ears so we can escape hearing it because it will lure us away from the foolish things to which we have attached ourselves. To save you from falling back into these attachments, into your self-centeredness, your self-importance, or your greed or vanity or pride, he draws you into his circle dance. You are one with all his companions. Sometimes he dances with everybody, he's everyone's partner. Other times he's in the center, and the big circle of dancers who want to be with Krishna dance around him.

This dance produces a divine ecstasy that will overrule all other attachments and that ecstasy will last. Even if the dance ends (because nothing is forever—even the sun goes down), you have a memory of the dance with Krishna, and a memory of this ecstasy. That memory is shared with all who were involved in the dance with Lord Krishna. It is *very, very important* that you keep that memory alive, even if your dance with Lord Krishna lasted only a brief moment. Once the ecstasy of being with Lord Krishna has you truly in its grip, you won't want to be anywhere else. Everything will seem pale, empty, false, an illusion. It's like having a heap of stones instead of true diamonds.

What happens when you experience that divine ecstasy? Does it do anything to you besides temporarily giving you a feeling of being elevated? The divine ecstasy, once it is experienced even for a brief moment, will give you greater understanding, and it will heighten your intelligence and your memory. In fact, to make room for that heightened memory, all those inessential and nonsense things that you really don't want to keep there will be crowded out, because otherwise there would be an overload in your brain. The heightened memory of the experience becomes nourishment for your continuing dance, and for your desire to dance with Krishna and with no one else.

We all know that one in particular fell under the spell of Krishna—that one was Radha. She had been warned by the other gopis, "Watch out! If you give him even your finger, he will take your whole hand. If you give him your hand, he has you because you can't tear your arm off. And then one day he will leave and you will have incredible pain and longing. Krishna is a stealer of hearts. He will steal your soul."

That warning fell on deaf ears as far as Radha was concerned. She would ask, "Why do you say that? All I do is long for Krishna and want to be with him. My mind can scarcely think of anything else."

The gopis said, "We know from experience. Be careful. Don't dance too long, don't dance too often. Krishna will not only steal your heart and soul, he will steal even your taste for life. You will want the divine life. No other life will be sufficient." The gopis told Radha of their own experience to convince her. They did their best to warn her. They liked the dance, but only a little bit at a time. The dance of life still had too much temptation and attraction.

One day, when the gopis were bathing in the river, they came out of the water and all their clothes were gone. Krishna was sitting in a tree with their clothes hanging all over the branches. He was saying, "Naked and unafraid you must come. No pretence." We use clothes to cover up our nakedness. Truth is naked. Naked truth is not easy to look at, or to expose to others. You struggle, you fight, you invent stories, you bring up defenses, often not even related to whatever you want to cover up. But if you want Krishna, there's no choice, except that you go, naked and unafraid and leave all your pretences behind. In fact, Lord Krishna commands you not to come any other way. He doesn't need all your covers. *You* need them. You hide behind them.

There are many different covers, many pretences about what you say you are doing for the Divine. For example, you say, "I practice so much Hatha Yoga, so many hours every day. I do rituals, and I chant hours of Mantras. I'm really somebody. And then there's all my work, not always selfless I admit, but most of it, at least I hope so." But you don't even really know whether your work is selfless because you are hiding behind all this.

You may sit and recite scriptures for many hours, and feel that's made your day, that you really have been with the Divine. But if you have only a tiny bit of awareness, you cannot help but recognize that you lack the feeling of ecstasy. If there is no ecstasy after the asanas, or the Mantras, or the rituals, or the selfless service, or the reciting of many slokas, what happened? Some other activity was going on in your mind, and *you* are now the thief. You have been stealing. You pretended to give yourself to the Divine through all this spiritual practice; you wanted to prove how holy, how spiritual, how religious you are. You put on this false garb, like a wolf in sheep's clothing.

In fact, by your pretence, you have even removed respect from the practice. It was mechanical, or your motivation was wrong. It was more fulfillment of ego, boasting how much you do. You cheat only yourself by doing that. Krishna is not to be cheated—ever. And he will not permit you to steal for very long. It's a useless game. It is much simpler to drop the pretences and come. Krishna will do anything to wrest you out of the powers that keep you bound.

Krishna is so clever that he could even deceive Yasoda. She believed him to be her son. It was baby Krishna, Gopala, who misled Yasoda, not the great powerful god. What would have happened to Yasoda if he had not done so? He could not have revealed to her the secrets of the spiritual world. In the story she tried to check his little mouth. She asked him, "Now, what have you got in there? Open your mouth, let me see if you are speaking the truth." She beheld the whole cosmos in his mouth. Yasoda was very surprised, and it was then that she had to change her thinking. What kind of a baby did she have? Where did he come from? And while she was guiding the little one, that little one became her great master, teaching her divine wisdom.

Krishna plays on our emotions, and that is good because most of the time we cannot handle our emotions. We put them in the wrong place, on some other individual. And then we pretend it's love. How do we know? If Krishna takes our emotions in his hands, they can become purified. If we hand over to the Divine whatever feelings and love we think we have—the way we understand love within all our limitations— if we hand that over to the Divine, then our feelings, our emotions, can be purified.

Krishna, if you ask him sincerely for divine help—not just in your head, and not just to get out of a tough or unpleasant situation, but really with a longing in your heart—Krishna will come and he *will* help you. But what you may not realize is that Krishna's help becomes also your tie.

When you think that you love someone, you create a rope between you and the one you love. You tie each other up in the belief of love and that rope is sometimes not very reliable. It's a rope of many strands, many gratifications, and sometimes it can unravel. All of a sudden it may fall apart because it has no true strings. When Krishna ties you, it's a very different kind of love. It's a rope that will *not* break. When Yasoda tried to tie baby Krishna so he couldn't steal the butter, the rope could not be tied, but he showed her how to tie it. If you will allow it to happen, you will be shown how to tie yourself to the Divine. If you're really clear and honest and sincere, you know very well that your weaknesses and your attraction to the world's pleasures are too powerful, so you had better ask Krishna how to tie yourself to him. If you can't tie yourself to him, then ask him to tie himself to you. When you allow the Divine, by whichever name you know it, to tie you by a rope, you will never get lost and the Divine will never give you up.

Baby Krishna was a butter thief. Why did he steal butter? First we have to ask, "What is milk?" In many of the teachings we hear of the milk of divine wisdom, the cream of the Vedas, the cream of the Puranas. Throughout Indian teachings milk and cream are separated. For some people there is only milk and for some people there is cream. To separate the milk and the cream—and maybe the water—in your own personal life is a matter of evaluating what is most important to you. Nourish yourself by that which is most important. Cream—you need only a little and you feel filled. Milk—you need more, but water will perhaps never be quite satisfactory.

Divine Mother is described in the scriptures of India as having large breasts, as if to say, "There's lots of milk, don't worry. Nobody will go hungry." But you have to come and get the milk. When you do come and ask, or even indicate that you want it, it's given freely, without end. But when pride and arrogance keep you from asking, then you may go hungry, and your heart and mind and soul will not have proper food and may starve.

So why did Krishna want to steal the butter? He wanted to give it to his friends. And who are his friends? The most important seekers. And why are they the most important? Because that's all they do, try to be with Krishna. And he in return makes sure that they get the very best.

If you think of butter as the essence of milk and if milk represents divine wisdom, then butter is that kind of wisdom which radiates from sources we cannot perceive through our senses. But we know it exists because we can experience it.

Butter stands not only for the wisdom emanating from some other source, but also for pure divine love which we can indeed call "unconditional." Human love is never, ever unconditional. Human beings are not capable of unconditional love. There's always some "because" attached to it. Something in us is gratified by the person we say we love. But when you turn to the Divine and you allow the Divine to gratify whatever your needs are, and you say that nothing and no one is good enough except the Divine, do not think for a moment that you will *ever* go without that divine food, that divine nourishment. You certainly will never, ever be undernourished.

The cow who gives milk is a holy animal. The cow is a mammal, and so are human beings. We are all mammals. Most of the time the mother has the milk even before the baby is born. It is the same with the Divine. That milk is there, waiting, and it is the true nourishment of human beings. If you can develop a taste for the milk of divine wisdom, what else would you want? What could possibly be as good as that?

Krishna's love for his devotees asks *everything* of you. He wants the highest love you're capable of. Little bits and pieces, fleeting moments, occasional thoughts, crumbs—that will not do. You yourself would not be happy if somebody you cared for just threw you a few crumbs every now and then, and made a few statements of love and devotion, and then took it all away by a display of arrogance and selfishness.

Krishna will not permit his devotees any barriers. He will tear them down, so often and so completely that you may sometimes feel the Divine treats you with ruthlessness. Why? Because if you're not ruthless with yourself, if you do not meet yourself on the gut level, Krishna has to do the job for you. He will not permit any barriers, and he can tackle any barrier that you might put up. The result can be devastating.

Yasoda tells how she put ropes around the containers of milk and butter and tried to hang them near the ceiling. This didn't work. Krishna could get to them. Then she put them in dark places, and that didn't work. He could see them. So we can put our egos, our vanity and pride, high up under the ceiling, but Krishna will get them down easily. If we hide them in the dark, he will find them. If we set up divisions, he will tear down our barriers. He may even, for our own good, lay some traps from which only he can release us.

Divine love doesn't play by ordinary rules. We know that Radha, his favorite, had been a wife and the mother of children, but she left it all. The rope that tied her to her husband didn't last. The rope that tied her to her children also unraveled. When she stole away to be with Krishna, when she gave heart, mind, and soul to Krishna, she could not really attend to her duties as a wife, or take care of the children, or have meals on time, or work in the fields. She was scolded, accused, and ridiculed for this, but divine love doesn't need to obey rules. Divine love is beyond rules, and the divine aspirant who is truly a lover of the Divine does not need to worry about those rules.

Rules are needed for ordinary people who do not have this intense love for the Divine. They need rules to keep things organized. These rules are also an oppression but they are needed because most people cannot handle freedom—there are too many interfering desires. We have to learn how to handle freedom correctly, and that is no easy lesson. We think we can handle it, only to fall into the ditches of our desires, of our pleasure-seeking ego, into self-deception and self-importance. That is true everywhere, in all walks of life, even in ashrams. Some people can handle the freedom given, but other people's freedom has to be restricted because they're not capable of handling it. When rules and regulations have to be set up to control those people, everybody suffers. But when the Divine—Krishna, or Divine Mother, or whichever divine aspect you choose—steps in to restrict your freedom, that can become much more serious. That can inflict very heavy pain.

We cannot take any liberties with the Divine. The lessons come very quickly—not in some other lifetime, but in weeks or months or a couple of years, sometimes in the next moment.

In order to handle the freedom that is given, we have to be on the alert at all times. We are given plenty of warning. Sometimes we hurt ourselves accidently, or so we think. Big or small, accidents give us a stern warning: "Watch out, or else!" We cannot play any games with the Divine. We can cheat those we live with, we can cheat those in charge, we can cheat the people we work with, we can cheat our superiors, our co-workers, we can cheat ourselves. We are very skillful in doing all that. But we cannot cheat the Divine. We cannot steal from the Divine. Your understanding may be too limited to recognize what you are doing to yourself, and how heavy the payment will be at a future time, most likely when you least expect it, but the law of karma is always on the alert. We cannot hide, however hard we may try.

We think we are so advanced because of our technology, but that doesn't mean a thing. If your heart and mind are not advanced, if your understanding or your awareness is limited, you can have *ten* computers, and they can't make up for your lack of awareness—for your stubbornness or your arrogance. In other words, technology can't change you; all it has to offer are more opportunities to tempt you to commit sins, because it helps you to gratify faster the wrong desires that keep you from the Divine.

Worldly success and its temptations make you a thief. That which belongs to the Divine, you steal. That is just childish, foolish, and very immature—like little children taking a candy from the dish and thinking it's a great triumph because mother hasn't seen them do it. But stealing from the Divine and from your own divinity will have serious consequences.

Your biggest thief is your ego. It scarcely ever lets you handle your freedom the right way or do the right thing. Whatever little wisdom you may gather over many years, the ego will turn into cleverness, so you only become more skillful in playing games with yourself and with others, more skillful in putting up the defenses to protect your self-centeredness, and your ego's desires, and your pride.

Remember, Yasoda put the butter pot in the darkness, yet Krishna found it. Krishna finds everything. There's no darkness so great that what you hide cannot be found. So all your efforts to hide are useless. Karma will catch you, if not now, then later. In the darkness of human existence, the Divine will find you and make demands upon you because you have not responded to the call of Lord Krishna's flute. When you hide from your spiritual responsibilities and from what you know is right, when you hide your love for the Divine, it is like watering milk down until scarcely any quality of milk remains.

Your foolishness and your greed cannot make any demands on the Divine. The choice is yours. You cannot say, "I didn't know." You do know, but the ego has taken over. That means Krishna cannot take care of you. You won't let him, and so you must deal with your self-created predicaments and pain all alone. All your pain *is* self-created. All your predicaments *are* yours. You have chosen intentional blindness. You are stealing away from the inner call you don't want to hear. You have closed your ears to the alluring sound of Lord Krishna's flute.

You may even have lost the memory that you did once hear that flute. There's only one remedy for that: restore your memory by your own efforts. When you start to do this, Krishna will come once again to help you. Invoke by your own efforts the longing for the divine sound of the flute. Follow the sound. Open your mind and your heart. Hear not only with your human ears, but also with your inner ear. And remember, the power that created the ear can hear even the finest whisper of your mind and of your heart.

Dealing with Injustice

IF WE OURSELVES ARE JUST, then we recognize the injustice of others. If we believe in justice, and we know somebody is being treated unjustly, we can sit back and pay no attention or we can scream and be angry or we can do something positive. There are a lot of positive things that one can do. It's a matter of brainstorming, looking at everything, not throwing away any ideas, making a whole list of possibilities. People often think it's a matter of having money—paying for somebody's education or travels, or helping someone start a business. That kind of help can be of great importance, but it isn't always the best thing. I have met a number of sons and daughters who were very well set up by their parents but they were not happy about it, because they had nothing they could look at and say, "Well, I did it myself!" They never got a sense of self-worth, of capability, of something they could be truly proud of. We have a lot of false pride, but having a healthy pride in a job well done is quite different.

There are many injustices where perhaps we can't do anything. But there are many organizations like Amnesty International which help people who are imprisoned. These organizations have the professional capacity to get the information and do something about it. You may not be able to do this yourself, but you *can* support organizations which make this their job.

I support many of these organizations. Some of them are probably on a government list of organizations to be watched. But I can't bother about that, because I can't be so protective of myself that I can't do anything to help.

There are many things you can do as an individual to support organizations. For example, when I was a new immigrant in Montreal, a little boy of five was run over by a car. The newspaper put his story on the front page and people sent money to the paper. A very elegant shop had a big notice in the window that said they were authorized by the paper to accept money for this boy. I went in there and said, "I don't have any money. I am an immigrant. But I would be happy to give my time." They smiled at me, probably thinking I was very naive, but they listened and took my address. I said, "I would be happy to give some dance performances, and all the proceeds can go to the boy."

The gentleman who ran the store looked at me in a very fatherly way, and said, "You are a nice lady, but my goodness, don't you know that Montreal doesn't have a single theater? Where do you think you will dance?"

I didn't know that. However, a women's organization picked up my name and address and phoned me. They found auditoriums in schools and colleges. These were dark, dungeony, dirty places. However, that didn't matter. After that, I gave many performances for the blind to pay for their dogs to be trained, and later for cancer aid, and for many other purposes. Very often these performances were out of town and it would take me an extra day to travel. I would say, "You will have to talk to my boss." My boss always let me go.

What I am trying to say is, if you want to help where there is injustice, you will find a way.

Once I helped an Indian dancer give performances in private homes in Montreal. She said, "Ah, social life. I have had it up to here."

I said, "But there isn't any situation where you cannot throw some seeds."

"How would I do this? Do you think I can tell people I do yoga and suggest they stand on their heads? They will laugh at me."

I said, "No, no. Ask them, 'Do you dream? Do you dream in black and white, or do you dream in color?' Startle them with questions. You don't have to talk about hats and the latest color of nail polish, or even about the latest novel. Bring something up that is interesting. However, if you have read the latest novel you will find something in there that you can use. You can throw a seed."

Of course, we could sit here all night talking about injustice, and what we can do. But what about anger? What's the root of all this anger about the injustice of other people? Find out if you have ever taken advantage of someone. If you never have, then you can be angry about other people doing so. But we have all taken advantage of others. If you think you have never taken advantage of someone, you have just totally forgotten doing it. So what's the point of being angry about this?

Also, we are angry and project this onto others when really we are not satisfied with our own lives. And when anger doesn't go anywhere and nothing gets done, then depression follows: "I can't even be angry any more. Nothing works. Nothing is worth living for and now I am very depressed."

Basically you know you aren't even looking at your potentials, never mind doing something about them. So you are angry. Find out what makes you angry. I say again, everybody at some time in life is taken advantage of. But when you have stopped taking advantage of others, or being unjust or supercritical, or tearing everything apart, when you have balanced your karma, when in your karmic book, good and bad, debit and credit, are balanced, nobody will take advantage of you. It is when we haven't paid off our own karma that other people take advantage of us and we become angry. So we are constantly being reminded through events that we are not balanced yet. We should be *super* careful not to get further into the red.

Karma

Many people have not suffered great losses in this life, and there are various reasons for that. What doesn't catch up with you in this life will catch up with you in some other life. Let us assume that Gurudev was correct in saying that in some past life in India, I was very attached to the family and particularly to the mother, as probably most Indian women would be. He said that on account of some of the merits from that life I was given the chance to break loose from attachment to a mother by being born to a mother to whom I wouldn't form any attachments.

Most of the time we function under the saying, "The echo returns what it receives." If you call into a grotto, the sound travels around and you get your own voice back, but it's not necessarily improved. Many of the things we get are the echo of actions or words that we sent out, and which may have taken a long time to get back to us. I think a lot of what comes to us is what we sent out, particularly if we have thoughts that we want to pay off karma, that we don't want to carry anything over.

In the Fourth Discourse of the Bhagavad Gita, Krishna says, "The approach of devotees decides what they will get." In other words, if you are taking small steps toward the Divine, then you will have only small insights; your rewards, your blessings, will be small. For a long, long time you may have nothing to indicate that you are really moving forward. This is because you have not taken into consideration the backlog of karma that you may have to deal with. When karma is balanced to some degree, at least, then the Divine gives you an opening in return. So sometimes it's good to plunge right in, and *not* say, "Well, I will go slowly, one step at a time." That can be a little overcautious, and also overprotective. It means you don't want to have too many inconveniences all at once. By going too slowly, however, we may tempt the Divine, who may say, "No, you cannot go that slowly. There's not enough time left. If that's the way you're going to go, something will have to speed you up." Then you may find drama coming into your life.

If you express the wish to pay off your karma almost right away, even if you don't have a conscious plan but just have that idea in your thoughts, it can come back very quickly. Then you will wonder why all these terrible things are happening. Some of what happens to us is a learning experience because we need that particular lesson, and the other portion comes because it's the echo of something that we sent out. It's probably half and half.

If you read the Gita carefully, it says that you will have an accumulation of good karma at one point, but you will lose that if you don't make the best use of it when it is given to you. If your life circumstances are not particularly difficult, your life is the accumulation of good karma, and you have the choice of undoing whatever has been done in the past. It's a matter of using your intelligence, using your understanding, thinking about it and not just skimming over it. People who have had a lot of bad luck and hardships from the economic situation right now are people who had a chance and didn't use it. So you can throw your chance away, or it may have to be taken away because you are misusing it.

If you make a great effort to understand the difficulties, tragedies, and pains of others, even if your understanding is only theoretical, you won't necessarily have to suffer those experiences yourself. Of course, at some time you may need specific training in a particular experience for some reason. Karma is really like bookkeeping. We run up our debts, and then we pay them off.

At one point I said to Gurudev, "But I'm really not good enough. If I were, the terrible things in my life wouldn't have happened to me."

He said, "You had to have these experiences to understand the experiences of others. You had to have stomach ulcers yourself to understand the pain and the humility."

I thought it could mean also that in some lifetime I hadn't taken enough trouble to understand the stomach, or the pain of other people's experiences. But in this life, I don't need to have cancer myself to understand the pain of those who do, because I experienced such terrible things in the war.

But my lesson in the war was probably not about the suffering of others. It was, rather, to see the tremendous guidance I received during the whole war and the Hitler situation. My first husband, Wolfgang, even said, "You won't be scratched." Even the loss of my valuables and furniture was probably not the lesson. That loss was not important. The learning for me was to see that there really is guidance—daily, hourly, and during the war, even from minute to minute. That is very difficult to see and to remember under shifting circumstances. Often I was prevented from leaving the house too soon, or too early, or from being in a certain place at a certain time. People would hold me back from going somewhere by asking me if they could stay with me. The next day I would see that if I hadn't said yes, I would have been killed in the bombing that hit the place I was going to.

This shows another aspect to my experiences. Both Swami Sivananda and Ramdas said to me independently that I was prepared for

this job from the day I was born. That was not always gratefully acknowledged because I lacked the memory that I had agreed to do this. Even now, however, I have often said, "If I can do it, you can do it," forgetting that indeed I have been trained and prepared. Perhaps the person I am saying this to didn't bring into this life all that I brought into it, so it is unfair to say, "What I can do, you can do."

Take heed of that. Think of how the idea of being

trained might fit into your life, because if there is conscious cooperation, you may not have to have painful experiences.

But it's not quite that easy. Gurudev told a story of all the saints
and sages, men and women, up in mid-heaven in a big meeting hall,
deciding the destiny of the people. The one closest to Brahman said,
"Help is needed on Earth. Who will go?"

Each of them knew what they would have to face. It was a time of
revolutions on Earth. There was a great silence. Then a few said they
were willing to go.

Being born in such bad times as these doesn't mean, necessarily,
that it's for your personal development or that it's a personal punishment. I think these things have happened many and many a time. There
are stories of the same kind about Divine Mother asking: "Who will go
and help and do my work?" I have often felt that I didn't know which
way was right or left, or up or down, and yet I have often felt that really
everything was laid out. I just couldn't see it at the time, and I didn't
have the background to understand it. The six months I had in India
with my Guru were not enough.

However, even if I had been able to spend much more time with
him, personal interaction with a Guru doesn't answer everything. You
must get clarification for yourself. It is important to try to get some
from your own dreams and by surrendering. Let your heart speak more
when it can.

If you do not develop the understanding of surrender, you will get
it in the next life. Be sure about that. You can avoid a lot of trouble by
saying, "I am here. What is it you want me to do? Make it very clear
because I am so wrapped up in my own thoughts. Give me the strength."
Pray for a clear dream that doesn't have many ways of being interpreted,
and for the strength to see in the dream.

I have often said in a prayer, "My mind is so clever, it can interpret
anything in any way it wants. Make it so that I won't have that chance.
Make it very clear, with no question about it." If it's too tough, then
it's a matter of humility to say, "I need help to see this. Please help
me." Otherwise you could really ruin the rest of your life.

I have been hammering at conscious cooperation for many lifetimes. Sometime, if you really want to understand and know, you may find out more about your life and how many lives have converged into this one to give you this chance to undo, to rebuild, and to build entirely anew.

Evolution and Maya

THERE IS A DISPARITY in the evolution of consciousness in human beings. Groups of people develop at different rates, side by side. There are on Earth right now some very primitive people who have still not developed a written language. Yet there were people living in the Middle East thousands of years ago who wrote works which later became part of the Bible's Book of Proverbs. They were people with very high ideals and insights on how to conduct life and how to take care of other human beings less fortunate in their grasp and intelligence.

But even inside a group, individual people develop at different rates. In evolution, a whole group of people doesn't start in one place and as a *group* move to another. This doesn't happen even in the school system of today. There are some bright students who can move on faster, and some who hang behind. You cannot shift any group of people as a class.

Some individuals have very little intelligence. They are literal-minded, and their whole way of thinking, their whole way of life, is very linear. But when sufficient experience comes into their lives, changes are bound to come. These experiences—particularly if they are painful—can create a desire to think life over, to think it all through again, and maybe to realize that things work quite differently from the literal. But is that evolution?

Even if the shift takes place, from the literal to something more elaborate, it is not necessarily better or more true, because everything we do is affected by maya. Maya is a tricky subject. I knew a swami who used to bring up the view quite frequently that all is illusion. I would joke with him and say, "Yes, swamiji, you are not here and I am not here, so where are we? Who is doing the talking and who is listening?" I feel that if you take the position that all is maya, you may as well not say anything because there is nobody who says anything, and there isn't anybody who is listening, and the whole world doesn't exist!

An example often used to explain maya is this: if you put a rose into a closed, dark container where no light falls on the rose, there is no perception by our sight that allows us to say, "There is a rose. There is an object that we have given the name *rose*." Fine, but even if the rose is in the dark, the rose does not disappear. We temporarily cannot see it, temporarily it is prevented from appearing, or attracting any of our senses, but it doesn't disappear.

There are many such explanations in philosophy that don't hold water, if you take them the way they are presented, reflect on them, and apply your own experience and understanding to them.

Let me explain that to you on a personal level. You cannot say, "I have cancer," because that wouldn't be quite correct. *You* are not the body and you are not the mind. What has cancer is the body. The *mind* can't have cancer because the mind has no substance. The mind is a process of functioning in the brain. So the brain can have cancer but not the mind. But the mind is not tangible and if you say, "I am not the body, I am not the mind," then as individuals, each of you has to figure out how to translate that thought into words of your own, which will give you a personal understanding of the idea that is expressed in that saying.

But there can be a disorder in the cells of the body because sometimes the proper consciousness is absent from those particular cells due to some other interference, and that interference comes from the mind. If there is an interference in the cells of the body, then one has to find out what the interference is. This is true with any disease.

The rose will only flower when it has all the ingredients that it needs: the temperature, the light, the nourishment, the air currents, and the water. If there is an interference in any of these, it can't flower. Those are the laws of its existence. If there is an interference of any kind in your life, you have to find out what law is being broken. If you think of yourself as a rose, then you have to find out under what conditions you flower and function best, and then you may find that the mind is somehow not functioning properly. Perhaps your body chemistry is in disorder. If it is, you have to think about it and see if you can correct it. To correct the condition, you have to change, either by correcting the chemical household of the body, or by correcting your mental-emotional makeup.

We are dealing with the very tangible body and with a lot of *in*tangibles that are connected and related to it. This indicates that there are different levels of existence. The course of evolution through these levels is determined by how you use the mind and how far you can train it to become flexible, and by how far you can train the emotions to become adaptable and flexible so they further your well-being rather than interfere with it.

If you have a pair of shoes that pinch you, there is no point in keeping them. You are wearing the wrong kind of shoes for the size or shape of your feet. Change. Clarify the problem and then change the situation to the best of your ability. The trimming of greedy emotions is very important, because the constant seeking of self-gratification will sooner or later hinder your evolution. It's the wrong focus.

It's not the *physical* that will grow through evolution. The physical will adapt itself to the process of your evolution which depends purely on the power of the mind. But the powers of the mind are not easily understood. We have to be extremely courageous to look at the powers of the mind as they pertain in our own life: what they really are, what it really is that we are doing, why we are doing it, what changes are needed. These are not very easy to see because the emotions create a filter.

I became aware of this particularly when I was dealing with people who were married to alcoholics and people who had relatives in prison. The need to survive in their own eyes and the eyes of others created thoughts something like this: "I am too good to be the husband of a woman who is an alcoholic," or "I am too good to be the wife of a man who is in prison."

The mind will construct something that is all maya in order to rationalize the husband being in prison or the wife being an alcoholic. Those constructions are purely maya. They come from carrying survival far beyond having your daily bread and a warm room and a comfortable bed. They come from the desire to survive in the eyes of others.

That desire to survive is why you try to please, why you are "nice." You want to be accepted. You want to be heard. You want to be listened to. You want your remarks and contributions to be appreciated. To achieve, that you will go through many complicated mental-emotional dances.

But that kind of survival in the family, in business, or in a group of friends is not satisfying. You want to survive also in your own mind, in your own judgment, in your own criticism. The idea in your mind of what you *should* be is a very complicated thing in itself. That you should be beautiful, intelligent, wise, six feet tall, have this nose or that color of hair, these are all very primitive ideas, but they are very, very powerful.

You want to survive in your own mind, and your own mind sets the criteria by which you want to survive. That's a very dangerous trap. It makes difficulties and creates a lot of absolutely unnecessary pain. Again, it's all maya. It means not having the strength, the courage, to

accept what *is*. You must deal with self-acceptance—the acceptance of your physical appearance and of your mental and emotional makeup.

Maya is a very complicated thing, and it is maya that prevents evolution. Whether you can accept yourself or whether you feel you have to do certain things in order to survive in the world—these are two quite different ways of thinking. Sit down and think them over. Find out where you are. Do it again six months from now, and next year. Find out again and again how much your thinking has advanced, how much stronger and more courageous you have become about accepting where you are, what you are.

In the *Kundalini* book I have said that you can create your own

worlds.* Think. Is that true or not true? Is that a fairy tale? I have said also that you can become invisible—not just by being ignored like a wallflower, but by your desire.† What does this mean? You can become invisible on a very tangible level if it doesn't matter to you whether you are seen or whether you are heard, and if it doesn't matter whether you are appreciated. When these things don't matter, you are pushing maya out of your way and saying, "I don't need recognition. I want to go right to the essence." Then other things begin to happen, and they have great significance. You will come in contact with part of that essence. You won't be able to do it every day, but if you truly want to move on the spiritual path, you should be able to do it once in a while. If you can achieve that contact, that's evolution. That's the evolution of peeling the onion, one layer after another, until you come to the essence that is you. It will take you some time, of course.

You can see this evolution beginning in the animal kingdom with monkeys. I once saw an experiment where monkeys were kept without food for two days, then taken to a beach where some food was thrown on the soft sand. The monkeys grabbed up the food, all covered with grains of sand, and stuffed it into their mouths. Then, of course, they had to spit a great deal to get the sand out. Next, the researcher put some of the food covered with sand into the water, and the sand fell off. Some of the monkeys saw this and grabbed the food quickly as it surfaced with the sand washed away.

Then a big basin was put into the water some distance from shore and heaped with bananas. Some of the monkeys walked on their hind legs through the water to get to it. But the moment they grabbed a banana, they reverted to their habitual way of moving on all fours, and had to run back through water with waves over their heads. Some monkeys took this chance, but there were some who would rather die of starvation. That's precisely the human picture, too. There are some people who will take the chance, and there are some others who would rather die of physical, mental, or emotional starvation.

---

* Radha, *Kundalini Yoga for the West*, chapter 10.

† *Kundalini*, pp. 179, 310.

We evolve through these various kingdoms—mineral, plant, animal, human. It takes billions of years, probably, and millions of births. Even at the human level, we see many people who are closer often to the animal kingdom than to what we normally call human.

We can only assume that consciousness came into existence somewhere, and then evolved through individuals who were willing to take a chance. We can only speculate that life has some sort of meaning within which we can make our own individual lives as meaningful as possible.

I find it tempting to say, "That's the way it is," but I have seen my own thinking develop and change, so I keep my thoughts suspended. I will never say, "*That's* the way it is," because at that moment I put a limitation on my development. I always hope that my mind can push any limitations further out. I got wonderful advice from my Tibetan Guru, who said, "Never, *ever,* think you are there, because at that moment you stop evolving." There is always something further. It becomes more subtle, it becomes more complicated. Eventually, it goes beyond language because language is limited. I have often felt that we cannot evolve much further unless language evolves.

Sex

IN THE FIRST THREE STAGES of human existence,* people live almost entirely by instincts. When you look at what is going on in the world, that can be seen very clearly, particularly with the sex instinct—hardly a day goes by, for example, without AIDS being reported in the news. In the next three stages of humanity, people come to understand that they should not live by instincts like animals, which cannot help living that way. They realize they are human beings endowed with reason and logic and that they have to apply these gifts.

Sex isn't bad, any more than food is bad. If we eat what the body

---

* See Radha, *From the Mating Dance to the Cosmic Dance*, chapter 1, for an explanation of the seven stages of human development.

needs, we will be healthy. But if we overeat and abuse our body, and don't respect its functions, if we eat only for pleasure, then food can be bad and we can get into all sorts of trouble. Sex is for procreation. If we don't accept that, if we insist sex is for pleasure, then we get into serious difficulty because nature cannot be turned into something it is not.

The purpose of sex is to bring a child into the world through the love and care of the parents for each other. The fruit of that love is the baby. The parents' duty is to bring the child up, educate it, and lead it to the glorification of the Divine, but this rarely ever happens.* We have to realize that although sex has brought us into existence it is not really the sex act that gives us life. Life is not given to us by other human beings. We owe our lives to the Divine, to the life force itself. That force is neutral and has to be handled with responsibility and great discrimination.

That is not how most people use this energy, however. Many use it simply to gratify the instincts. We have prettier words for instincts today. We call them biological urges, and we speak of the biological clock, but those words don't free us from the responsibility to use our common sense and our discrimination.

I have met many women in the middle of their thirties, and even older, who suddenly say, "I think I should have a baby."

I ask them, "Why? You were happy without it. You have a career. Are you going to give that up?"

They often say, "Oh, these days, you can have a baby and a career."

Yes, of course you can, if you have a high income. Do you? It costs a lot of money to hire someone to look after the household and the child, *if* you can find someone who is reliable and will stay with you. Too often a couple finds a woman to look after the child, then in three or four months, her boyfriend leaves town and she wants to move with him. So she quits the job because it's very easy to get another one. There are many desperate parents looking for someone to care for their children.

---

* The Bhagavad Gita says it is very good fortune to be born into a family of yogis, but very rare; Bhagavad Gita, Sixth Discourse, verse 42. Yogananda said his parents came together only when they wished to have a child. They were not ruled by instincts. Paramahamsa Yogananda, *Autobiography of a Yogi* (Los Angeles: Self Realization Fellowship, 1975) p. 7.

At first, having a new baby creates great excitement, but by the time the child is three or four or five years old, the mother may be saying, "I wanted to be a writer and I had a good start before the baby arrived, but now I'm too busy, too tired, too tied-down to write."

All I can say is, "Why did you listen to your biological clock? Didn't you know yourself? Did you make no effort to think through what your life would be like or what you would have to give up?"

You always have to think your actions through no matter what it is you wish to do. You cannot suddenly simply stop something you have put in motion without cracks and breakages occurring in your life or someone else's.

People speak of their personal freedom and rights, but they do not take responsibility for what they put into the world.

A man who was president of a large organization told me in sad tones that he was adopted. I said, "Perhaps you were fortunate. The couple who adopted you must have really wanted children." And he answered, "But there's no dignity in being a sexual accident."

Now, how many people think about that when they are engaging in sex? How many take responsibility for each action? Most are seeking personal gratification only.

People breed cows and horses for high physical quality, but give little thought to the well-being of the children they may produce. There are institutions full of children with congenital afflictions because people will not awaken to the fact that they have a responsibility for what they put into this world.

And we do not even ask ourselves why we seek each other out, what is it that makes us seek union with another human being.

Getting Married

Most people have a marriage partner in life, and sometimes after a divorce or death another partner will be sought. Children are born to most of these relationships and, of course, many children are also born as the result of very temporary relationships.

Couples may enter relationships for a long time or a short time with very little idea of why. Very few people know what it means to enter a relationship in the full knowledge of responsibility. Little or no training is given to young people in this aspect of life. So they get married, not knowing how to make a marriage a success or what to do when it becomes rough. There may be children who are not really wanted, and the couple may not understand the responsibilities involved in being parents. And many are not sufficiently educated to deal with other very important questions, such as birth control and health safety.

Most of us have entered relationships in ignorance, and we may go from one relationship to another repeating our mistakes. Marriage and children need to be given the same serious consideration we usually give to starting a new career or choosing a house, but too often we rush headlong into marriage or parenthood driven by instincts or thinking only of emotional gratification. There are very, very few people who go to work on their relationship in full awareness, with full intention. I think I can count on the fingers of one hand the ones that I know.

There are many motivations for entering a relationship. We may just want to leave home, or to do things we think only married people can do. Perhaps we want the respect or adoration we think we will receive from a husband or wife. We may want the social acceptance that goes with the married status. It could be that we want somebody who will take responsibility for our own individual happiness, not realizing that this is an impossible demand. It sometimes takes much disappointment and heartbreak before we realize that each one of us is responsible for our own inner peace and happiness.

We may also be looking to satisfy our need for approval. We may have ideas like this in mind: "If somebody says I am wonderful, my life is worth living. If I have somebody important in my life, that makes me important." We may not even know these thoughts are in our minds, but many of us strive all our lives for the approval of our fathers or mothers, husbands or wives. We cannot believe that we will be all right unless we have it.

We cannot expect this from anyone—wife, husband, son or daughter. If we think others can provide our happiness or make us feel accepted, we are pursuing an illusion. We have not looked clearly at what we think about relationship and why we want one. Nobody is required to provide happiness for another. We are responsible for ourselves. This is unfortunately not generally understood and much pain results. Pain is a great teacher. It takes a lot of disappointment, a lot of puncturing of our balloons of illusion, before we can be free of childish things, before we can look at things for what they are, not for what we wish they were.

So you are happy one day, unhappy the next. You argue, then you make up, and everything is wonderful again. Then soon you are hurt and disappointed again. You move between happiness and pain, back and forth, back and forth. You are on a teeter-totter, and unless you move to the center, there will always be this up and down movement, because your emotions are not controlled. They will always be there, but you have to get control of them. As you move toward the center, your emotional reactions will become shorter and shorter, until finally they will just last a few minutes, or a few seconds.

We often look for social acceptance in marriage. People may say, "If you are not married, you don't really know how to accept responsibility." Years ago, when I worked for a large company, I saw that preference in hiring was always given to married men for that reason.

So we tumble into a relationship, driven by social pressures, by instincts, by biological drives, and by old habits. We have no idea how much factors like these contribute to what we think is our own personal, freely-made decision.

Does this mean that we shouldn't have relationships? Not at all. If we can bring out the best in each other, then a relationship is appropriate. But if we want the other person only for our own gratification, entertainment, or needs, then it's wrong. And if we keep the person away from spiritual practice, we become demons. We cannot bring out the best in each other if this sort of thing is going on.

Before entering into a relationship, we have to ask very soberly what it is we want from that relationship. What is the motivation for entering into it? We have to look at things really clear-eyed and ask: "What am I seeking? Am I hoping my partner will fulfill or satisfy something that is lacking in me? What do I want satisfied?" The same questions can be asked about a relationship that already exists.

You must be very clear about what you need and what you want, and how far you are willing to go in giving up your personal desires and needs. You must know, also, what draws you to this relationship. Is it that you have something in common? Do you share a desire to have children? Do you want to go into business or a career together? Have you come together because you both want to live an unconventional life?

Companionship is one of the things most often looked for in a relationship. It is a word loaded with desires so deeply buried that we don't really know what we mean when we use it. Maybe what we mean is just that we are afraid to be alone. Maybe we really mean we want sex, but we say companionship because it is a nicer, more acceptable word.

The sexual relationship, too, has to receive clear-eyed investigation. What are the needs there? Is this the driving force for entering a relationship? Is it the sole purpose of being together? We have to be very clear about these matters.

When we look at our reasons for wanting a relationship, we may find that what we really want is something temporary: "*Now* I need you. I want you right here next to me. Oh, now I *don't* need you. Let me put you on a shelf where I can get you again when I *do* need you." Men and women both do this.

We know little about how much self-interest is involved in our relationships. Suppose someone hasn't looked at you for two days. You begin to wonder, "Is there something wrong. Doesn't she like me anymore?" So you go to work to make your presence known to this person, and when you get a friendly word or a smile in return, you feel settled and secure again. It is very difficult to be truly concerned about another person without the monkey of self-interest putting its head through the back door and saying, "What about me? Am I getting something out of this, too?"

There is probably no way of living in which we do not seek the fulfillment of our self-interest and the expression of our own personal needs. We have to accept that, and be clear about it. When we are clear about it, there will be no false expectations. When you know what you want from a relationship, you can ask yourself right at the beginning: "Will I get the satisfaction that I want? Can I make such-and-such a demand and expect it to be met?" With the answers to those questions, you can make a clear decision about entering the relationship.

When you have this clarity, you have to accept what you are, and what you want. It is no use trying to be somebody you are not or chasing after something you think you ought to want. You have to be clear, also, about what you are able to give, and what you are able to forego in the relationship. When you are as clear as you can possibly be, you will avoid the heartbreak and disappointment that comes from expecting something of yourself that you cannot do or asking for something that the other person cannot give.

The demands you make of your relationship come from your illusions. You believe you have the power to change your partner so that he or she will provide what you want. "Then," you think, "things will be all right." Or you think changing the circumstances will improve the situation, so perhaps you decide to have a baby: "*Then* everything will be all right." But that won't improve anything, and it is a very unfortunate way to bring a child into the world.

Another word that needs to be examined carefully is love. We continually abuse and misuse words. If you look at the word love, we say we love potatoes but we don't love green beans. This has nothing to do with love. Friendship is another word we abuse: "Come and meet my friend. Now, what was your name, please?" We have stripped the meaning from very important words that express the most beautiful and valuable and refined feelings just by overusing them and misusing them until they have nothing to say anymore. What word would you use now for a friend or for true love? There is no word for you to use.

The Devi of Speech—the power of speech—is extremely important. When you understand this, you will also recognize how you manipulate yourself with words, particularly emotionally and mentally. You will see how you hypnotize yourself into ideas.

So what do we mean by love, particularly in regard to sex and marriage? Each one of you has to have a correct definition of that word. Clarify to yourself what it is that *you* would call love. For example: How much does being accepted come into your definition? Is what you call love only a matter of convenience? There is no harm if you *know*. The harm comes when you start deceiving yourself into thinking there is no self-interest in what you are calling love. When you do that, you are putting a skeleton into your closet, and one day it will rattle.

If love means somebody has to push your buttons, that has nothing to do with love. You may as well say, "I like to imagine that you love me. To help my imagination, this is the button you should push." You don't really investigate how somebody shows love; you just ask to have your buttons pushed. If I determine what you should do to convince me that you love me, there's nothing you can do unless you know what button to push. This has nothing to do with love. It's very difficult for human beings who love each other to recognize this.

Love is also not the result of the satisfaction of biological urges. Everybody knows that. Why keep on playing that game? Why go on saying, "I love you" when it's not true, when all you want is to have your emotional and sexual needs fulfilled?

If you are carrying out a relationship as a moral duty, don't fool yourself into believing that it's based on love. Don't carry and nourish illusions that you know are not true. When the illusions are gone, you can be grateful for whatever the relationship gives you instead of complaining about what it doesn't give you. Then you can be *truly* concerned about the other person, because you are no longer putting an imposition on him or her to fulfill your illusions.

You have to look the facts clearly in the face and rip out all the illusions. It is a very brutal process. But if you do it *before* you get into hot water, you will avoid a lot of problems in the future. Once you are in a difficult situation, it's very hard to look at the facts, because all you see is your loss or your pain or your feelings of emptiness.

It is hard to live with no illusions to soften the facts, whether in marriage or in spiritual life. I used to think everybody coming to a spiritual path would be very committed, that they would live a certain way, do certain things, and think a certain way. I found out that was not the case at all. Sometimes it was just like a temporary affair. They would leave, suddenly, saying, "Now everything is better in my life. Thank you.

You have helped me through a bad time. Good-bye." Sometimes I would think the Divine had provided something permanently, only to find everything changed a few years later. It wasn't permanent at all, and that's true wherever there is human life.

The only way I know out of the dilemmas of human relationships—and I have given forty years to thinking about them and wrestling with them—is to dedicate whatever you do to the Most High. Dedicate *everything*, and make that surrender to the Most High as complete and perfect as you can, whatever perfection means to you. You may slip every now and again. You may have the desire to go on what I used to call a sightseeing trip—to do something you know you should not be doing. If you go ahead and do it, don't lose your awareness. Know *exactly* what you are doing, and remember there is nothing for free. I have occasionally eaten something I knew would not agree with me, and I have said, "Well, enjoy now and pay later." You always have to pay in one way or another.

You have to be really, really clear about everything you do. I cannot remind you of that enough. Every night, go over the day, go over what happened. Find out where your awareness slipped. By reflecting on the daily events, you can catch your slips. If you don't catch them, you just go back into your bad habits and do the same old things over and over again.

In the end, married or not, we have to make our way alone. As the Christian teachings say, it is you and you alone who will stand before the throne of God and give witness of the life that you have lived on Earth. There will be nobody holding your hand. It's the same with Self-Realization. It is attained by you alone. Another person can be a helpful influence, perhaps creating favorable circumstances for you in a personal relationship, but you achieve this state of awareness alone.

So take your heart and your prayers and put yourself thoroughly in the Light, and be on your way.

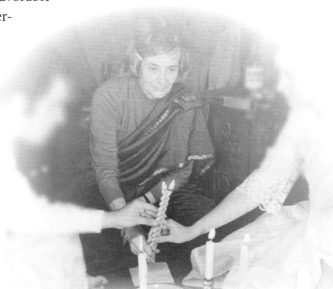

Fulfillment

PEOPLE SEEK FULFILLMENT in many different ways—in relation-ships, friends, relatives, family, work. Many people pursue it that way for years and years, wondering when it's going to happen, and why it really never comes.

A husband has his own inner life, even if he doesn't know it. His career—making money and providing for the family—is only tempo-rarily a fulfillment, which he may realize when the children leave home and there is no reason any more to strain himself to make ends meet or to be an excellent provider.

But men do not learn from their parents, or anywhere else, that they have a right to find fulfillment in the same way women have. How-ever, men mistakenly think their wives have fulfillment through having babies and bringing them up. If fulfillment is really in marriage and raising children, why do we see more than fifty percent of marriages breaking up?

The idea of seeking fulfillment has to be explored. Where is it that we should look for it? A raise in salary or escalating profits don't seem to supply it. That satisfaction is temporary. It lasts only a short time and afterwards there is a great emptiness which people try to cover up by going out to eat, or having expensive holidays, or watching television.

Even in this covering up, a man and a woman may not share inter-ests. He watches sports on television to cover up, but she couldn't care less about sports. Their personal temperament and makeup are very different. If you are in an intimate relationship with somebody who does not care for your interests, then you will be reluctant to care for the other person's interests. In a marriage, she may use his energies and he may use her energies. For what? Why do they use each other's energies? To forget, to sidestep knowing that there is an emptiness. These difficul-ties can remain unchanged over many years of marriage.

And why is it that people can barely stand to be alone unless they are busy with something? Is it so they don't have to look at the empti-ness that stares at them in moments of aloneness? The fulfillment that is sought cannot be found in all those activities.

We are seeking fulfillment and we don't know where to find it; neither do we know how to go about it, so years go by and we are still searching. If you don't want to let more years go by, then it's very important to sit down and ask, "What is my idea of fulfillment?"

Many people have found great acclamation for their work in the theater, in movies, in art. They can make people laugh or cry, they can overawe people with the products of their art. Yet even the most accomplished and celebrated artist is not fulfilled. Any writer will say, "I could have done that better." Any painter will say, "Next picture," until he or she again sits in front of the empty canvas and is terrified because there is that knowing: "No matter what I produce, however beautiful, however great a success, I will not be able to do what I want to achieve." An actress may have tremendous successes, and then we hear that she is going to a psychiatrist because she has states of deep depression, and she may even end up in a mental hospital.

What is it that people seek? You must ask yourself that question. Otherwise your life goes by, and death will be a terrifying moment, because you have not done what you took birth for. It's extremely important that you formulate something in your mind, however faint and weak your idea is, that will express what you are after.

Let's look a bit more at fulfillment in relationships. First, there is acceptance. You say, "Well, if you accept me, then it's easier for me to accept you." Do people accept each other? How long does that acceptance last—particularly when your partner is not doing what you want, when you are uncertain about your expectations, or when your expectations are left dangling. You have to look at all the "becauses," too: "I love you because, because, because. . . ." Relationship is a two-way street. That is true between partners, and it is true also between children and parents, because no one really knows the expectations of others. This is the first mistake we make in relationships: we really don't know what the expectations are.

Then there is the fact that life has become very complex in modern times, and presents us with a lot of challenges. Can you accept the challenge? Is the challenge too big? Is the acceptance of some very daring challenges a price too high to be paid? Will these challenges bring you closer to what you think you are here for? Will they give you that fulfillment? No. Even the greatest challenges you can accept will give you only temporarily a sense of fulfillment.

Let's look at togetherness. You may say, *"Together* we will do things, *together* we will build a career, *together* we will build a business." Sometimes this togetherness is done even at the cost of the family. The children are sometimes left to themselves while the parents build a family empire. Even though it may be important to the parents, it should not be built at the expense of children, whether they are small or whether they are teenagers.

Then we can look at needs—his needs and her needs and the children's needs. Accepting challenges and wanting to be accepted by another are really just ways to provide for our needs. They are really a disguised form of self-gratification. When those needs are not met, trouble is right there, waiting. The breaking point is often reached very quickly between a husband and wife or between parents and children when needs are not met. The parents will say, "You are on your own. I have had enough of you." Or the children will say, "You cannot run my life. I want to run my life myself," and so they may have to learn the hard way.

The togetherness that was envisioned was really only a dream. We all dream, not just at night. We have our daydreams, our expectations. Clarify your expectations, and be as straightforward and as honest as you possibly can! Don't just say words. Don't intellectualize. I have seen all these things happen. People make beautiful vows to each other on the wedding day, but in only a couple of years they don't even remember them.

Those expectations—those vows—need to be discussed. They look fine on paper and when you pronounce them at your wedding, but what's going to happen afterwards? How will you accept each other when some of these promises become shaky, or disappear, or there is an unwillingness to meet them, or when a sacrifice is demanded by one party and the other will not make that sacrifice?

You see, before we can really become spiritual people, we have to look at who we are, we have to look in the mirror and see ourselves as clearly as possible. I have met people who tried to meditate for years but did not really succeed. They read in a text about Kundalini that there are great spiritual powers, but they haven't attained these powers because you have to come face to face with yourself first, before you can enter that spiritual temple.

This is very well illustrated in a lovely little story about the devotee who sang his heart out to Lord Krishna, singing bhajans and Mantras and even just Krishna's name. Finally, one day after a number of years, he said, "Lord, I always try to come to you. You never come to *me*. I am getting discouraged. Do you really hear me?"

Lord Krishna said, "Yes, I will come. I have heard you. I will come on such-and-such a day, such-and-such an hour."

The devotee began to clean up his house. He opened doors and windows and threw everything out, as is traditional with many people. If you drive along their roads, you see them littered with all sorts of things. Then came the appointed time for Lord Krishna to appear, but he didn't. So the devotee waited one day, two days. Maybe he hadn't heard right. Maybe he had made a mistake about the time. After a week he was sure that Lord Krishna would not come. So, again, in his chanting he approached Lord Krishna and said, "Lord, you cannot break promises. You wouldn't want me to break *my* promises. You tell us always how serious it is to break any promises. You promised to come and you haven't."

Lord Krishna said, "Oh, yes, I came, but there was so much garbage lying around your house, I felt disinclined to step over it."

So, you see, we are not ready if we are surrounded by our resentments and anger, and by a lot of old stuff from the past that we should have been finished with years ago. We are not perfect. It would be good if we looked at our own shortcomings and then said, "Well, the shortcomings of So-and-so (my wife or my husband) aren't all that much worse than mine. In fact, perhaps they are pretty much the same. So what's the big deal?" Where's your generosity? If you are so spiritual, then you should be able to be very generous with other people and say, "It's okay. I have made my mistakes, you make yours. We have our weaknesses."

But let us deal from a point of strength, not from the point of our weaknesses. If we deal with each other in any human relationship from a point of strength, we are on the right track. If we deal from a point of our weaknesses, we aren't.

There is a story of a great artist whose name you may know: Anna Pavlova. She was a great Russian dancer. When she danced the dying swan, you could have heard a pin drop in the auditorium. Then one day she thought she was missing something: "Women should be married, should have babies. And maybe I will miss all that. What's my life going to be without that?"

She had a friendship with a man that she liked and felt she could live with, so she said, "Well, he would be as good as anybody." But she acted at that time from a point of weakness, from her need as a woman for companionship. She got married. Then came the division. Yes, she was going to be a great wife and fulfill all the wifely duties. But after a short while she felt she just couldn't do this. It was leaving her empty. There were no challenges. Being a lovely, dutiful wife did not give her any fulfillment. But her husband, who was also quite successful in business, felt it was wonderful. He had this famous woman—the world lay at her feet—and she was *his* wife. But we can get used to anything, even marriage to a famous person. After a while, it's not so special any more.

Finally, this man could see that his dutiful wife was doing things with much resentment, so they talked it over, and she said, "Let's not get in each other's hair. Your world is business. My world is dance. I can give inspiration to people when they come to a performance. They can forget their worries, their troubles. For a couple of hours, I can still something in them."

What he thought about business has never been told, but I can imagine that he stepped back into a man's world of business, free of the obligation to entertain and be a super husband to a famous woman who had given up her career. He was paying too high a price for this marriage, so after a while, when his vanity had been gratified, he was not willing to pay the price. Marriage to a ballerina, adored and worshipped the world over, was not giving *him* any fulfillment, either.

There are women who are born for a career. There are women who are born to be mothers. But they should be clear which way to go. Motherhood should not be just a temporary delight. It should not be only a temporary response to a biological urge. To put a new life into the world means a great deal of responsibility. That responsibility should be looked upon very clearly. Many a young girl dreams she is going to sit in a rocking chair with her baby like a Madonna, and her husband will sit at her feet adoring her and being grateful forever. If she marries with this dream, she very soon finds out this is not the case. It's a fantasy that has little reality, if any. This loving husband, this loving wife, these are fantasies.

We are often in love with the *idea* of marriage. That's different from really wanting to be married and accepting all the ups and downs and everything that comes with it. We are in love with the idea of love, but we really don't know how to love. We say, "Oh, I fell in love with this man or this woman." Or, "No, I fell out of love. Terrible things happened." We say we "make love." You can't make love. Love is a force and it can flow only through a heart that does not demand. But it's not one heart. It's not just hers or just his. Love cannot be at the cost of one or the other. But love that really flows through *both* hearts—his and hers— is very rare, probably one in ten million. But we want to believe that everybody can grasp that for themselves. It is a deep-seated desire.

You have to find out what your desires are, where they come from, and if there is a reality to the fulfillment of those desires. Why do we have these feelings and urges? Why do we have these images of the dream woman, the dream prince? Because there is some divine spark in us, and we are seeking union with that. Even the best of husbands and the most ideal of wives cannot provide that. Human frailty, human weaknesses, will keep you from that fulfillment.

Freedom is another idea. People often think, "I will be a fulfilled person if I have freedom and independence." Freedom from what? The freedom you need is probably not freedom from the duties of being a husband, a wife, or a son or daughter. The freedom you need is freedom from your limitations, from your weaknesses that need really to be dealt with seriously, and not just tinkered with a little bit here, a little bit there.

And what is the independence you are seeking? Emotional independence, financial independence? Emotional and financial independence go hand in hand, something simply not understood by male psychologists and psychiatrists. But now many men, because of work situations, have become economically dependent on their wives, and they are beginning to realize that they are also emotionally dependent on them. And they don't like it, because it's not the image that they have of themselves. That's not the tradition. Now what?

You see, a person who is dependent—and most of the time, for the last few thousand years, it has been women who have been dependent—a person who is dependent says, "I love you. Oh, you are so great! You are wonderful! There is nobody who can do things that well." And in the other person, there is a tiny little voice that says, "Why do you tell me this so often? You are telling me this again. Oh, of course. You are trying to make me emotionally dependent, because if I am not you will be left in thin air."

If one partner says to the other, "I love you," that love is already indicative of dependence. But if a partner is independent and says, "I love you, but I can also live without you," that love can be trusted. There is no "because" attached to it, and no heavy dependence.

Will love like that lead to fulfillment? No. It will give you an inkling of what fulfillment could be, but that isn't it. It's a gateway to that fulfillment, but you have stepped through only the first gate. There are a couple more to come.

Next comes self-expression: "I am a loving wife and a loving mother, and I try to wash the dishes, do the cooking, and all the rest of it with all the love possible." But there is a limit to how much you can put into that. Later on, the food may become poisoned with resentment.

Many a mother has said to me, "Three months for a course at the Ashram! I can't desert my husband for that long! I can't leave my children!"*

I have said, "Why not? You think they are happy with such a resentful woman? I have to step back from you because your resentment hits me right in my solar plexus, it's so obvious. Perhaps if you do the course you will come back a different person, with a little more knowledge of yourself and a little more self-control, and perhaps with an inclination to look at the facts as they are, not as you want them to be." Usually, if they come, it has worked out that way.

---

* The Ashram's Yoga Development Course is a three-month long intensive personal and spiritual development course.

Looking at facts, at truth, is very cruel. Self-expression says, "I want to paint, I want to be an artist, I want to be a dancer, I want to be a great actor or a great actress, I want to be anything that gives me fame." When I was twenty-seven years old I was at the height of a career as a concert dancer. I was one of the first European dancers to present Oriental dances. Like any other artist, particularly of my age group, I wanted to perform in *the* most famous theater. When that day came and I was finally there, I said, "Here is the great moment! But where is the great feeling of incredible happiness and fulfillment? What happened to it? Where is it?"

The applause of the audience didn't move me, because I realized at that moment that through my art I could manipulate them. I could create responses of an emotional nature in them that anybody who acquires the same skills can do. I was terribly disappointed on that evening of my greatest success. People couldn't understand that. *This was it*—and it wasn't enough.

So I began my own search and for many years I could not find what I was looking for. I saw friends getting married, having babies. I got married, too. I could see that this was not it, but companionship is very nice, particularly if your husband adores you. It takes a while before you know that he really is in love with the dancer or with the artist, that he knows very little about who you are as a person. When that penetrates, it is the next disappointment.

I was an only child from a very wealthy family and like any rich girl, I didn't marry a poor boy. I married into another millionaire's family, so I knew all about what money and social status can do. But the fulfillment wasn't there, either.

It took a long time for me to find what I was looking for. It was not until 1954 when I was in Canada that I had the experience in meditation of meeting my Guru, Swami Sivananda of Rishikesh. I didn't find out who he was for some time after that, but when I finally did, I wrote to him, and he replied, "You are coming home." From then on I could see that I was on the royal highway to fulfillment of a very different kind.

When I met Swami Sivananda Saraswati, he opened the door and my life began. I was already forty-four years old. Until then I had been like everybody else—a zombie, going from this thing to that, thinking they were the right things to do. I really didn't know that there could be a purpose in life, and yet there was an undercurrent that was always saying, "There must be more to life. My God! It's just constant repetition. This cannot be *all* there is to it."

Tradition, of course, had blocked the way for me. Traditionally you don't do things that make you an outsider. People say, "You belong to a cult. That's awful." But I said, "I have to find out." I also wanted to know where I came from, I wanted to know about Western spiritual philosophy, what was behind it. So after studying many things of the East, I went into the history of Christianity. I think any Christian should do that, or any person who has a Christian background. I studied the history of Christianity, only to find out it was a cultic offspring of Judaism. And then I found out Judaism was also not a new religion. It was an offspring of ancient Egyptian religion. Many things in the Old Testament, I was shocked to find, had been written a few thousand years before by Egyptians. So where did it all begin?

For a while, I was very confused. Then I said, "But in all those thou-

sands of years there have been people upholding ethics and ideals. They have tried to search for the Most High in a variety of ways. In nature, there is not just *one* flower, there is not *one* type of tree, there is not *one* type of insect, there is not one type of *anything.* And there is not just one type of people. There are many types of people, and so there are as many ways to approach the Most High. The symbol of Light was a very appealing one to me. We cannot count the rays of the sun, but if we could, we would see there are many rays and we can use each one of these to travel to the center from which the light has emanated. I think this is the greatest promise, that this great divine Cosmic Intelligence, Energy, whatever you want to name it, has so many rays to be perceived, has so many forms, so many names, that you can choose whatever is best for you at a given time in your life.

As you progress, as you grow from a spiritual birth into spiritual life, your approach to that divine Cosmic Energy is bound to change. It's like going to school. You learn to write the alphabet, then you learn to form words, then sentences. Then you learn the intricacies of grammar so you can write stories. One day you can even write poetry. So, a tradition is a good place to start, but we must not be imprisoned by it. However, we must not destroy it at a cost to others. The tradition that has no more use for you is still very helpful for someone else. Don't interfere. Let it happen.

When you start your spiritual journey, you are like a little toddler. You toddle around confused for a little while. But as you pursue your path, you will experience in your own way, within your own makeup and temperament, that the Divine is ever available, regardless of what shape and form you give it or what name. And you can increase and deepen your faith only when you allow it to be tested.

People sometimes think they are being disloyal to a particular group of people if they leave the group. Sometimes, when I meet students from years back, they do not want to see me, but I walk up to them and ask, "How are you doing?"

They say, "Well, you know. . . ," and they stutter around.

I say, "It's all right. It's all right. Wherever the seed of the Divine has taken root, that's all right. I'm a sanyasi. I am not here to collect the fruits and count the membership. If you have found a place that you need for now, stay. Be the best. *Do* the best wherever you can."

When we seek the Divine, only the approach is different. You may call the Divine by the name of Jesus and the Virgin Mother, and I may call it Lord Krishna and Radha. Somebody else may call it Siva and Parvati, or Buddha and Yasodhara. These are just different names for the same thing.

We make things so complicated, yet it's very simple to understand. Let me give you an example from our own Western background. We talk of Jesus, the Son of Mary, the Carpenter, the Galilean, the Crucified, the Shower of the Way, the Healer, the Speaker of the Sermon on the Mount. I don't remember all that he is called, but we are always speaking of the same person. These different names only represent different aspects.

When we call him the Carpenter, we mean the man who is practical, who can do things with his hands and who will honor any kind of work. When we speak of the Son of Mary, we are speaking of the little baby aspect that she gave birth to, or the man who was taken down from the cross that she held in her arms. It is always one and the same Jesus.

Bear this in mind, because you often create your own confusions. Communicate within yourself well. If you learn to communicate with yourself, you will also communicate well with others. The communication between your mind, even your doubting mind, and the Most High in yourself, is a very fruitful and rich communication. Don't choke it.

In other words, in your communication even with your most beloved, be honest. But you can't unless you are first honest with yourself. How much do you want to give? How much are you really trying to get? Unless you know where you stand, on which end of the pole, you cannot meet with your beloved, whether it's a human being or the Divine. You cannot meet in the middle, in the center, unless you know who you are. You do not find yourself by *going* somewhere, by leaving your house, because wherever you go, you take yourself with you.

To men who want to leave their wives, or women who want to leave their husbands, I have said, "Why?"

"I want to find myself," they say.

I say, "What will you find? The same person that you are here to-night you will find wherever you go." Some people who did not choose to listen have met with great disappointments, because finally this truth became clear.

Fulfillment is a very important word. It has to have meaning. You have to know where in your life it is, and where you seek it.

Be more generous, be more of the giving type. Think about the beautiful Saint Francis Prayer where Saint Francis asked not to be understood but to understand, not to be comforted but to comfort. If you can give freely and generously, you have the first experience of inner fulfillment. The joy that you give to others, that joy reflects back to you. That is pure joy, and it is that joy that will give you fulfillment.

The Prayer of Saint Francis

Make me a channel of thy peace;
Where there is hatred, let me sow your love;
Where there is injury, your pardon, Lord;
And where there's doubt, true faith in thee.

Make me a channel of thy peace;
Where there's despair in life, let me bring hope;
Where there is darkness, let me bring your Light;
And where there's sadness, ever joy.

O, Master, grant that I may never seek
So much to be consoled as to console,
To be understood, as to understand,
To be loved, as to love with all my soul.

Make me a channel of thy peace;
It is in pardoning that we are pardoned,
And giving unto all that we receive,
And dying, grow into eternal Light.

Spiritual Life in the Family

THERE ARE GREAT SPIRITUAL OPPORTUNITIES in the family. People often think they can start on the spiritual path only when they have achieved purity, or their children are grown up, or they have left their husband or wife. This is not so. My own Guru never said to anybody, "You must walk out on your family," nor have I ever told people to walk out on their children or spouse.

When I asked Gurudev Sivananda about this, he said leaving was not the point. He used to say, "Why do people want to walk out? Let them become free of all their attachments and emotions right where they are!" The point is to perfect yourself wherever you are. Make your situation, whatever it is, the battlefield of the Gita. Then in due time, when you are sincere and earnest about what you want to do, the circumstances will develop in such way that you can achieve it.

Having been a medical doctor, he would often use examples from medicine. He would tell people who were dissatisfied with their situations, "If you are a very skilled surgeon, or very good diagnostician, you won't be asked just to roll bandages, because there is other work where you will be more useful, more needed." It's the same on the spiritual path: if a man makes himself a perfect father, or a woman makes herself a perfect wife, the door will open for them.

What kind of person you want to be—physically, mentally, emotionally, and spiritually—is your decision. Make that decision. Put it into action and achieve it. Set goals for yourself about what kind of a person you want to be, and about the things that make your life worth living. Then live in the family accordingly.

Attachment, self-importance, and possessiveness have to go. It is only then that you can truly love your partner or your children—or anyone else for that matter. Your ideas about what people should do or what they should want do not express your concern for others. They are only products of your self-will. What *you* want for another person or what *you* think your children should want for themselves is nothing but an attempt to impose your will on them. However, once you reach a state where you can love someone without being possessive, without attachment, you may at first think you have lost the capacity to love, that you don't care for anybody any more. But it is only your attachment that has disappeared.

People often complain that all their time and efforts are taken up by their family. If you find that your life is entirely focused on your husband or wife or your children, it is because that is where you have chosen to place your focus, so don't complain about that. Instead, decide how you want to shift it.

I once spent the morning in spiritual discussion with a woman who had four children, the youngest being a boy of fifteen. She told me she was happy that I had come because she had no spiritual nourishment in her life. Yet the moment the boy walked into the house, she got up and asked him, "What would you like for lunch?" The whole morning of receiving the teaching had meant nothing to her. Making lunch for her fifteen-year-old son was what she was focused on, and she had probably been thinking all along, "What is the time? He will be home soon."

You can make having a family the excuse for not living a spiritual life, and you can make spiritual life an excuse for leaving the family. Neither is necessary. You can live a spiritual life wherever you are. All you need to do is shift your focus to the place where it should be. That is your decision, nobody else's.

You can decide instead to concentrate on purifying your conduct and emotions. In a family it is particularly important to purify the emotions to avoid possessiveness. Concentrate on activities of loving kindness, compassion, joy, and equanimity within the family. Possessiveness has no place in a family. Every mother or father has to set the children free eventually. You cannot live through your children. You cannot have them do precisely what *you* want. Everyone has his or her own karma. Where your children are concerned, you are only God's caretaker.

Also, possessiveness and self-importance can wipe out all your attempts at spiritual life. Get rid of them.

To purify your emotions, you need to know yourself. It takes a lot of self-searching to know where you are spiritually, and why you do what you do. If you haven't done this searching, you don't really know whether what you think is real or not real. You don't truly know what your feelings are, or whether they are free of possessiveness. If you do not know these things about yourself, you will beat out all your problems on someone else's back—your spouse, your children, the people at work, the Guru. That is very hard on everyone around you, and it isn't much of a life for you either.

Whatever your situation is in life, however, you must make the best of it, even without help. You can do the work of purification on yourself and gain self-awareness anywhere. The *Kundalini* book* contains many methods for dealing with problems. Although I have put it as simply as possible in that book, most people sense the difficulties of putting these methods into practice, so they read the book and find it fascinating, but they don't try to do what is suggested. However, even a small amount of work is a gain. You can start getting yourself out of the deep shadow into more Light, and you can make your life better by working on yourself. Even knowing what you are attached to is a big advance in itself. Make lists of your attachments as you understand them, and then every day in your reflection map your progress in becoming free of them.

Or you can reflect on positive mental states, such as confidence, trust, self-respect, non-hatred, alertness, equanimity, and nonviolence. If you take even one of these and look at your day in relation to it, you will see many positive places where you did the best you could. You will also find other times where you were thoughtless, careless, or forgetful. Remind yourself about your goal and keep going.

Perhaps one day your husband, or your wife, will say, "You are so pleasant, so thoughtful, I hardly know you any more." But it will take time. It will take more than setting a good example for a couple of days or a couple of months, or for that matter a couple of years, to make a change in the family, because for many years you have put out an image to your family that is not easily eradicated, and you have to take responsibility for that, too.

If a departure from family life is unavoidable, you should part as two friends. Say to each other simply: "I cannot give you what you hoped

---

* Radha, *Kundalini Yoga for the West.*

for and expected from me, and I am sorry to say that you cannot give me what I need. Let's not quarrel. Let's be friends." A legal divorce may not even be necessary. Try taking an absence of six months or a year to find out what spiritual life is really like. Life in an ashram or a monastery may look very glamorous when you are in the family situation, but it can lose its attractiveness very quickly because, as Indira Devi says, in an ashram you live in a greenhouse. You are constantly watered and under observation, so you grow faster. And you may not want to grow that fast! You may have illusions about what spiritual life is without understanding the facts. For example, you will have to give up a lot. Money is the least of it. You may find it very difficult to wear only the clothes that are given to you, and to eat only the food that is given to you. There are also emotional attachments which can be hard to deal with—for example, the first Christmas or the first birthday that you spend alone in a spiritual life, away from family. Also in a spiritual community, there is really nobody to talk to, because when you are meeting yourself at the gut level, nobody *really* wants to hear about the pain and agonies you are experiencing. It's a very lonely road.

But if you have to walk alone, within a family or without friends, that's your karma, and you can do that, too, if you have to. There are many women who live a secret spiritual life. Their families know nothing about it. These women don't need to talk about it, or argue or be opinionated about it. They just quietly do their job. Then the time may come when their Divine Committee says, "That's enough now," and sets them free. I know one woman who was dropped after many years of marriage. When the first shock was over, she said to me, "You know, I'm really glad it happened, because I was too duty-bound. I would never have even thought of walking out because I had taken my marriage vows so seriously. Now, one part of me is hurt, but the other part knows *I have been set free.*"

When your time comes, you can be sure the Divine will have work ready for you. But you must know what you are offering, what it is that you want to give, and you must have the humility to wait and to ask for help. It will come. No amount of talking about it will bring you to that point. It is practice and study, hand in hand, that will do it.

Companionship

COMPANIONSHIP IS SOMETHING many people search for without really asking themselves what it is they want from the other person. This is a very great mistake which leads to misunderstandings and pain.

First, you must clarify to yourself what your needs for companionship are. You may not have many needs and some of them may be quite simple, but they may be extremely strong. You may have a need simply to touch someone. Often people who have a need for touch will acquire an animal they can pet.

Once you have established what your need is for companionship, find out also what your expectations are. In a companionship between two people, there are many expectations. Most are emotional. The usual answer is, "I want a friend." If that is so, you then have to ask yourself, "What is a friend? What does it mean to have a true friend, or to *be* a true friend?"

When you investigate companionship, you may discover a number of things to which you have been blinding yourself. Sometimes companionship is based on blackmail; sometimes on bribery. Very often it is a matter of playing games. There is a certain excitement in playing games, but if the companionship is not well-balanced, one person becomes the victim of the other.

There are also many false beliefs about companionship, especially where love and marriage are concerned. Love, like companionship, has many facets. We can talk about mother's love, divine love, romantic love. It is important to know what you mean by love, and whether you truly love, or whether you are only in love with the *idea* of love, or the *idea* of marriage. Being in love with an idea can be very deceptive. To be in love with an idea of marriage, for example, does not make you capable of truly being the other half in a marriage. It does not make you capable of taking the other half of the responsibility, and it does not make you capable of being accommodating, understanding, and compassionate. To be in love with an idea, *any* idea, is to maintain intentional blindness, supported many a time by the power of self-suggestion. We tell ourselves that we love the other person, or that we are happy in the marriage, when really the power of suggestion is preventing us from looking clearly at what is actually going on. We blackmail ourselves when we pretend that something is a certain way, while deep within ourselves we know it is not so. A needy personality aspect can bribe us to stay with a false belief for a long time.

You also have to look closely at the companionship between yourself and those who you think are your close friends. How sure are you that you really are close friends? Very often closeness in a friendship is only an unacknowledged desire, one that may not even be fulfilled. There can be much pain in having a desire you do not admit, and even more pain if that desire is not being met. The companionship may be one of convenience, or it may be simply a bond involving mutual gratification of emotional needs. It may have come into existence to take care of fears, such as economic fears, fear of getting sick, fear of being alone, fear of not having anybody to talk to, fears about safety, or even fear of being alone with yourself.

For these reasons, close friends, or people who consider themselves close friends, do not necessarily understand each other very well. You may discover this in your own friendships and it comes as a real surprise, but it is necessary to strip away the illusion of what you would like to believe, so you can see what *is*. How do you define the word *friend*? What do you expect from the person you would call your "best friend?" What would you have to offer as another person's best friend? In a friendship, you have to leave aside as much as possible the demands that your own needs be filled, because otherwise you are just making friendship another opportunity for self-gratification. This is seeing the naked truth, this is meeting yourself on the gut level.

True friendship is not always a parallel relationship, because there is much giving and taking in life. But if you can give happily at one time and take willingly at another, then your friendship has a future. When your relationship with the Divine takes over, however, even that kind of friendship may end, because we can find Realization only as individuals, not with another person.

Sometimes we have an inkling that things are not quite as we believe them to be in a relationship, but we prefer to ignore that vague knowledge. There can be an attachment even to our *mistaken* love, to the belief system which created it, and to the self-suggestion which sustains it. Our attachments are not just to money and possessions, or to people, or to conveniences. Attachments can be *extremely* subtle, making it difficult to discover them all, and attachments that are mistaken for love in companionship can be deeply disappointing.

Because of the attachment to intentional blindness, we do not recognize our mistakes. However, one day we will wake up to our own self-deception, and then we may respond by feeling deceived or betrayed by the other person. We may even begin to feel betrayed before that day of awakening actually arrives. But it is our attachment to a false belief system that has deceived us, and not the other person.

It is of great importance to discover all these things, because they are a weight that presses you down. It is harder to focus on the Divine when your focus is all on your companion and on the hopes, attachments, expectations, and conveniences that you have invested in the companionship. These are what keep you from truly knowing.

There is also a kind of strange, unhealthy, almost compelling loyalty in some relationships. It is a perverse loyalty often acquired by people in a relationship to make their own feelings acceptable or legitimate. This can turn into a real merry-go-round of justification and self-deception. But true loyalty can come only from a pure heart, from a true conviction, not from a false belief system.

Some of the games played in relationships are really deadly, both to the relationship and to the individuals in it. What lies behind these deadly games is a tremendous effort to be liked and accepted. That effort exacts a price far beyond any return that it ever gives. If you have to make such acrobatic efforts to please, to be accepted, you may be again submitting to a mistaken belief—the belief that what you do will make you accepted. If your efforts have to be that strenuous, however, your situation may be very delicate. It could be that you have only to make one mistake that is emotionally displeasing to your companion, or create only a small inconvenience, and you will be rejected. Then all your effort will have gone for nothing. We have all seen this many times in our own lives and in other people's lives. The value system that has created these unhealthy situations has to be investigated keenly and in great detail. You may find that you have to abandon it completely.

The effort to be accepted has to be directed somewhere else. You cannot get the acceptance you are looking for from other people. All human beings are born alone, and we must accept being utterly alone. If there is anywhere that we can turn for companionship, it is nowhere but to the Divine. Your need for acceptance has to be turned to the Divine. Being accepted by the Divine is your true goal.

The mistake you make in your tremendous efforts to achieve acceptance is that you have not respected your own sincerity and your own honesty. In the need to be accepted, you may have sacrificed your hon-

esty and sincerity for the sake of an unproven belief system, one that is built only on imagination and emotional greed. When honesty is not included in your interactions, the companionship is unhealthy. One person is arrogant and dominates the other.

On the spiritual path, one can claim to love the Divine, when one really wants only to catch the attention of others. Honesty on the divine path, with love for the Divine, has to be right to the bone. Otherwise we live a lie. If you seek spiritual life only to get attention, you fall between two chairs. You are neither following the divine path, nor seeking a successful life in the world. You are nowhere, and that is not a good place to be. Your decision has to be clear-cut. Success on the spiritual path is irrelevant if you measure it by what is recognizable to other people. Success can be measured only by divine inspirations. And these have to be true, not born of a fertile imagination.

So is there a right kind of companionship? Before we can ask that, we should ask: "Is there a right kind of love?" I think there is. Love is where there is forgiveness, where there is understanding, where there is giving, and where there is being undemanding—and where there is no expectation. You cannot ask, "If I give you this, what do I get in return?"

As Gurudev Sivananda used to say, "Some people give a cup of water and expect to get a cup of coffee in return. They always want back more than they give."

The true aspirant gives all, and asks nothing in return. That can be very hard, particularly in the early stages of development. We want in return some confirmation from the Divine that we are doing the right thing. In the very early stages, that is acceptable, or at least excusable. But to expect something in return for what we give to another person, that is no true giving. That is bargaining. Be clear about when you are giving, and when you are making a bargain. Don't say, "I give," and then start bargaining about it later.

So what then is the right kind of companionship? In the end, no companionship will sustain you. Being alone has to be faced. You were born alone. You will die alone. It is the Light that will sustain you. What good does it do to surround yourself with something other than the Light? Friendships come and go. People come and go in your life. Have a companion on the royal highway. Have the Light. Turn to the Light, because it is Divine Light that will lead you from darkness to the true Light. It will begin with the light of understanding of yourself: Where am I? Who am I? And then with understanding others. And from there to more and more awareness.

Inspiration will come from the Divine Light, or your ishta devata—the symbol that you have chosen to represent the Light: Tara, Siva, Krishna, the Virgin Mother, Jesus, Buddha, whatever suits you best, whatever you are closest to. When you have received this inspiration do not talk about it too easily and readily with others. Keep it sacred in the tabernacle of your own heart. Don't put it on the marketplace. Put your faults and shortcomings on the marketplace instead, because if you pretend you don't have any, you will be locking up tremendous power in keeping that pretence alive, in trying to be somebody you are not. Use your willpower to direct that energy toward the Light, and surrender it to the Light. That will get you where you want to go.

If you can make your total being follow the Light, you can overcome all obstacles. The words of the Divine Light Invocation Mantra are a perfect road map.

I am created by Divine Light
I am sustained by Divine Light
I am protected by Divine Light
I am surrounded by Divine Light
I am ever growing into Divine Light

To direct yourself really well, or to overcome whatever your shortcoming is—your arrogance, your anger, your resentment, your jealousy, your fear—make a very firm decision: *"I am ever growing into Divine Light."* Instead of talking when you walk from one place to another, recite the Mantra. When you are listening to somebody else talk, recite the Mantra in your heart.

Be accepted by the Divine. Struggle for *that,* not for somebody else's acceptance because that doesn't help you to surrender; it won't take you to Cosmic Consciousness. Very soon that person may be out of your life. He or she may move away, or find somebody else, or your companionship may lose its meaning because the other person's life may take a turn that you cannot follow. Your companionship should come from the ishta devata. Then you will have no disappointment, no letdown. And keep that relationship a secret. In secrecy, the power will grow.

Spiritualizing Marriage

PEOPLE OFTEN ASK ME if there can be a "spiritual marriage" between two people.* I am always careful about saying yes. The two people in any couple are individuals, each with his or her own past, which also includes individual past lives. The purpose for which each took birth can be very different, one from the other. The desire for the spiritual goal may not be equally strong in both of them. For one or the other, the spiritual journey may be only a small part of life. The equal desire for spiritual life is an ideal condition that you will probably never encounter. In any attempt to live a spiritual life together, these differences have to be accepted.

To live a spiritual life through marriage, you must both—husband and wife—be willing. If only one of you wants this and the other just goes along to please, it won't work. There has to be the desire for the Divine in both. If you are the one who is more interested, you must work to inspire your partner, but do not make it too hard a discipline or your partner will lose any interest in a spiritual path. And you must remember at all times that courtesy and friendship must never be dropped from the relationship.

Even if you are both interested in the spiritual path, you may not move in step. You may do different practices. Remain understanding and courteous toward each other, and let time bring the two of you into step.

If a couple is willing to acknowledge these differences and work

---

* For a full discussion of marriage on the path, see Radha, *From the Mating Dance to the Cosmic Dance.*

together, how should they go about living a spiritual life within their marriage?

The first and most important thing is this: in marriage on the spiritual path, both individuals have to put love for the Divine ahead of love for the other person. Your first love must be your love for God. If God doesn't come first with you, then someone else does, and that means you have put the Divine in second place. That is a great loss. Only when your love for the Divine is established can you turn to a more human type of love.

People often worry that this will break up their marriage. They say, "We have a good marriage, it's nice and peaceful, we are good friends, we have come a long way. Is spiritual life going to break all that up?" No. From what I have seen, people who draw together in spiritual life come together and meet on the top of the mountain, although they may go around the mountain in a serpentine way and there may be many tests to see if they are really putting their love for God first.

To help couples to begin spiritualizing their marriage, I suggest that before engaging in sex they chant Mantra or meditate together for half an hour. Any kind of spiritual practice that you do together in order to spiritualize your relationship before you engage in sex will definitely help you to get a rein on passionate feelings.

Spiritual practice can also bring together couples who have serious marital problems. They may have reached such an impasse that they face each other with a whirlwind of accusation between them and there is no way to talk sense with them. But if they can be brought to do some spiritual practice, the power in that can help them to move a little. They may not go in step, but there are many paths up the mountain and when they meet at the top they will be together in a different way.

On the spiritual path, everyone goes through times of dryness. Even the greatest of saints have experienced this. Marriage also goes in cycles and periods of dryness will occur. After between eight and twelve years of being married, you will experience a personal dryness in regard to the relationship. Then you need a time to be by yourself, to develop yourself, to be alone, to look inward instead of being always outwardly ready to provide for the happiness and peace of the other person. If a

couple can acknowledge that after ten years of marriage they are entering a different phase, instead of quarreling or parting, they can agree to explore the phase and discover how to deal with it. They may need to grant each other more freedom, although people do not always have enough trust in themselves to accept the gift of freedom—or to give it to another person.

After ten years, one of you may want a new partner, but let me tell you that new partner will just have different problems. The cycles will simply continue and in another ten years, or maybe much sooner, you will be back in the same boat. It is not so easy to find someone you can trust the way you have trusted a person you have been with for many years. You may want to part because the romance is gone, but you have to grow up. You cannot be like a child, always wanting fun. When the romance is gone, you have to mature within your relationship, and that maturing process will, of course, bring changes in the way you are with each other.

It is the same on the spiritual path. You have to become mature here as well. You may have been thinking of yourself as Divine Mother's

child, but one day you will have to say, "It's time to take off my baby shoes because Divine Mother needs the work done *now*. She needs somebody who is serious and willing to grow up." When that time comes, you have to take even more responsibility spiritually, you have to try harder to understand, and go deeper in your time of reflection.

When you want to bring about changes in your relationship, be very clear what you are doing, what your motivation is, and how you will actually proceed. Observe yourself, and know your methods of control and manipulation. To know yourself, you have to be ruthlessly honest. You cannot blame anyone else. You have to take responsibility. Every marriage experiences outside pressure; there's nothing unusual about that. It's how you *handle* that pressure, that makes the difference. You may sometimes complain just to get something off your chest, but that's as far as complaining should go. Challenges come to give you the opportunity to grow beyond the limitations that you have drawn around yourself, to give you the opportunity to go beyond yourself. You can go as far as you want to go. You can push out your self-created limitations so that you can know more, understand more, and make it to the top of the mountain.

If both partners are spiritual and make that their real bond, their marriage will change. They will become less possessive. There will be more trust and confidence between them. One will not always be watching the other to ensure that promises and marriage vows are being kept. Then there can come into the relationship a true deepening.

And when you get to the top of the mountain, then what? Wait until you are picked up by the Light. Maybe a great spiral of Light will come to you, or maybe your dreams will make an announcement. How it comes is different for everybody, but once you have even a little taste of that divine love, tenderness, sweetness, I can assure you nothing else will ever be good enough. The greatest love affair in the world ends, by physical death if by no other way. But a love affair with the Divine really only begins when you leave this Earth. So why be satisfied with less if you can have so much more?

Love

LOVE IS NOT EASY to define. You may love somebody because that person accepts you, is nice to you, does you little favors and pays you compliments, or gives you presents and invites you to parties . . . because, because, because. . . . When you love, there shouldn't be any "because" and *that* kind of love is very difficult to imagine, never mind to live.

Mainly what we consider "love" is a certain closeness with somebody or some people. That closeness we interpret as "love." But if the closeness ceases, we feel we have lost all love. A great sadness occurs when somebody dies or is lost, because at this point we lose the gratification we were getting from the closeness.

But was that closeness truly love? We see situations in life all the time where two people love each other and everything is great. But it takes just one incident, one displeasing action, one thing that is deemed unacceptable, and "love" goes out the window. Is that truly love? I wouldn't call it love. How many times does a woman reject a husband because he continually displeases her in one area, or a husband reject his wife for a single displeasing characteristic? They no longer see the love that still exists in many other areas of the marriage.

The love we seek as human beings is an illusion. It's the fulfillment of the concept each one of us has about love. Instead of pursuing this illusion, I usually suggest that couples be good friends. If you can be each other's best friend, you will have achieved a lot.

I am amazed how quickly people will walk out of a relationship. Their idea of love is satisfaction, and they say, "I am not satisfied any more. I have a need you don't meet," and they walk out.

Imagine if the Divine did that to us. We wouldn't survive. Do we please the Most High? We do many things from a certain sense of duty or as obedience, but that's not doing them for the love of God. We do very little for the love of God, and that is why we have so many squabbles.

I think the moments in a lifetime when we do something really for the love of God are so rare that you can count them on your ten fingers. These are moments when we rise above our personality aspects and really function through our essence. That's a particular state of mind and a particular state of consciousness, where we don't interact with anybody. When that happens, it's like a love affair between you and the Divine. But the rest of the time, you can only say that you are making the effort. Your effort is sometimes enough, and sometimes not enough, but you can't really say that you please God.

Perhaps there isn't any love other than truly divine love, because to love us God or Divine Mother constantly has to overlook all our faults, mistakes, shortcomings, broken promises, and broken intentions. We are either scattered or we are rigid. When we are scattered, our devotion is just here and there, now and then—nothing, really. When we are all persistence and regularity, our devotion becomes routine and loses depth.

So what is our love for God? That is very difficult to say. We are of two natures. We have a tangible, physical body that lives in a tangible, physical world which has its own reality. Then we live also in a mental world, where with our invisible thoughts we create a world of the unseen. We live in these two worlds, but most of the time we are not aware of doing so. When we go beyond our ordinary thinking world, beyond the world of our ordinary stream of thoughts, then we come more into a world of consciousness. But would you call it "love for God" if you are very attracted to that other stream of consciousness? I'm not sure if I would use the term "love." If you have an experience of that other state of consciousness, even just once, then that becomes *knowing*. You know that state exists and you want to experience it again. But I don't think we can compare that to what we call love.

When you are in a state of divine ecstasy, the word doesn't really matter. You have physical sensations, but not what you would normally connect with love. Your body temperature may change and you may have little awareness of your surroundings. You have an emotion that may express something of the separation of ordinary life. Certainly you have an awareness of how long you have been "away." You may feel ecstatic, happy that you have made it back again, because you haven't been in this state since yesterday, or since this morning. You become more aware and conscious of the time of separation, and then you experience a happy emotion. You think, happily, "Oh, I'm back again." It's as if the sun has just come out.

But you can't love the Divine as you can love an object or another person. You might say that you love the sun, but what you really mean is "prefer." You don't love the sun, because when the sun is really hot, you run away from it, seeking shade. It's very difficult, and sometimes quite ambiguous to talk about love of God.

When I look for Taras or Buddhas, I look at all the faces very carefully because I know how important beautiful faces are. Our sense of beauty needs to be satisfied. But then, you see, where's our love? We are now concerned that the face should be inspirational, should accord with our concept of beauty. Is this love of the Divine or love of beauty?

Most people say, "I can love only beautiful people. If a person isn't beautiful, I have to make a particular effort." I met a man once in New York who talked all evening about his beautiful master—how handsome he was, how well-proportioned, how beautiful his beard. There was nothing spiritual in his talk. He was in love only with beauty.

To Sarada Devi, Ramakrishna was God. Ramakrishna was not a handsome fellow, so it would take a lot, indeed, to discover the spiritual beauty on the inside, and to bypass entirely the human form of the man himself.

We all have a love for beauty. You have to define what beauty is for you. Then you can use it as a tool. Whatever is not beautiful within you, you can develop into beauty. You can also develop a means of expressing this beauty on the outside. But only you know whether the beauty you express on the outside is truly beauty from the inside. Only you can say if that beauty is a true reflection, an echo, of your inner beauty, or whether you are expressing beauty on the outside only to impress or manipulate others. This is very difficult to ascertain because you can flip-flop within seconds, depending on who crosses your path from one moment to the next. And the question of love is still not answered.

The only permanence in love is from the Divine, even when you don't recognize it, even when there is a separation. As long as you don't turn away, the Divine is facing you all the time. It's not the Divine who turns away. The sun doesn't disappear from the sky. It is only covered by clouds. It is usually the clouds of your own thinking, your own emotions, and even the feeling of "love," or whatever you want to call it, that comes between you and the Divine.

Pain is also part of the experience because pain is necessary in order to get out of duality, to escape the pairs of opposites—and we do not like pain. But the opposite of divine ecstasy is separation from the Divine, and that is painful so it is very difficult to get away from pain. We can escape pain only when we know that pleasure and pain are the same. We label an experience "pain" because we are moving from one opposite to the other. If we stand still, pain and pleasure are two sides of the same thing. We cannot have all pleasure and no pain. If I stand in shadow, there still has to be light because there wouldn't be any shadow otherwise. The light isn't there on my terms either—all light and no shadow. But we still try to love people on our own terms—because, because, because. . . .

Our aim has to be to come closer to accepting the Divine for what the Divine is. That's really the crux of the matter of love.

The evidence of divine love that we are all looking for is really not so difficult to find. Just look back in your life at all the dangerous or very unpleasant things that you have escaped. You may have been just on the edge, and then by some good turn of destiny, you avoided a disaster. You can see that grace has been functioning in your life to a large extent. If you look at where grace has worked for you, you will find there the proof and the evidence of divine love. Try to recall every situation in your life where you can clearly see how grace was operating (but don't bend anything to make it look like grace). When you have looked at these situations, you may also recognize that you haven't done anything specific to deserve this grace.

So how did it happen?

If you have received a lot of grace in your life, pass a little bit on to others. Have patience. Have understanding. Be kind. Be considerate, even if your patience is tested to its utmost.

Practical Aspects of Spiritual Life

WHAT IF YOUR IDEAS of spiritual life are only a dream? The dreams about spiritual life are manifold. People may say to themselves: "I may be clairvoyant, I may be clairaudient. People will admire me, people will pay more respect, perhaps people will worship me," and all this sort of thing. That may all happen. But be *extremely* careful. Realize that your human personality is little more than a ghost. In other words, it has little or no reality. The ego has no manifesting power. What is sometimes called manifestations of evil are really the manifestation of the accumulation of all negative, selfish gratifications. To clear them out, you have to do a lot of housecleaning, particularly in the mind. Ask many, many times: "Where are my thoughts? What am I thinking about?" Investigate the contents of your mind.

Have you ever looked at your dream of spiritual life to see what can be realized? Have you ever asked yourself how much you would give toward the manifestation of that dream of spiritual life? The power of the mind to manifest is enormous.

Of course, the karmic situation in your own life has to be correct. In other words, you cannot dream about what spiritual life will give you the way you dream about what money or love or success will give you. In spiritual life, you are dealing with a powerful reality, much more real than the life you generally think of as real.

And you have to plan for the future. In ordinary life, if you expect to live another ten years or twenty or thirty, you have to plan to take care of your health. Spiritually speaking, you have to do the same thing. You have to create a situation for yourself where you can continue to live a spiritual life. If you have just a few dollars in your spiritual bank account, that won't carry you very far. You will need to become not only a millionaire, but a spiritual billionaire. Then, as with any capital, you can live off the interest. There is no question about that.

What is a spiritual bank account? First, there has to be an understanding that you can't expect to get great rewards for a small effort, for a decision to be a little bit less selfish, a little less attached or less possessive. If you get any reward, it will take a long time because you have a lot of backlog to pay off. That backlog of karmic debts can be in some cases enormous. You can only hope that perhaps your dream of paying it off is indicative that you are nearing the end of it, or that you are at least halfway through.

In spiritual life, live as openly as you can. Have no secrets, nothing that you have to hide, whether it's books, magazines, pictures, visitors. Anybody should be able to walk into your room at any time. Living in the marketplace like this is not easy, but doing it for a number of years can be extremely helpful, because finally you will get over the need for secrecy.

Secrecy is really nonexistent. Gurudev Sivananda used to say, "Everybody has secret sins. But everybody else *knows* these secret sins. So where's the secret?"

Living this openly may be a little uncomfortable for a while, particularly for someone like myself who came from a very small family with no brothers and sisters and from a social level where everything was kept secret. Hypocrisy is all that emerges from that.

Learn to be alone, but learn to be with others as well. Because the oneness of all cannot be experienced when you are protecting your privacy too much. Of course, you have to do spiritual practice alone. Nobody can do it for you, and it's much more intense when you are by yourself. But have the right reasons for being alone and for doing practice.

When you do the Divine Light Invocation, do it with the thought in mind that, wherever you are, there is enough Light that everything you have and do can be seen. You don't even have to feel that you have to defend anything. If others don't agree with what you do, that's their business. As long as you are in your heart and you know what your number one commitment is, it cannot be violated.

So, it's very important that you find out what your number one commitment is. Don't dream about it. But be as specific and clear as you can. I have said this a thousand times, but I will say it still once more: "If the Divine comes first in your life, everything else falls into place." Then you have nothing to worry about, and there are no secrets. But if you have secret dreams that you keep to yourself, and you scheme their manifestation, things will not fall into place.

You see, you can cheat me by pretence, and you can cheat people who are trying to help you. But you can do this only for a certain length of time. You can cheat nobody forever. And make it known to your silly mind that you can never, ever cheat the Divine. That is sin. Your mistakes are one thing. But trying to cheat the Divine, *that* is *sin*.

You simply have to get that monkey mind disciplined. I feel sorry for those who have never been disciplined at home because they have to go through quite a process when they come to the Ashram. The same is true for those who have made little use of their intelligence. It doesn't matter whether you have a degree or not, or whether you are a self-made person. I expect you to use the intelligence that you have, to listen to what you hear, to think about it, and to reflect and understand. Otherwise, it's just hopeless to expect any progress.

In the courses and classes at the Ashram, if you haven't learned it before, you learn to use your intelligence. The use of intelligence is not a matter of I.Q. It's a matter of awareness and of learning from the mistakes of others. If you don't like criticism, then when you see somebody else's mistake, say to yourself, "I am not going to do the same thing. I am not going to invite this criticism."

If you have deep within yourself a little child who throws tantrums to get its way, you will need a lot of discipline to bring that under control—and the sooner the better. The circumstances under which you came into this life are all your own. Only you can bring discipline into your life.

Self-expression is another thing you must discipline. When there is too much emphasis on self-expression, your personal interests become too scattered. You can express yourself anywhere: how you organize things, how you run a house, how you cultivate a garden, how you cook—anything. But minimize self-expression where your work is intended to benefit others. That is very important. Benefiting others means being more giving. If you are focused on yourself, on self-expression, you are indulging in the kind of self-love that is a most destructive power. Do away with it as fast as you can.

If you do not have discipline, you cannot handle freedom properly. I sometimes have to clip people's wings when they come to the Ashram because they don't know how to handle freedom. But you will learn how if you are truly, honestly committed to that greater awakening to the Divine.

Self-importance is a wonderful tool for you to investigate yourself. That investigation can be part of your commitment toward discovering your truly divine nature. That you will wrestle with a lot of difficulties, there is no question. But you have to find where your priorities are. You need loyalty and commitment to the work, and you need respect for anyone who is honestly contributing to the divine work, never mind what the work may be. There is a certain strength in an individual who can do the work quietly, without hankering for recognition and show. What you *want* to do is one thing, and what you *ought* to do may be something else. Find out what you ought to do. It may not be what you already can do quite well, what comes easily.

On the spiritual path, people should not become dependent on me or on any Guru. They should not be here because I am here. The work is the divine work and it should not end when the Guru's life ends. Anybody who is truly committed will keep carrying it out.

I can imagine quite easily that some people have considered me fanatic because for me the work needed in the Ashram comes first. Some people have said to me that I sacrificed them to the Ashram. But I didn't. I cannot sacrifice anybody. I don't have the power to do that. What I do is use my best power of persuasion to keep people on the spiritual path, but that's as far as I can go. The rest is like planting seeds: I can water them, but it is the Divine who has to make the plant grow. And you have to allow yourself to be nourished, to be taken care of, so that you can grow.

Sometimes spiritual life and spiritual practice are not what many people expect. I wonder if anyone who knows me has ever asked, "What did Swami Radha do? Her days had ten, twelve, fourteen hours of hard work. When did she have time to do spiritual practice?"

Many a time in the early days of the Ashram I didn't have time to sit down for formal spiritual practice because I had to do all the domestic work myself. So domestic work had to be my spiritual practice. If you peel potatoes or wash dishes or make beds or whatever, and if you are truly committed to the Divine, you will be given the help and shown how to do it.

One way was shown to me by a young woman who spent six months with us before entering a monastery.

When I said to her one day, "Sometimes I fall asleep in the middle of my practice."

She said, "But you know, you can use all your work as spiritual practice. This is what they do at the monastery I am going to. As you straighten out a bedspread, you ask Divine Mother to straighten out all the wrinkles in the back of your mind."

"Terrific!" I thought.

Later on, I found many other ways. For example, for years before we had a dishwasher we often washed dishes until eleven o'clock at night, so I learned to do this: polish a glass, hold it up and say that I would like my thinking and my life to be that transparent. If you can become this transparent, you have nothing to hide. No secrets. Nobody needs to agree with what you do, as long as you know that whatever you have done, it can all be in the open.

Your commitment to spiritual life is something that has to be reviewed every now and then. You have to look at it as you look at your resolutions at the New Year. You can't say, "Oh, I did it once and it hasn't changed. I don't have to do it again." Find out. Watch yourself. What has first place in your life? If you don't think about your commitment and review it, you are less than lukewarm.

I warn you also not to switch schools of thought too quickly because you think one sounds more intelligent, or has a famous name, or because someone you know is a member or follower of a particular school. You can become very confused. You have to be clear about yourself first: What's in your mind? How well do you know your mind? Where are the impasses? How do you go in and how do you go out?

The decision about spiritual life lies with each individual. You may meet a teacher once in your lifetime for a short period of time, and that meeting turns your life. You may live in an ashram for years and years and years, and never do anything. I have seen this in India and I have, to some degree, seen that here also. If your desire for spiritual life is just on the surface it will run off. You have to take the teachings right into your heart. You have to put them into the tabernacle, the Holy of Holies. Constantly in your reflection, you have to examine what you have done each day against the decisions that you have made about spiritual life. Are you really fulfilling your aspirations? Are you really listening? Are you really surrendering, or are you just covering up for self-will?

Spiritual life can be a very exciting life. But too often, we seek excitement somewhere else, and that gets in the way.

Difficult Times on the Path

WHEN YOU UNDERGO times of difficulty, it is necessary to sit back and wait. Don't act. I have frankly admitted that sometimes I have felt like walking out of the Ashram. I haven't done so. I'm still here. At those times, I have had to assess my situation and say, "I'm not committed to *people*, because they change. They come and go. I am committed to the work, and to whomever Divine Mother sends me. If I walked out, I would be letting *her* down, not *people.* They will find somebody else. Or maybe it's very good if they have to stand on their own two feet."

You have to be true to that first love that was spoken of in the Book of Revelation where Jesus said to John, in that great visionary experience, "You have forsaken your first love."* Indeed we have. We have lived for our own pleasures. We have given up that first love, the love for the Divine, the source of all creation.

Temptations of any kind are tests to strengthen our faith. How would we react? What would we do? We can't be in life-threatening situations all the time to strengthen our faith, so we are given temptation and the darkness of not knowing how things will turn out.

There have been no great saintly people who have not experienced

---

* Revelation 2:4.

this darkness. Saint John of the Cross had *ten years* of total dryness where all his great visions, all his insights, all the songs of angels and whatever he had experienced, meant *nothing.* When I read about this, I was shocked! How can this mean *nothing*? What's left?

The indulgence in visions and beautiful feelings *is* an indulgence, and indulgences have no place when you are with the true Light.

People in the East have dark times, too. I met some who had been in this darkness for years, and this almost pulled the carpet from under my feet. I thought, "If this person has been living in the Ashram in Gurudev's presence for eighteen years and still has this darkness, then I don't have even a chance!"

That's not so. We all have the chance. We all have to go through that test. We all go through a desert. Even Jesus went through the desert for forty days. Let's remember that. Let's not have superhuman expectations. We become superhuman only by meeting the demands in the proper sense of not giving up. Even if you have to hold on by your teeth, your fingertips, or your toenails—just hold on. Wait.

When it ends, it's like two lovers meeting after they have been separated for a long time. What great joy! What a sparkle in the eye! What a smile! Let me tell you, when you meet the Divine again, on the other side of the desert, there is *no* description for what you experience then. And there isn't anybody who does not have to go through that desert. It's a very tough time. But hang on, however tough, because the tougher the time, the greater, also, the reward.

Jesus says if you get your reward on Earth, then you have had your reward.* But if your suffering at being separated from the Divine was so great that acknowledgment and praise meant nothing to you, then you *truly* get your reward from where it counts, from the Divine. That is permanent, and nobody can give you that.

Human beings will hate you one day, love you the next. The teeter-totter of love and hate can be very trying. You think, "Oh, here is somebody who *really* understands me, somebody I can talk to." It won't last, but we are always seeking something that will.

---

* Matthew 6:1, 5.

Turn to that one thing that *will* last. Nothing else does. Even if you stuff yourself to the point where you could burst, you get hungry again. You may have all sorts of spiritual entertainments, visions, or whatever you want to call them—"How fascinating, how interesting! Look at this!"—then they're gone. Then you wait for the next entertainment, and it doesn't come fast enough to please you.

As Jesus said, "Unless you see wonders and miracles, you won't believe."* It's not a matter of believing. It's a matter of an inner knowing. Don't ever deny that inner knowing. It's wonderful if you are a believer and have blind faith. But you can only go through life with blind faith for so long. Then it has to be verified.

Verification is there for the asking. You just have to ask for the right gift. There are many Mantras that give you all sorts of promises. You can have a son, a daughter, riches. You can conquer your enemies or your illnesses. You can know the future. All sorts of things. And then what?

That's the question that is always there. You always have to go a step further, and ask, "And then what? What happens after I have that? What is the next step?"

Teenagers have come to me and said, "I want to know what sex is, from *my* experience. I don't want just to hear about it, to read about it."

I say, "Yes. I understand that. The only thing is once you have had it, then what? What comes after? What if. . . ?"

---

* John 4:48.

I help them look at the consequences very, very clearly, and then I say, "If you can answer those questions, go ahead. But remember those consequences are going to take place."

When you go through the desert, you look for water. Water is symbolic for whatever you need to quench your thirst. Make sure that the water is crystal clear.

There are people who come to the Ashram for only a couple of years, and when they have what they think they need, they leave and go back to the world and keep on living. They have definitely become a little better, a little more honest, a little more straightforward, a bit more dependable, and that's all they want. It's sad that they don't ever ask themselves, "What next? What is the next step? What's going to happen now?"

You can cooperate with the Law of Evolution. That choice is available to each one of you. It's not a matter of how good you are, or how bad you are. Even if you are the greatest of the sinners, it's available.

Temptation

WE GO THROUGH LIFE with many temptations. There is temptation wherever you are, not only on the spiritual path. Handling food or money is a temptation. You may be tempted to eat an entire bowl of cherries and then say you don't know who did it. Everything is a temptation. I remember one time when I was just a little thing, between three and four years old. There were guests expected. Some special cherries with the stones removed were set out on a sideboard. I managed somehow to reach up and get a cherry. At that very moment, there was a tremendous clap of thunder, and I said, "For *one cherry*?" We get our warnings.

Temptation is always with us, and as we learn to deal with the smaller temptations, the object of the temptation gets more serious. After his enlightenment, Lord Buddha said, "Now I can leave my body. I have achieved what I labored so hard for. There isn't anybody here who really wants liberation, Self-Realization, so I can prepare to go, to leave my body."

Then he heard a voice—I think it may have been his own Higher Self—saying, "No, no, no. Don't do this. There are some people whose consciousness is covered with just a very thin layer of dust which can be wiped away with one stroke. For the sake of those, you must stay here and help them and teach them."

For the Buddha, the temptation was to leave Earth.

Temptation for Jesus was very different. First he was tempted to throw himself down from a high cliff, because the scripture said he could do this and never a bone in his body would be broken. But he realized one must not tempt God.

Then he was tempted by the devil who said, "If you will worship me, I will give you all the world, and all the power in the world."

Jesus said at that time, "Satan, get behind me."*

If we read about the lives of saints and yogis and yoginis and saintly women, the temptation for each one was peculiar to their individual circumstances.

On my first trip to India, I visited an ashram where I was invited to become the holy mother. I took that to Gurudev Sivananda, and with his mischievous manner he confirmed my suspicion that it was just all a temptation of the ego to test me. The funny thing is, when I returned three years later and I was wondering what had become of this ashram, the man who tried to persuade me to do this didn't even recognize me. The Divine had used him as an instrument because he was handy. We are often used as an instrument for conveying the divine message, or even delivering a temptation, because we are suitable or handy. To be a divine instrument has nothing to do with being particularly holy.

Yogananda liked to think of a saint as a sinner who never gives up.† I like that definition. I don't like the word sinner. I don't like the word saint, either, because there are all sorts of meanings attached to it.

---

* Matthew 4:10.

† Paramahansa Yogananda, *Sayings of Paramahansa Yogananda* (Self-Realization Fellowship), p. 6.

I think the term genius is better. There are people who are geniuses in science, in literature, in philosophy, in mathematics. I think what we usually term a saint is just a genius in a different field. To call them geniuses allows them to remain human and to accept their humanness.

We must accept our humanness because if we deny that, it means we have not understood the message and we have no true insight. We can never deny our humanness. We are what we are. Sylvia had to be incorporated in what has become Radha.* You can never deny what you are. That means you always have to accept your humanness in total, and not say, "Oh, I am not good enough, I am not pure enough."

Define purity to yourself, what you mean and understand by that word, and what you want it to mean. When I asked the very illustrious people that I met in India, "What is purity?" the general conclusion and message was the same: share what you have; do not keep things exclusively to yourself.

You must share what you have. But you cannot speak of sharing your heart or your thoughts and feelings. You can talk about them, but you can't share them. And you cannot share the solution to temptation, but you also cannot share the responsibility for giving in to temptation, either. You can drag somebody in, but that is not sharing.

Temptation is found in things of great magnitude, and it's in the smallest of things. There is always a temptation to take more than you need. You may put more on your plate than you can eat, and throw the rest away. You have to watch for greed of all kinds. But if you have some treat that you like, eat it as a gift from the Divine, with a feeling of gratitude. Then you won't have any regrets. Eat it also with the idea that you are giving what you eat to your body—sometimes to nourish it, sometimes as enjoyment—for a very definite purpose. That purpose is to serve the Most High. If you do things with sincerity in the service of the Most High, you will never make a mistake. Let your dedication be very clear, very direct. That way you will be putting yourself under the Divine's grace.

Many temptations have come my way, and by no means have I

---

* Sylvia was my name before sanyas; Radha means Cosmic Love and is the name my Guru gave me.

conquered them all by myself. I was given lots of grace. Suddenly, at the very last minute, I would realize, "Oh, my God. No. I can't do this." It was grace giving me that last minute recognition. So while temptation is always present, there is also the means by which we can win over it. The effort we make brings that special state of grace. There is very little that we do by our own powers, by our own insights.

Some scriptures say you will be tempted twice in your weakest spots. If you resist and conquer the first time, you will be tested a second time. If you can resist the second time, you will not be tempted a third time. I understand that to be connected with the polarity of the mind: one part of us can reject, and the other part can accept, so we have to be very alert, and very aware.

Once again, I would like to remind you of dear old Papa Ramdas' prayer: "Ram, hold onto me. I am too weak. I cannot hold on to you."

When I heard about that at Ramdas' place during my second visit to India, I said, "If *he* is saying that, what about me? I am just starting on this great journey." I decided I had better adopt something similar. My prayer was to Divine Mother asking her to make sure to hang on to me, particularly in those moments when I couldn't hang on to her.

The Earth with all its temptations and the temptations of our surroundings and our lives are just tremendously powerful. The Tibetan teachings say that everybody surrounding a person who seeks spiritual life is a demon, a monster, a wild beast who will distract you from the spiritual path. These are all symbolic terms and must be understood metaphorically. We live in a jungle, and we must not surrender to the jungle if we want to survive on the journey toward Higher Consciousness. If we want to go back to our heavenly home, we have to conquer our earthly nature so that we can claim our spiritual nature. Our spiritual nature is the only thing that we really have. We are trapped on the Earth.* We are the fallen angels, we are the gods who came down here

---

* There is a legend in the East that human beings are really inexperienced young gods who once lived in mid-heaven. They saw the Earth and were so tempted by its beauty that they came down to see it. They began to enjoy its temptations, but when they wanted to return to mid-heaven they suddenly found that they had become too heavy and that the Earth was so sticky it held them to it.

from mid-heaven. That has to be remembered, because temptation comes in many, many ways. To be declared the holy mother of an ashram is just a temptation for the ego.

But we have very human physical needs and the temptations that arise from them are much more difficult to handle. We have to guard the senses very carefully and that is a difficult thing to do. The capacity our five senses have to trap us can only be assessed in our time of reflection. We really have to sit back and reflect very carefully to see how our senses lead us into laying traps for ourselves that we then fall into. If we could turn every one of our actions, including eating, drinking, and everything else, into a kind of worship, then we would be reasonably safe.

The power of the Mantra can be accumulated to the degree that it becomes a protection. When we become aware of our own weaknesses and of being trapped by any of the senses, there's only one solution and one recourse, and that's the power of the Mantra. Resort to the Mantra. Make it a habit to have the Mantra going in your mind at all times, as a constant reminder.*

Temptations assail everybody. Clarify them to yourself in your diary or by writing a paper on them. What are your temptations? You often make life very difficult for yourself by not clarifying what your temptations are, and by not staying away from them.

If you are diabetic and you want to stay alive, you have to stay away from sugar. No question. If you have temptations that are strong and powerful because of the emotions, that is *worse* than sugar is to a diabetic. If you want to keep your spiritual being alive, you have to stay away from temptations. Don't use temptation to create your own traps. If someone is diabetic, it would be foolish for that person to buy a couple of boxes of chocolate because, eventually, of course, he or she will eat them, with disastrous result.

Replace that term *sugar* with whatever you are very, very tempted by. And become clear. Yoga is a process of clarification. Be clear what your temptations are. And also be clear what you have to be grateful for.

---

* For instructions on Mantra, see Radha, *Mantras: Words of Power.*

If you want more, turn that urge for more into becoming a more disciplined, more powerful person, because that makes you more realized, that makes you more aware. All your striving for things is really just because you want to achieve self-control. And that's where your effort should go.

In your time of reflection, you have to clarify constantly (even if it's only intellectually): "Why was I born? Why am I here? What is the purpose of my life?" Then keep on asking, "Am I pursuing that purpose? And how am I pursuing it? Is this the best way to pursue it?" If you need help, have the humility to ask for it. Resort to prayer, worship, meditation—whatever will help.

Clarify your mind again and again. All the papers written for classes and workshops at the Ashram have no other purpose than to help you clarify the mind and remember your true nature. It's often that we are trapped by our senses not because we are so weak but because we are so forgetful. It is forgetfulness of our spiritual nature, of our divine nature, that we have to overcome. Make it a point at least once every day to do the Divine Light Invocation, with every bit of concentration you can put into it, so that you will remember and experience your divine nature.

In Eastern teachings, we are called the young gods from mid-heaven trapped on Earth, and in Christian teachings we are called the fallen angels. Either way, we don't belong here. Our body has not the power that the mind has. So whether you think you are a young god from mid-heaven or a fallen angel, make sure you are on your way back home!

The way back home is available to every single one of us, if we apply ourselves to it. The Gita gives this promise, Jesus gave it, and all the Gurus have given it. That's the only promise you can really count on.

Accept that promise.

Image and Tradition

✳ IN THE FIRST FEW YEARS on the spiritual path, you should follow the basic yoga tradition, using Hatha Yoga, Bhakti Yoga, Jnana Yoga, Raja Yoga. This will give you a solid foundation and, eventually, you can put all this experience together into a very harmonious development. This first period can last anywhere from five to eight years, depending on your temperament. There is no definite time that applies to everybody.

During this period, you use an image of the Divine—the ishta devata—as your focal point to keep the wandering mind, the monkey mind, still. If you have some experiences with the image, if your mind embellishes it, then the image becomes your very own. It doesn't matter if you begin with an image which you have bought, or one you have painted yourself, or one which has been given to you, or if it is entirely a mind-created image. None of this matters. What matters is that the attachment to this image can be very elevating and supportive in the pursuit of spiritual life. If you put the image into the Light with the Divine Light Invocation, you need not worry that you will get stuck in the worship of an image, because the image will, in due time, dissolve into Light. You will not get stuck unless you want to. If you insist that this image has become the Supreme Being in your life, then the idea of a Supreme Being is essential at that stage in your life. That's all right. Let it be. One day perhaps the Light will dissolve that also. You do not need to make any particular effort to dissolve the image—just keep putting it in the Light.

However, if the mind says, "But I know this is only an image," and then the critical part comes in and says, "It's all your own mind. You have created all this with your own mind, and there is really nothing in it," stop for a moment and think: the mind constantly creates and all criticism is the product of the mind. Let the criticism be and observe that at least the mind has evolved from pure fantasy, from pure illusion, to the desire to create an image of the divine power.

Of course, that power has really no image, no shape, no form, no name. We use an image only because we have to have something to communicate to each other. If your image dissolves into Light, that's fine.

But if the mind keeps making that image into more beautiful shapes and forms—smaller and more intricate, bigger and more overpowering—let all this happen. It's much better that the mind is busy doing that, instead of scheming all sorts of self-gratification and speculating on all sorts of achievements of a more worldly nature. If the mind has begun to take delight in creating a spiritual image of the power you are pursuing, it has made some progress. Don't let the critical aspect of your mind throw that away.

However, at some point, the image may not be satisfactory any longer because, somewhere in the back of the mind, the yogi or yogini is aware that this image was chosen. It has served its purpose.

There are those of us who are not concrete thinkers, but more abstract thinkers. Such people will reject any image. But then their emotions and mind may become focused entirely on the teacher, or the Guru, or the roshi. That, unfortunately, does not always create a closer relationship with the teacher. The relationship can become very authoritarian, very disciplinarian, without any overtones of personal contact, personal interest, personal care, and what I sometimes call "the shoulder to cry on." In effect, the answer given to the student who comes with personal problems is, "I am not interested in your problems. Your problems are yours. Don't bother me with them." If the practice is a disciplinary practice only, the mind has to be held very tightly. Some people can handle that, but some people's minds become so seriously disoriented that they require help from psychiatrists.

At this Ashram people are free to choose any image that they wish, according to their temperament. There is the worship of the male aspect: Siva, Krishna, Jesus, Buddha. There is the worship of the female aspect: Divine Mother, Mary, Tara.* People choose the image that is closest to their hearts and to what the Divine represents for them. As long as we continue having to receive the teachings through a mind that reveres and takes on the color of what it reveres, the teachings themselves have

---

* To my mind, it is quite possible that deities like Krishna or Tara were once people who lived like you and me, but they realized their potential. Certainly, all the great sages of the past were people who realized their potential.

to take whatever shape and form we give them so that we can understand them.

That shape and form will change every few years. Sometimes the change will come in four or five years, sometimes in eight, ten, or even twelve years. Ten years is a very important cycle. At that time, you will want a change. People who are associated with this Ashram don't have to go somewhere else. They can pursue that change in their own way and still remain connected with the teachings.

But I would not want anybody to think that the field is greener and the fruits are bigger on the other side of the fence. This is not the case. If by your temperament and mental makeup the change in your practice comes naturally, I would be the last to stand in your way. But you cannot be running all over the place and thinking, "This tradition is easier, that one is more entertaining, here is one that is more satisfying." You will never get anywhere looking for emotional satisfaction in spiritual life, and you must never, ever seek entertainment. If you think that way, it's better to choose one tradition and stick with it, because that will give you a solid foundation under your feet.

This brings us to the idea of commitment. If you are committed to one type of spiritual life, make it a whole commitment. Don't be lukewarm. Swami Vivekananda used to say that even Divine Mother can't do anything with people who are lukewarm.

If you are a passionate person, you can turn that into passion for the Divine. Yoga permits you to turn your passion around, to turn it to the Divine. Most of the time, the things we put our hearts into are only illusions. If they are only temporary gratifications of mental, emotional, or physical needs, what happens after they have been met? Often at Christmas people overeat. Then they say they won't need to eat for another week. That isn't true, of course. In fact, you can very easily develop into a glutton if you don't watch the desire to fill emotional and physical needs. Instead, shift your needs to the Divine or, if you can't handle them, give them back to Divine Mother, and say, "You gave this to me for whatever your purpose was, but I can't handle it. You had better take it back. You take care of it. And then we'll go from there."

It is very important that you be true to yourself. You should not run away from your responsibilities, but when these have been met, you should not stay if there is no chance for spiritual life. People who have a family have to wait until their time comes. There are a number of women at the Ashram who have experienced that. They fulfilled their family responsibilities and are now free to pursue their spiritual life. Not everybody goes to an ashram because of a great longing for the Divine, but if the pain is great enough, hard enough, deep enough, stirring enough, it may make individuals realize that they have to look for something else in life.

Look at the uncertainties of life, and look at the changing nature of people, even of loved ones. If you look at things clear-eyed for what they are, there isn't much that lasts. So if you need something to focus on that will last over a longer period of time, then it's better to take that step toward the Divine. Escalate your very human longing from the level of constant change to the level of permanence.

It's not a matter of this tradition or that tradition. It's a matter of what you want. And it's a matter of pursuing what you want with all your might, whatever it is. It really doesn't matter whether you use Tibetan yoga, Tibetan Buddhism, Indian yoga, Indian Buddhism, Judaism, Christianity or Islam, or any other spiritual tradition. The clarity you need, the ingredients you need, to attain to Cosmic Consciousness are the same in any tradition.

You do not have to adopt the cultural habits of a tradition. You don't have to be absolute vegetarians, you don't have to go barefoot and chew betel nuts just because it is done in the culture where a tradition began. You don't have to follow any tradition, even in regard to family life, because life moves on, and traditions are constantly challenged. The deadwood needs to be cut out, but before you do this, be sure you have the sword of discrimination in your hands, and ask very carefully, "What am I doing?"

It's you, your future, and what you want to attain, that are at stake. You have to sit down and really think, "Where do I want to go and what steps do I want to take to get there? What will be, so to speak, my marching gear?" That is very, very important. You can dance for Krishna or for Divine Mother, you can chant for Siva or for the Virgin Mother. You can think of Krishna Consciousness or Christ Consciousness. You can say the rosary for Mary. You have all the spiritual freedom you need. The only direction I will give you is: "Get there!" That's my concern. Get there!

Using an Image

I WOULD LIKE to give you an example of how an image can be used to focus the mind. If we look at the Om Krishna Guru Mantra,* we can get some understanding of where to put our attention and what the Mantra is really saying.

The Mantra starts with Om. The cosmic sound of Om contains all the names, all the forms of the Divine. Krishna is a personalized emanation that we create in order to grasp the unexplainable, because the Cosmic Om, Cosmic Energy, God, is not something that the ordinary human mind can understand. Even the well-trained mind can have only a faint idea. We need a personal aspect of this Cosmic Om or God or Cosmic Intelligence because it would otherwise be impossible for the mind to focus its attention for more than a brief moment. To hold even an abstract thought of Cosmic Intelligence or Energy in the mind sufficiently long is not possible without a long time of preparation.

So people create a symbol or an image of the Most High in their own minds. I'm sure if fish could think of God, a little fish would probably think of the whale: "Dear God, so great, so huge, so powerful."

---

* See Radha, *Mantras: Words of Power,* revised edition, which includes the music for this Mantra on page 71.

Human beings do the same thing. We think of the Divine in the form of superhuman beings who are illumined or realized. What we mean by superhuman being we don't really know, because most of the time these are only random ideas that we do not clarify to ourselves.

Krishna then is a personalized aspect of the immeasurable power that we call God, or the Absolute, or the Most High. If you think of the Absolute, Cosmic Intelligence, Cosmic Energy, as being just what it says—energy—how would you understand this energy taking any personal interest in you? How would you address yourself to this energy or avail yourself of it? The solution is to create a suitable image that has meaning to you, in which you sum up the Most High of your understanding—the most perfect, the most beautiful, the best, that perfect divine love without human frailty. All these are attributes that you give to the idea of God, or the idea of Cosmic Intelligence. There's nothing wrong with that because this creation shows you your mind is capable of creating something higher than the millions of little ideas and desires which only gratify selfishness and show off the ego. *That* is not the mind in its creative aspect of the Most High.

The mind and its creative ability are tremendous. The mind never rests. Even when we sleep, the mind is active. We dream, even if we never recall our dreams. We dream a minimum of ninety minutes every night. The best and highest way to use the energy available to us creatively is to create an image of God.

The danger is that in the pressure of events you forget that you created this image for your own convenience, to fulfill your need for personal contact. You forget that Cosmic Energy or God, itself, has no need of your creation. If at some point you fall in love with your creation, if you forget that it is your creation, then this image becomes the rival in your mind of what God really is.

On the daily level, if I have an idea about a friend, this is *my* idea. He may have contributed something to it through his speech or his actions, but nevertheless, it is *my* idea. This image that I have now of him might be correct, but it might be quite wrong or it might be only partially right. If I'm in love with the idea that I have created, if I am attached to it, I will never know him, because the image has become his rival.

We create an image of the Divine and call it Lord Krishna or Jesus or Buddha or Mary or Tara. We can take Jesus as an example. The image that you have of Jesus is just as wrong as the image you have of yourself, if you are not aware of your own creations. And the image that you have of Jesus is his rival. He can never make himself truly known to you. The image that you hold in your mind prevents you in the end from truly knowing Christ Consciousness.

The danger is to say, "Oh, yeah, very interesting, I never thought of that before," and then to forget about it. Your mind constantly seeks new entertainment: "Oh, I already know that, I've heard it before. What else? Something new, please." But have you digested it? What are you doing with it? It is entirely your responsibility to do something with it. There is a Western tendency to cut everything apart and fit it into neat pigeon-holes. This is not possible with the Divine, because it is all one thing.

In the Om Krishna Guru Mantra, Guru includes the aspect of the human Guru challenging you with such ideas, tossing you into deeper levels of thought, into new avenues, challenging you to look into greater depths of life. Acceptance comes.

Have I been mechanical? Have I been a robber? Have I been a sleep-walker? Never let your practice become a mechanical habit. That diminishes the sacred practice and that is sin. Making mistakes in ignorance is one thing, but once you have the information, once you have the instructions, you cannot afford to make mistakes. If you realize after your practice that you have really not put your heart and mind into it, pray and say, "This was all I was capable of today for whatever reason. You are Divine Intelligence. You are the loving God of which I am created. This is all I could do today." This way you are practicing humility and honesty at the same time, by admitting to yourself and to the Most High that this is all you had today. Be it the Divine Light Invocation or Mantra chanting, it is not expected that you will be one hundred per cent in your practice, but you must try. You must bring the wandering mind always back to what you set out to do. That concentration and mental discipline will also give you benefits in many other walks of life.

Try to chant Om Krishna Guru, and put your attention on the word Guru. Then after a few minutes, put your attention on the word Krishna, the God in the image and also the God within. And then feel your attention go to the Om, the cosmic symbol of all energy.

There is an old saying that is still valuable: when the student is ready, the teacher comes. When the student is ready, not only for the teacher but also to listen to the teachings and to put them into practice, then there can be an experience of Krishna. This means that in the way in which you have created the image, the image becomes something very real. It takes on a life of its own. Finally this image will, if you can let go of it, dissolve into Light, the finest image that the human mind can hold on to, and yet an image that no longer needs any substitution. Then, if the student has learned to listen which is only possible through an act of surrender and by stilling the mind—getting rid of all the mental background noises—then the Cosmic Om can be heard. This is an experience beyond your wildest dreams, something you will never forget, when you may forget all else.

Each time you chant Mantra you will have some result, some benefit. This benefit comes in stages. Whenever you have reached one stage, never think that is the last. There is always something more.

The Purpose of Images

THE WORD GOD does not have any particular shape or form unless we give it shape and form. But if I say to you, "Close your eyes; now, tell me what comes to your mind when I say the word *God*," you create in your mind an image. This is what each individual does in the same way with the words *Virgin Mother*. Not everyone thinks of the Virgin as being clad in blue robes. Each person has his or her own creation. But it very rarely happens that an image comes into your mind entirely on its own account. The image which comes is usually something already embedded in your mind. Most often it's the way you perceived the Divine the first time you were ever made aware of the Divine.

But most people are at a loss when I ask them, "What is your soul?

How do you think of your soul?" The soul is the one thing that is not pictured in the mind. If people feel a need to have an image, perhaps because they want to say something like, "I wish my soul could go right now to Divine Mother and bring me messages," the only image they have is the one of the dove, because that's what is pictured in books to represent "the holy spirit."

All cultures have an idea of something indescribable that is in some way inherent in the human being. When we want to talk about it, we give it a name, even though it has no particular shape or form. We call it soul, oversoul, Higher Self, the divine Atman, the Absolute, but it is something that we can't really fasten to an image in our mind.

The images of the Divine that are presented by various religions have an overpowering influence and we accept them without question. From a yogic point of view, that is fine—to start with. It is fine to have an image in the beginning, but as my Guru would say, "It's fine to be in kindergarten, but you have to get out of it sooner or later." You have to deal with this on a very personal level, and really ask, "If I say *God* or *Atman* or *soul*, what do I mean?"

When you begin to think like this you will begin to understand that the Divine is neither male nor female and has no shape or form. It's very helpful to find out just what exactly your mind is doing with this idea of the Divine. I avoid the word *God* here because God has already been assigned the image of an old man in this culture, and we talk of "He" and "Him." If you want to break loose from narrow images, you must think only of the Divine, of the divine power, divine forces.

Also, you have to recognize that the idea of God is something that has already crystallized in your unconscious, and you have to give it time and freedom to emerge. You cannot put restrictions on it to make it what you want it to be. You have to give it the freedom to emerge from your unconscious.

Only then can you attach a statement like *reality* to it—and there are, of course, different levels of reality. There is the level of reality of your physical existence, and there is the reality of your mental world, and there is another reality beyond that. You can give a name to that reality beyond for the sake of communication. You can call it "the celestial world." But when you use such terms, you need to clarify to yourself what you mean.

Why is it necessary to clarify and think so intensely, to pin yourself down so closely? It is not that you want to get away from images necessarily, but you must first have a grip on a starting point for thinking of divine forces. Otherwise, it is very difficult, if not impossible, to go beyond name and form.

We cannot force ourselves to renounce a shape and form that has become meaningful to us. But we can renounce our insistence that the Divine reveal itself (neither "himself" nor "herself," *it*self) to us in the way *we* want, or the way *we* find suitable. If you can renounce that, then something will emerge from the unconscious that you have been bringing along for many lifetimes, and that will help your continuing evolution.

In this life, you have again started with an image. This helps the mind to be more steadfast, more single-pointed, more focused. Then, when you have learned to focus better, you can help yourself to break away from dependency on the image by putting the image itself into the Light. And when you are ready—when your mind is courageous and powerful enough—the image that you have been using will dissolve in the Light.

It is not something you can force. The intellect cannot come along and think, "Well, I'm too advanced. I don't need this image anymore." This is perhaps the best sign that you *do* need it. You

The Divine Light flame over the reflecting pool beside the Temple of Divine Light

have to surrender your self-will about this. You have to renounce your insistence that you will recognize the divine presence only in the way you want it to appear. If you do not, you may wait for the rest of your life, and it may never happen. You *must* recognize that by your insistence you are trying to command the Divine. Impossible. When egocentricity comes in and pride of intellect—"Because I'm here and I call Your name, You ought to come"—you will never make contact with the Divine. The practice of surrender, which begins in daily living, has to lead eventually to surrendering your ideas about how you want the Divine to be.*

Images are only a reminder. Keeping them around, particularly if you are very work-oriented, will remind you of the divine presence. Any kind of image—thangka, painting, statue, embroidery—can help you to remember. Tell yourself that each time your eyes fall on the image you are maintaining contact with the Divine. This will help you to keep a level of awareness of the Divine as you go from one job to another, or from one room to another, or from one building to another. If you use it that way, the image serves a marvelous purpose. People sometimes ask me, "You have a thangka here, you have a statue over there. You have two altars in this room. How many special places do you have?"

I say, "You know, I am so busy, so much work has to be done, and I have to change from one job to another so often, but every time my eyes glance over an image, I remember I am only the head and hands of the Divine." We are not all that bad, but we keep forgetting because of the impact of life.

For going beyond image, the Light is the best help. And the starting point is yourself. If you do the Divine Light Invocation,† with utmost focus and attention and put all your emotions into it, it will transform the image you have of yourself of being unworthy, or incapable; or of being so great, such a winner. Both will dissolve in the Light.

To transform yourself into a being of Light is a marvelous experi-

---

* You can practice surrender in very practical ways. See the section called "Practicing Surrender," page 99.

† See Radha, *The Divine Light Invocation.*

ence. It will transform you tremendously, but because of your human nature, you will not be able to hang on to the experience. You cannot possess or own what I will term "mystical experiences." But they can be an inspiration to carry you further, to help you take the next steps, and make greater effort, so that finally *all* your imaginings can be put aside.

Put yourself in the Light.

Visions

THERE ARE TWO OPPOSING views about visions. One is that visions are true and are a direct contact with the Divine. The opposite view is that they're all in the mind, something produced by the creative power of the mind.

I went to Swami Sivananda about this one day, because it troubled me, and I didn't have enough understanding of my own experiences. I said, "Now, in Montreal I had a vision of you, but you knew about it even though you were all the way over here in India. How can anybody say it was just my mind? I had never seen you. I didn't even know of your existence."

He then gave me a short discourse on visions. He said, "There is a distinct difference between kinds of vision. If you have a vision of a high spiritual nature, you will be turned around a hundred and eighty degrees, and it is almost impossible for you to remain the same person." He said hundreds of people would tell him their visions, and ask him what he thought about them, and he could tell by the tone of their voices that they were looking for confirmation that they had had a spiritual experience. Today many people come to me and say, "Can I tell you my experience, my vision?" Then they ask, with that same tone in their voice, "Do you think this was a vision?"

This question is easily answered. When you have what I call a real vision, you don't need to ask anybody for confirmation. The experience is, by itself, so powerful that when you close your eyes and think about it ten or twenty years later, it's almost like making a leap in time back to that moment. A real vision makes a tremendous impact. It takes you pretty much out of your ordinary attention and behavior for a couple of days.

However, both schools of thought are right, up to a point. Most people do a lot of wishful thinking and have good intentions. There is no doubt about that, but they do not yet have the experience necessary to have visions. After giving this much thought and dealing with many people, I now try to help people understand their experiences this way. First I ask, "Where do you think your mind is most creative?" Then I say, "If your mind can create what you are calling a vision, then you may be very close to a real vision, because you are opening the door. If the mind is so creative, what more beautiful thing can it do than create a vision of Divine Mother, or Lord Krishna, or Siva, or Parvati, or Mary? You are helping the mind to create the best thing it can."

From my observation of people over many years, I have seen that self-created visions can lead in the end to a transformation of their personalities, and that can open the door to a true vision.

If you are not sure whether you had a true vision, that probably means your mind is still producing the images, but it is using its creative ability in the best way possible. Perhaps this kind of experience is a preparation process that you need in order to deal with the impact that a true spiritual vision has.

It is wise to look at visions from both these angles. If your vision doesn't turn you around a hundred and eighty degrees, don't just write it off and say, "Oh, well, I'm just left out by the Divine. I just don't seem to be worth anything." Think instead that your mind has used all its creative power. The mind's full creative power is usually used only in sexual activity, but you are now using it in a much, much higher way. That may be a wonderful preparation for having a vision of high spiritual quality over which your mind has no influence. *That* vision you can't create.

What the mind has created, it can always recreate. If you make one painting or one sculpture, you can make another one. But if you have one true spiritual vision, you cannot create another one. It is not in your power to do that. But through your own creation, you can make yourself receptive. You become then a sort of vessel into which the divine energy can pour. That alone is wonderful.

One day in Germany during the war when the raids were heaviest, I went to the apartment house of some friends of mine. The door was open, and the Jewish star had been placed on it, so I knew that they must have been taken away to prison. I stood there wondering, "Should I walk in or not? Is there anybody watching the place, or not?" In that moment, everything fell away from me. I had no trust in life, in people. Nothing mattered. So I went in and, of course, the apartment was empty. They had gone. There were baby napkins soaking in the sink. There was food on the table—they had been taken while at dinner. I remember myself walking down the steps and down the street. I had about a twenty-minute walk back to my place, and I was thinking, "All this talk about God and greatness. There is just nothing. There is just nothing. There couldn't be, or these things wouldn't happen."

This total negation was particularly intense because this family had a small baby. This baby had nothing to do with the war or Hitler. What sin could this baby possibly have to be punished for? Who knows whether it even survived the journey to the camp. I made up my mind there was no God. It was only people's weakness that made them create their own God because they had to hang onto something. But I thought, "When these things can happen, there is *nothing* to hold on to, absolutely nothing."

There was a little park nearby and suddenly I had an urge to sit down on one of the benches, and just be in that utter despair where there seemed to be no point in living. It didn't make sense for me even to go into a shelter during the next bombing raid. What point was there to living?

While all this was going on in my mind, a Buddha image suddenly appeared just before my eyes. It started to grow as I watched. It became bigger and bigger and filled the whole sky. There it was—a seated Buddha on a large lotus like a tremendous roof over me. It filled all the sky that I could see.

Suddenly a voice said, "Under the Buddha you can take refuge. You are safe." And I saw myself somehow stepping out of my body and running over to the Buddha. I sat on the ground and did something very peculiar that I had never heard of, never read about. I felt I must sit in a place underneath the Buddha where my spine would continue in his, and then I was just totally absorbed.

I recalled that experience very vividly when I was in India. Gurudev Sivananda very rarely sat in a cross-legged position, but one time he did, and because he was so huge, this brought back to me that experience with the Buddha. Somehow he knew that. When he got up and walked back to his kutir, and I followed him, he said to people, "Radha has a very soft spot in her heart for the Buddha." You can't recreate a vision, but the memory is very powerful. It was so powerful in my mind at that moment that Gurudev could easily pick it up. It is something that has stayed with me ever since. When things were really bad, and I didn't know whether to go right or left, or forward or backward, or what was going to happen next, the memory alone of that experience so many years ago in 1944 would return powerfully to me.

In any war, in any country, innocent and powerless people are sacrificed to the power structures. When you turn to the Light and try to attract the Light, you have to realize also that where there is a lot of Light there can be a lot of shadow. The sun is not in the zenith for very long.

Once in Montreal I was invited to a spiritualist church. I wasn't quite sure what would transpire there. Across the room, there was a very big man who appeared to me to be physically very strong. I was somehow very much afraid of him, and I didn't know what to do. He got up in anger and came toward me, and stood in front of me. I just looked down. I couldn't look into his face, I was just too afraid. And then I saw blue feet with ankle bells and orange cloth around them. As I looked up—I could only see up to the shoulders—I saw Lord Krishna holding the flute with the golden tassel hanging down. The melody didn't have any words but it seemed to me, in that moment of fear, to be saying, "But I am here. I am here. I am even in this evil man. Don't worry."

It is the focus that you have to remember. What are you focused on? It's only the focus on the Divine that will open the doors for you. Nothing else. A single-pointed mind is the key to any door to the Divine.

Speech and Mantra

THERE IS NO MUSICAL INSTRUMENT ever created that has the same power as the human voice. By the way you use your voice and your breath, you can say the name of a person—just one word—and express as many emotions as there are keys on a grand piano. The human voice is capable of a tremendous range of expression and intonations, and it resounds in your own body, as you may have already discovered with Mantra. In Indian philosophy the power of speech is called the Devi of Speech. *Devi* means power or goddess.

If we look at the expression of emotions, we can see there are many ways of speaking. We can cover up what we don't want to let another person know by the emotions we express in our speech. And we give ourselves away. When we cry, we make a sound. When we laugh, we make a sound. When our laugh is cynical, others can hear that in the sound. When our laugh comes from the heart, that can be heard in the sound, too. We can hear in someone's voice what is being said, besides just the words. Or we can hear how the words disguise what the voice really conveys.

We can have a very arrogant tone of voice. We often talk down to children, patronizing them. We may discover old emotions which are only revealed to us when we hear them in our speech. Our voice can imply violence, hidden anger, but also hidden pain and fear. There is no emotion that we do not, in some way or other, express through our voice. Even if we suppress the voice, the emotion will come through the breath. We cannot entirely hide it.

Once we begin to pay attention to our voice, we become aware of how enormously skillful we have become in our ability to cover up. We can be very diplomatic in our choice of words, and extremely careful in sounding someone out by the way we speak. We can put a certain casualness in our voice when really we are in a high state of tension because we are anxious to know what the other person is thinking.

Sometimes we might make remarks just for the sake of saying something, to keep a conversation going, or as a way of saying, "I am talking to you to show you that I like you." Our intentions may be quite good, and yet, with our speech, we may also sometimes condition a person to look at something differently from how they have been looking at it.

When the Ashram was new, and Siva House was our first building, one of the young men who helped build the Ashram worked on a survey crew. He had two rooms in Siva House. One was his office with his drawing table. The other was a little room beside it, with a small balcony looking over the lake. This was his bedroom and living room. He was very happy with this.

Then a fellow came to the Ashram who had never made it anywhere because he didn't like to work. He stood around a lot, looking very grim. He was expected to help with the firewood but, of course, he had to have a cup of coffee first. Then, two hours later when the firewood was all chopped, he would show up. This is the kind of person he was. One day, he came into the room of this young man and he said, "My God! How do you stand it? You wake up and you have *all* this work right in front of you!"

Now, if he had lived like that, *he* couldn't have taken it, because his attitude to work was catastrophic. But ever after that, the young man who lived in those rooms hated the work and the Ashram. A very sensitive spot had been hit there, and unfortunately it was the worst in him that responded to it. If his attitude had been one of selfless service, he would have said, "Have you an office like mine, looking over the lake and so comfortable? I don't need to get a car going in the winter or take a bus." But he didn't. His self-pity was aroused, and that stayed with him for years.

We have to be careful with all we say because we may just nourish the self-pity or anger or jealousy in people rather than elevating them. The Devi of Speech is very powerful. If you don't know what to say, but you want to show somebody friendliness, smile and let it come from your heart. Words alone, just to keep something going, don't necessarily convey what perhaps you intended to convey.

You can find out who you are by watching yourself act and by hearing yourself speak. Listening to yourself is very revealing, and there is plenty of opportunity—there is a lot of talking going on in everybody's life. Find out who you talk to, what you say, how you talk, why you talk, and what you are expressing in your talking.

The sound of your voice expresses numerous emotions. Try to become aware of how you express them. Find out how you feel when you hum, when you whistle, when you chant. Find out if it makes a difference if you hum, or whistle, or chant as you go from one place to another, or when you are working, or when you are by yourself. Are you expressing a happy mood?

There is a story told in India of a man who had a wonderful meditation in which he had contact with the Divine. Afterwards, he walked briskly along the road humming to himself. Another man came toward him and said, "You sound happy."

"I am," replied the first man.

"Why are you happy?" the other asked.

"Oh, I feel wonderful. The air is so soft and the sun is shining. Everything is wonderful."

"Is that why you are humming?"

He thought for a moment and he said, "Yes."

Your innermost experience tries to find expression, even if there is no witness of what you experience except your own mind. And if you love the Divine, it shows in your voice, in the way you chant. Don't let your spiritual practice become mechanical.

In the yogic tradition, there is a difference between emotions and feelings: feelings are cultivated emotions. When emotions are uncultivated, we are pretty much under their influence. But when we cultivate our emotions, they become refined feelings. Then we are capable of having a certain warmth in our voice, a certain softness and a loving tone. We can kindle hope in another person in the way we express our consideration, our concern. The voice can become very melodious, and very clear and steady in tone, whereas the voice that is vibrating with emotions is anything but steady.

The human voice has a range from very low to very high, and vice versa. The voice can bridge between the high and the low, between your higher and your lower nature. When you speak, your own voice can tell you where you are at any given moment. When you are in a certain state of harmony, when your feelings are their finest and least self-concerned, you may speak to somebody, and that person will say, "You know, you really struck a chord in my heart." This means there was no manipulation in your voice, so the other person could be very open and responding. In fact, you *resounded* in the person's heart.

Laughter is an important part of the voice. If somebody is very down, you may be able to ease the situation by pointing out what's funny about it. You can say, "Oh, it's really more funny than serious. Look, it's just your perfectionism that makes it seem so dramatic, but it's really very funny." That way you can completely change a situation from depression to relief, to hope.

From the way other people respond to our voice, we realize we have tremendous power. We can upset people, and we can also elevate them.

The most important sound is the sound we make with our voice. The most sacred speech is Mantra, and the greatest purification of speech comes through the chanting of Mantras. The only Western music that comes close to the effectiveness of some Mantras is Bach. Bach's music has a mathematical precision underlying it. It is not an expression of emotions. Some Gregorian chants—but only some of them—also come close.

Sounds are symbols, and some symbols can manifest. Sounds of the human voice are, like any other sounds, vibration. Sometimes this vibration can be very subtle, depending on the contents of your emotions.

The human voice is then a bridge between the world of daily chatter and a world of utter silence and aloneness. Pilots who use gliders say that once they are up in the glider, all they can hear is the wind, their own breath, and their own heartbeat. Except for that, it is absolutely silent.

Such an absolute silence is what we would like to acquire in the practice of meditation. In that moment of absolute silence, you may hear something within yourself. Let us call this "the divine word," or "the divine sound." The sound of the ocean gives you some idea of the divine sound, because the Cosmic Om sounds like a roaring ocean. If there is no sound being produced within yourself, then you can hear this "divine word," leading you to Mantra.* And, of course, Mantra is really the crown of the Devi of Speech.

---

* For basic instructions on Mantra practice, see Radha, *Mantras: Words of Power.*

At this point, you become quite aware of the vibrations of your sound—the sound of your voice, the sound when you sigh, and when you take a deep breath, and you may hear the sound of your heart. You may have an urge to speak, but this great silence embraces you, and you find it superfluous to say anything even silently in your own mind. It's a beautiful experience. The real meaning of the Devi of Speech suddenly emerges, like a very clear-sounding thought. It is also at that moment that your feelings are so refined and the vibration within is so strong, so high, that you don't want to use your human voice and so the tongue remains silent.

It's a wonderful state to be in. Then you come again to a point of chanting the divine word, where again breath, vibration, and rhythm are created intentionally by the use of the voice. That is when you begin to understand that Mantra is above all the chatter of daily living.

The chakras have a sound, a different one for each, and you may experience these. They sound a little like musical instruments, such as the flute or a bell. In the cave of Swami Purushottamananda, I heard birds singing but there were no birds in the cave—only rocks. Rocks, too, have a voice.

Sound has a purity that does not depend on your voice. The purity of the sound comes from your heart. And when you have achieved purity of mind by reciting Mantra with the visualization of the deity which belongs to the Mantra you recite—when you *experience* the sound of that image—then you will understand what some scriptural texts call "the sound without a sound." This sound without sound is like the stream of consciousness. It takes quite a bit of practice to come close to such experiences, but when you can do so, you achieve a state beyond mind.

There are direct instructions of how to achieve this result in many Indian scriptures. Here are the directions from one of them.*

The Devi says:

"Oh Siva, what is your reality? What is this wonder-filled universe? What constitutes seed? Who centers the universal wheel? What is this life beyond form pervading forms? How may we enter it fully, above space and time, names and descriptions? Let my doubts be cleared."

Devi, though already enlightened, asks these questions so others throughout the universe may receive Siva's instructions. Siva replies, giving the one hundred and twelve ways, of which nine deal with sound.

"Devi, imagine the Sanskrit letters in these honey-filled foci of awareness, first as letters, then more subtly as sounds, then as most subtle feeling. Then, leaving all of them aside, be free."

This is the first instruction. It is a very direct process using Sanskrit letters. AUM is a Sanskrit letter. Aum or Om embraces all shapes and forms, all names that we give to the divine power. Now, if you speak, whisper, or chant Om you must use your breath. You cannot do this without using the breath. That sets the pranic current in motion in yourself and that will help you to become aware of refined feelings. Then the sound will come from the heart, rather than from your throat or your

---

* Paul Reps, ed., *Zen Flesh, Zen Bones* (Rutland, USA: Charles E. Tuttle Co., 1957), p. 191ff. This is part of a passage entitled "Centering" which was compiled from a translation of ancient texts called the Vigyan Bhairava, the Sochanda Tantra and the Malini Vijaya Tantra.

mouth. Your voice will become silent, and the Om will become a self-generating sound, to which you don't attribute anything. At that moment you are free.

Even one such experience will create some difficulties in the future when people ask you to answer basic questions that are of emotional importance to them. You will feel reluctant because now you know these questions have no importance whatsoever. An experience like this will make it difficult to live in the world. Everything sounds gross and unnecessary. However, it takes quite awhile and quite a lot of practice to achieve this.

Here is another paragraph:

"Bathe in the center of sound, as in the continuous sound of a waterfall. Or, by putting fingers in ears, hear *the sound of sounds.*"

Here Siva speaks of the twelve sounds in the human body. You can hear any one of them, depending on the state of your development. Then you hear "the sound of sounds"—you meet yourself, your own essence, and suddenly you know what your essence is.

Siva says:

"Intone a sound, as A-U-M, slowly. As sound enters soundfulness, *so do you.*

"In the beginning and gradual refinement of the sound of any letter, *awake.*"

Be really present. Have no other thoughts in your mind.

"While listening to stringed instruments, hear their composite central sound; thus *omnipresence.*"

"Intone a sound audibly, then less and less audibly as feeling deepens into *this silent harmony.*"

"With mouth slightly open, keep mind in the middle of the tongue. Or, as breath comes silently in, feel the sound *HH.*"

This passage means focus your mind on the middle of your tongue. It means *concentrate* so that when you speak, you will have to watch how you speak. When you speak, you use different parts of your mouth. Some words are pronounced right on the tip of your tongue, others in the back of the throat as in the guttural sounds of some languages. But how do you pronounce anything on the middle of your tongue? Silence. The *H* sound is the sound of exhalation.

People call me "Swami Rad-a." Indians do not say "Rad-a;" they say "Rad-ha." They pronounce the *h* between the *d* and the *a*. They do not say "Budd-a." They say "Budd-ha." The breath plays a great part. It is the most subtle thing in your speech, the refined part.

Here is another paragraph:

"Center on the sound A-U-M without any *A* or *M*."

This means only the letter *U* [oo] is left. In practicing Mantra, a Guru will instruct you that *A* [Ah] is sounded just below your navel or around your navel, *U* is at your sternum, and *M* is in the throat. In this way, you are instructed to leave your emotions in the area of the navel and your self-will in the area of the throat. You are then in your heart.

In English the *U* is shaped like a vessel you could put something into, so I have often said to Western people, "Think of the *U* as your heart, and put as much as you can into your heart, where it will undergo a process of purification. That will give you control of emotions, and it will give you control of your self-will, which is seated in the throat chakra.

Now here's another instruction:

"Enter the sound of your name and, through this sound, *all sounds*."

The Indians are in a habit of very quickly giving Westerners an Indian name. Sometimes the reason is that the person becomes more acceptable to them by having a name that is familiar to them. Another reason—and this is the reason of more highly developed Gurus—is that by adopting this new name you are to become aware of the meaning of all the letters. Also you change your identification slightly. You don't see yourself only as the person that you were, but as the one you are going to be, too.

There is a meaning in every name. If I take my names, *Sylvia* means a little imp of the woods, while *Radha* means cosmic love. The subtle psychological influences of the name *Radha* are much more helpful than the idea of being a little imp of the woods. I may be both, but I should focus on the one that is more beneficial to my development.

Names have meanings. There may be more in your name than you think. Maybe you have been given some sort of a message along with your name. It's up to you to discover if there is a message.

Myth and Symbols

WHEN WE HEAR OR READ stories from a different culture, we have to ask, "How did these stories come about? What can they mean to us?" The traditional stories of India have their human level and they have a deeper meaning. If you look for the deeper level, you can discover the meaning of the stories.

When I was in India, Swami Chidananda told us a story about Ram and Sita.* Sita was kidnapped by the demon, Ravana, and taken to Sri Lanka. She dropped pieces of her jewelry in order to let Ram know where she was being taken. Hanuman brought the pieces to Ram as he found them, but Ram didn't recognize them until Hanuman brought him a ring that she had worn on her toes. This little bit of story has significance. There has been a tradition in India that men should not look into a woman's face. The eye contact of a man looking into a woman's eyes, or a woman looking into a man's eyes, gives the power of human creation a greater strength than people can handle. So all Ram knew was the jewelry she wore on her ankles and her feet. When he saw them, then he could find the way to her.

The feet are the foundation that you lay, and that the Lord or Divine Mother helps you to lay, by pushing you, directing you where to walk, and by putting you into some really difficult positions so you can learn not be sidetracked. The Divine may also put a lot of pain on you to make you think about the things that are essential. All the time this is going on, the real issue is the search for the spiritual principle. You can call it God, or Goddess, or Divine Mother, or Rama, or Tara, or Jesus. It is all the same spiritual principle and you have to be connected to it, so you must always be searching for it.

Then there is Hanuman, the Monkey God. Hanuman is a very tricky thing to understand. For instance, the mind in many ways can be compared to a monkey: restless, looking here, looking there. Monkeys are curious, like the mind, and because they see everything going on around

---

* From the *Ramayana,* one of India's great epic scriptural texts.

them, they can give warning of potential danger. If you watch monkeys, you will see they are constantly on the lookout. And they are all over the place, eating. One moment they are eating here and then they are over there, stuffing themselves, like the mind always stuffing itself with new desires and ideas.

Hanuman is also Ram's devoted servant. The mind is *your* most devoted servant. It's always with you—there is scarcely a situation, there is scarcely a moment, where your mind is not with you, except in a time of what you might call reverie. You may look into the sky and see clouds over the water or over the horizon, or you may look at a big tree, or a flower. If somebody asks you at that time, "What are you thinking?" you don't know. You weren't thinking. That is the only moment the monkey mind is not with you.

To recapture these moments is to recapture the original state of the mind. But when the monkey mind becomes greedy, then that part we call "the inner Self," the soul, becomes sad because it has lost contact with us. When that contact is lost, we go into moods where nothing is right, everything is wrong, life is miserable, and we have a string of complaints. We know that these complaints have little truth. Sometimes we throw them outward just as a relief from the imagined pressure created by self-importance, which also comes from the monkey mind. You say, "I'm working under so much pressure," because you can feel important if you stress that all the time. But you may also condition yourself, and your monkey mind then brings all these things into existence.

There is no way that we can cut the head off the monkey mind entirely, but we can push it into the background by giving more power to that other part of the mind—the inner Light, the eternal part. If we don't do this, we will get lost. We will lose another lifetime, and we can even make ourselves sick by poisoning our whole system with that negativity. You have to be extremely careful not to fall into that trap. It's a very bad trap. Anyone who has come to the spiritual path in any way has been guided by Divine Mother. Once you are on the path, you have to find out how far you will follow it, or whether you will just let the monkey mind resist and indulge in the other aspects of mind. You have a great deal of freedom. You can take either way.

One part of the story of Ram and Sita has a clue that is particularly important. Sita cries, "Am I forgotten?" when Ram doesn't come to rescue her. This is the clue: there is pain and there is joy, there is love and there is separation, and both have to become the same for you. You can become indifferent to pain and indifferent to joy, because pain is one extreme and joy is the other. You run first to this extreme, and then you run to that extreme, you are here and then an hour later you are there, and in five minutes you are back again. You are constantly on the run. That is not a good state to be in because you are making your life extremely difficult. At some point you have to make a decision, otherwise you feel like a leaf in the wind, blown here, blown there, and belonging nowhere. That is the greatest state of unhappiness. There is no question that making a decision for the spiritual life demands a lot of commitment, a lot of strength, but it has at least a purpose. You are not thrown here and there, and you know that eventually, in proportion to the effort you make, you will reach your goal.

Sita cries, "Am I forgotten?" We go through this life thinking often that our mother didn't love us, or our father didn't, that nobody does— our husband or wife, or our brother or sister, or friends—nobody loves us. That may be quite so, and it's not necessarily only a negative psychological attitude, because as your awareness grows, you see that often what you considered love wasn't so. It was attachment. People were convenient to you, and you were convenient for them. In the end, everyone is really only concerned about themselves. So where does love come in? That understanding has to come to you, because when there is nobody left to love you, there is only one place to turn, and that is the Most High.

When I was first in Canada, I felt very sorry for myself, because here I was in a country whose language I didn't speak well, in a job that didn't even pay my bills. I had to work evenings, I had to work weekends. What was the point of all this? I had no loving family to return to or to get letters from or be in contact with. My mother didn't want children and told me that quite often. Then one day in a meditation, I had a very wonderful experience of Divine Mother saying, "But you didn't *need* a mother, because *I* took care of you. *I* guided every step from the moment you were born. *I* directed you. You didn't need anybody but me."

When you have no way to turn, you are bound to turn to the Most High as you understand it. You have at some point to accept that there is nothing left, not your health, not your well-being, not even any kind of possession. There is really *nothing* left. This is how we human beings are. If everything is wonderful, if we have no needs, if we have food, and if we don't have to worry about bills, then we don't worry about turning to the Divine. We do not yet understand that cooperation with the Law of Evolution is our duty, and if we do not do this, then we have to walk through the valley of tears and death and deprivation.

We are like a friend who comes to see you only in great despair and need. At other times you never hear anything or see anything of this friend. Would you consider that person a friend? No. But the Divine loves you more than you love, more than a friend loves. Your love is very little by comparison. The creative forces that have put you into this world watch you with tenderness and care, but how much do you care? That is not a question you can answer easily. How much do you really care? Easily hurt, easily insulted, easily pained, you want to turn away and say, "Oh no, I don't need God any more. What is the use?" You don't realize that it is really the monkey mind in a negative sense (not in the sense of Hanuman, the faithful servant) that has turned away. It is as if you helped someone you called a friend over and over and over, and then your friend didn't acknowledge the help received. It's very painful for the Divine to give you a lot of things and then hear you complain it's not enough and you want more.

If you complain because you want to release tension—fine. But there has to come a time—five minutes later—when you say, "Okay, I relieved some of the tension, but now I have also to see the blessings."

If you do your share, the Divine will come. There is always a hand if you take it. Are you going to take it? If you don't take it, you cause pain to the Divine again, because you are letting the Divine down. You have to remember. You have to acknowledge the divine gifts that you have been given.

Reading myths and legends is like reading a fairy tale unless somehow you get an understanding of the symbolism. When you have a grip on symbolism, you can also understand your own dreams much better.

Think of the symbols for thoughts. Can you imagine that you have a grain of rice for each of your thoughts—just one grain of rice? If you put all the thoughts you have had up to this point in a room, how many of these rooms would you need? Garuda, the eagle, is the symbol of thoughts. Thoughts have wings. The elephant is the symbol of memory. It never forgets anything. You are weighed down by memory of the past. Then there is the tortoise who carries the world, and has markings on its shell. Those markings need to be deciphered.

These stories were a message given to people who couldn't read. They had to rely on the unconscious and on what would emerge from the accumulation from many lifetimes of involvement. The message is one. The message is the same.

Christian Myth and Symbolism

THE PARABLES OF JESUS occur with very slight differences in many other cultures, so much so that when I came to India, I was terribly upset. I thought that the Christians had stolen everything almost, because many of these stories that we hear about Jesus, Saint Francis, and other saints are very common knowledge. They are gathered in the Tantric tales which were recorded before Jesus was even born.

But after thinking about this, I thought, "What does it matter who started it? The *message* is the important thing. If I have a road map, the important thing is that it can help me to locate the road and pursue it. If the map is copied or dirty, it really doesn't matter, because the map is *not* the road. Now, I frequently use citations from the Christian teachings because they are almost identical with the Eastern teachings.

In one of these parables of Jesus, there is a master who has to go away on business. In the sense of Eastern psychology, this may be interpreted as follows: God has withdrawn from your consciousness because now for a while you are on your own. But before that divine power goes, you are given something to sustain yourself.

Human fathers and mothers, when they go on a trip, bring something when they come back. But your *divine* father and mother give you something that will sustain you in their absence.

The master gave his ten servants ten gold coins. So everybody had something to start with. After a while, he came back or, in psychological terms, the divine force made itself known to us again. In Jesus' story, the master was happily greeted by everybody. One said, "Master, I increased what you gave me tenfold." That means that person applied the divine inspiration tenfold.

Another one said, "Oh, I increased it five times."

And then the master asked a third servant, "What did you do?"

He said, "Oh, I was very afraid somebody would steal it, so I hid it away."

"Well," said the master, "if you are not doing anything with it, why should you have it? I will take it back."*

---

* Luke 19:11–26.

At some point, every one of us will get some divine inspiration, some guidance, some pointer, meet somebody who can help, or receive inspiration through poetry, that we will not allow ourselves to use. Instead of doing anything with it, we may say, "But my life is so terrible. I am so upset. It's so hard, all these obstacles. People say it is a challenge. I don't see the challenge. I am just breaking down. For me it's the last straw breaking the camel's back." Here is a great warning: Do you think that the intelligence you have now will be yours in the future? In another life you may be born with a lot less. I have never found a century, in all my search in the history of various religions and various schools of thought, in which there are so many mentally retarded people as there are today. Christians often say, "God is love." The Divine loves you so much that it takes away the intelligence you won't use so that you don't *mis*use it. Those who have misused intelligence will lose it.

We all have a certain level of human frailty, but there is no way you can go on doing things which are greedy and selfish beyond that level. There is today so much *intentional* greed, so much jealousy, so much hate, so much self-importance taking on incredible shapes and forms. This cannot go on forever.

This is why it is impossible to create peace on Earth. All these intentionally greedy, selfish, jealous, self-important people have to be reborn. They are the doers and they must be given a chance to redo, start all over, do it again. *That's* God's love.*

---

* I do not think, as many Eastern people do, that you will be thrown back as far as the animal kingdom. It's bad enough to lose normal consciousness and be born a sort of imbecile, and there are many degrees to which one can be mentally handicapped.

Killing

❁ THERE ARE MANY PEOPLE who have a human body but are not yet truly human. Hitler and people like him have senselessly killed millions of people out of their own fanaticism and from a desire to punish those who try to do what is good and right. Even though such people are not truly human, it would be almost an insult to compare them to animals. An animal doesn't usually kill unless it's hungry and wants food. Then it goes by its instincts and hunts. But people do the most terrible things. Tigers, pumas, lions, and most other so-called fierce animals only kill when they want to eat. So there is perhaps a nobility in animals that many human beings have not achieved.

You need to investigate the idea of killing on a very individual and personal level. What is it that everyone has to kill? As we become aware in the First Discourse of the Bhagavad Gita, the issue of killing is not quite as simple or limited as it looks. We see from the dialogue between Arjuna and Krishna how difficult it is for Arjuna to make the decision to kill his enemies, whether you think of them as his family or his personality aspects.

The devotee of Krishna, or anyone on the spiritual path, really has to think about this, and ask, "What does killing mean in my own personal life?"

People are killed in the flare of passion—hatred, anger, jealousy, greed. These are the motivations that lead to war, but they always begin in one's own personal life. It is very difficult to kill somebody if you have already killed your ego and all its negative characteristics. If the ego is dead or nearly dead, you feel there is no need to kill anybody, because all your real enemies—the ones within yourself—have already been taken care of. You have to kill those personality aspects which are the strong filter preventing you from recognizing the Divine. They make it impossible to really see, to really hear, to truly feel, and to have a taste for the Divine.

The body can be killed by the violence of another person, but we also can kill our own bodies by bringing discord into them so that they can no longer function properly.

I once knew a woman who controlled the world around her by

intentional wrong breathing. She would pretend to be very ill by forcing a labored breath, making it appear that she couldn't breathe. When she was taken to the hospital, however, the doctor could never find anything wrong. But eventually her lungs accepted this extraordinary activity, and a few months later she died of a lung disease.

She had a husband who treated her very badly, so I can understand why she had recourse to illness. But in the end she killed *herself*, because she didn't have the courage and the strength to stand on her own two feet and say to him, "Look, if you don't change your life, I will leave."

We can kill ourselves with excessive emotions. Anger and jealousy can poison our bodies, so that finally they can't handle it anymore. They don't know how to throw off the poison. Of course, we can also kill our bodies by eating the wrong food.

There are many ways of killing. A bomb or a shot are perhaps only the fastest methods. However, the ending of a life prematurely before the individual can find Higher Consciousness may be much more devastating than the act of killing the body.

It is worth thinking about how we kill many things in ourselves. But we can also kill things for other people. We can kill other people's honor or reputations by making false statements or by not correcting false statements made about them. We can undermine a person's reputation by just being flippant. We don't have to do or say anything harmful; all it takes are gestures or body language which convey a message, such as, "My God, have you ever *known* such an idiot?" An undermined reputation can ruin many years of a person's life. And one day, all these things will come back to us.

We can kill somebody's hope with one word. And how many times, particularly in marriages, do people kill each other with completely unnecessary remarks or attempts to have revenge? Whatever we criticize in someone else—even if it is never said aloud—we will have to face at some time in our own lives. I have seen many situations in the Ashram where one person criticized another person's handling of some situation, and then had to go through the same kind of difficulties caused by the same kind of personality aspects he or she had criticized in the other person—often handling the difficulties no better.

We also have to look into how we use the word *killing* in our everyday speech. We say things like, "making a killing" or "I could kill myself." We have to observe how we condition ourselves by the way we use it. If we understand how we manipulate ourselves with wrong words, we will have to acknowledge the importance and the power of the Devi of Speech. With the wrong word, we may kill our intuition and our enthusiasm for spiritual life, and perhaps even the still, small voice of conscience within,

as well as that divine inspiration which can be best termed "the Guru within."

The ego is a great killer. It always wants to reign, and the best in us can be very easily killed. We do so very little to nourish it. Yet that little flame of divine inspiration and love for spiritual life has to be very carefully protected.

If you have even a few experiences on the spiritual path, be very careful whom you talk to. You should talk to perhaps no more than one other person, someone who also has experienced something of a similar nature, because showing off will quickly snuff out that little spiritual flame. Sometimes it's best not to talk at all. Sometimes it's even wise not to let other people know that you understand the word *yoga* unless you are in the company of people who are seeking—and then make sure that their seeking is sincere.

Sincerity isn't always easy to distinguish. In 1959 when I was in Indira Devi's ashram, she said at satsang, "A lot of you are not here because you are truly seeking Krishna. You're here because you don't have enough money to do something else." She had really hit the nail on the head about a lot of the people who were there. They just had nothing else to do: "Let's go to satsang at Krishna Mandir. Dilip Kumar Roy sings so beautifully, and we can watch Indira Devi going into a state of trance."

Making spiritual events a kind of entertainment kills the very spirit of them. Watch that you don't kill the true spirit in yourself by carelessness.

Let's consider the expression *to make a killing*. This is competition. Competition is another way of killing. We see it everywhere. Mothers often regard their daughters as competition and become jealous of them. A father is jealous of his sons because they are young and strong and he sees them as competition. We can compete with others in work situations by holding them back, thereby stunting their development. Or we can do it by withholding necessary information. We can do it also by not recognizing another person's achievements, or by taking everything on ourselves so others don't get a chance to achieve anything. All this causes inhibition and lack of self-worth in others. We can belittle a talent which isn't yet developed so that the person never develops it into full bloom.

With all these things, we are killing indirectly. And that's really much more dangerous than direct attack, because there's deliberate intention and scheming in it, and much hidden jealousy and competition in ourselves that we are not acknowledging and correcting.

When you are in competition you fight because you want to win. When you want to win, you kill. If it's your ego and your egotistical personality aspects that you want to defeat, chop their heads off by all means. But that's where killing should end. We all experience competition and jealousy at some time in our lives, but we must root them out and we must be willing to correct our faulty thinking and wrong assessment of others.

We can also kill by unusual and unnecessary criticism of a characteristic that someone has. This criticism is not meant to be helpful. It is not offered to help the person overcome that characteristic. It simply stunts the person's growth and development, and that is a very destructive thing to do. Criticism is very treacherous ground. We always want to know if we are making progress, so we continually compare ourselves to others in this kind of indirect competition. At such a time, we can quickly say something about another person, which one part of us knows isn't right. When you do that, you can counteract what you have said by putting the individual in the Light as quickly as possible so you won't forget.* And then see that you don't repeat what you said. We have many, many bad habits, and they are best overcome by putting the individual we have hurt into the Light. But remember there is often the opportunity for you to balance what you said by saying also something very positive. There is a vast area in which we can do good and be helpful, if this is what we want to do.

You might find it helpful to give more thought to the word *killing*, especially for further reading in the Gita.

But you can start right now cutting off the heads of all your personality aspects. Throw them in the lake. Then you can nourish the baby Krishna that you have in your heart.

Fear

☸ WITHOUT THE EXPERIENCE of fear, we would not know what courage is. Without fear, courage wouldn't even be necessary. Most of us experience fear when we enter the spiritual path. We think that we face some tremendous unknown thing, some great danger, some frightening changes, some overpowering destiny that will get us.

One day my Guru asked me, "Have you ever been to Dattatreya?" Dattatreya is a temple in the hills, probably not more than two or three miles from the Sivananda Ashram. We had walked there several times, and once he pointed to a cistern in the ground for collecting rainwater. It was usually empty and had an iron grill over it.

I said I knew where the temple was. He said, "Very good. Very good. I want you to go to the cistern. You can open the grill, and you will find some hooks in the wall, so you can climb down to the bottom. When you are down in the bottom, close the grill and you will be quite pro-

---

* For the practice of putting people in the Light, see Radha, *The Divine Light Invocation.*

tected from wild animals. I want you to stay there and meditate until just before sunset."

I thought this was absolutely outrageous! What if a wild beast came, smelled something eatable in there, and waited until I came out of the hole. And how would I get to the Ashram fast enough before the sun went down? The sun goes down very fast in that part of the world.

So the question was: Should I or should I not do it? It was a very difficult decision to make. But I went.

Once I got there, however, I couldn't get the grill open. This was almost a relief. But then a man came along and said, "What are you trying to do? Oh, I see. You want to do some practice. What's your Mantra?"

"I'm not supposed to talk about my Mantra," I said.

"Oh, so you are serious," he said. "Well, do you know there can be all sorts of little vipers and big spiders and scorpions down there?"

He really fired up my imagination! In my mind's eye, all those things were down there. I began to wish he wouldn't help me with the grill. But he did.

It was damp down there. It was nice and cool, no question about that, but it was also damp. And I was still worried. How would I know when the sun was setting? I tried to find out how I would be able to tell. I was so nervous, all I did really was look upwards and watch for any little bit of shadow to fall on the grill that would tell me it was time to get out. Then I realized that I was not meditating, I had no concentration, nothing. I was just sitting there in fear, worrying about whether there was a wild animal waiting for me, whether I would have to stay there all night, whether anybody would remember I was there. What if even Gurudev had forgotten me? What would I do? At the first inkling that the sun was setting, I got out of the cistern and ran as fast as I could through two or three miles of bush along a narrow path to the highway.

There are many kinds of fear besides the fear of physical harm. One day Gurudev invited me to go for a walk. We came to a small hut, built almost like a cave. The man who lived in it had a sign on the wall.

Gurudev said, "You go over and look at it. Come back and tell me what you read."

On the board was written in English, "In the last thirty years, no woman has seen my face. If you wish darshan,* sit across the river."

I told Gurudev this, and he said, "What do you think?"

I didn't know what he expected me to say, so I just came out with what I felt. I said, "This poor fellow, he must be terribly afraid."

Yet, this man was also saying, "If you want to worship me, sit on the other side of the Ganges." Why should anybody worship someone who is so afraid?

Gurudev was very happy that I understood. You can practice all kinds of austerities, simply from a motivation of fear. For this man, the temptation would be too great if he saw a woman's face, but that note was also a way of catching women's attention. He was looking for the worship of women, so what was going on in this man's fantasies? That is a question that is easily answered.

The need for that kind of seclusion to break temptation is quite obvious and, I'm sure, very helpful. At some time in our spiritual evolution, we will have to dedicate a life to breaking the attachments that are strongest, so that we can walk more freely on the spiritual path. Then, in some other life, we won't need to be so rigorous.

At one point, I had been thinking if I could stay in a cave, I would surely find Realization. When we are quite innocent and naive and ignorant, we think if we can do the opposite to what we always do, we will gain something. There is no question that we gain, but it's not necessarily Realization. What I gained by sitting in a cave was overcoming my fear, and particularly so in that situation because I had to face a big python, not knowing if it was poisonous and could harm me.† So I overcame my fear. But that was only fear in one area. You may have a little wooden door on your hut with a couple of iron bars so a tiger can't come in, but a lot of other animals can come in: scorpions, snakes, rats.

You learn through circumstances where you are confronted with what you fear, but you don't really need to be exposed to those things.

---

* To offer darshan is for the Guru to offer him- or herself as a focus for the disciple's devotion.

† See Radha, *In the Company of the Wise*, p. 109.

You can sit down, take a piece of paper, and make a list of your fears. Look at them one by one. Sometimes fear is simply your uncultivated imagination. Then you need to work on the cultivation of imagination. It's like working the soil and then putting some good spiritual thoughts into the imagination. Let the imagination dwell, rather, on a spiritual image that is meaningful to you.

I met somebody who had not left the Sivananda Ashram for about twelve years—twelve years of tapas. By this time I was no longer so strongly impressed by this kind of action. I said, "If I took that person to Montreal, and had him cross the street, I wonder how he would react." We can handle what we are used to. That's not what we need to work on. We need to work on what we can't handle. If it means staying in a cave to face the fact that you are dependent on having someone to talk to, having lots of opportunity for self-expression, do this. Do it to find out where you stand, not necessarily for the expectation of great Realization, but just to know yourself. It's very important that we know ourselves.

In the Himalayas where a lot of people live in tiny little huts and in caves, they are very much on the alert for every unusual sound. I noticed that I listened like this when I stayed in Purushottamananda's cave for three days, and also whenever I stayed in someone else's house. Many people can't sleep in another place because of all the many new, strange sounds. It's not necessarily that they don't have their own bed: it's also that they have to get to know all the noises, and interpret them—find out if they are familiar or, if not, what they are. We are creatures of habit, so if we invite changes to break our habits, that is very helpful.

Death

DEATH IS NOT LOSING consciousness. It is *gaining* consciousness, and being aware of the Light, *if* the preparation for the physical death has been done correctly.

If we are so much absorbed in the Light that little else has a place in us, then at the time of death we will pass into the Light. In such a situation, the decision not to avoid death is not really all that big.

More than once I have gone through stages where I could not know how long I would be living, but I was determined not to avoid death because if the time comes that one can pass into the Light, why struggle for living? Unless there is the commitment to the Most High to do the work, what is there to live for? When there is such a commitment, you can think, "As long as this body functions and can do the work, I will do it. But when that changes, I shall have no regrets if I can leave." There should be no regrets then, because our daily consciousness, our body consciousness or body-mind, is mainly what keeps us from the Light. It is the body-mind that creates all the clouds so that we can't see the Light, that makes us forget, that creates our illusions. In fact, an old text says that if you achieve even the first stage of samadhi, the body may not live longer than twenty-one to twenty-four days after that, and then it drops off like a ripe fruit from the tree. It is with dedication to the work—to do Divine Mother's work—that one can stay alive and live longer. But as Jesus said, "There is much to harvest, but there are few workers who want to do the work."* This is because everybody is exercising self-will, and self-will dies very hard. Because of self-will, it's very difficult to die. Self-will fights back by any means it can find and prevents death. Self-will keeps the door to the Light closed.

However, when self-will dies by divine grace, there is a time of freedom, of jubilation. It's like stepping through a door, or coming out of the grip of iron tongs. Only then can you take a fresh breath of air, or a fresh breath of Light. The memory of that great moment is everlasting, it will dazzle everything else with Light.

After that it is sometimes difficult to do the work and to fulfill the promise given to the Divine, because the world and what it consists of may be losing its grip on you, and your interest may be fading away. Even a sense of duty is not compelling enough because, after all, the work was going on before this physical body came into existence and had the awareness of doing the work. You may also think that by dying you will be giving place and opportunity to others. This is good because it is up to each individual to develop this Light and carry the torch and bring Light to other people. So with all this to think about, it can become very difficult to stay and do the work.

The mind is a phenomenon, and so is the body. This whole world is a big phenomenon. You will realize soon that what you consider real today was just your own illusion, your own expectation, your own desires to have it be that way. When illusions about the mind and the body and the world burst like soap bubbles, what's left? Not much. There is not much left then that binds us, so why not go home?

Ramakrishna used to say to Sarada Devi, "When I am dead, I will

---

* Matthew 9:37.

not be gone. I will only be in another room. I will be gone only from the perception of your senses." If you can cultivate thoughts like this in your own words, you will have no fear of death.

When someone close to you dies, think that this person has only taken off earthly clothes. He or she hasn't died. There's no need to be sad because someone has taken clothes off that no longer fit. Death is not a going away. Death is only leaving illusion behind and going on to fulfill a much greater duty.

When your time comes, may you all pass into the Light, because only there can you find immortality.

Time

IN THE *KUNDALINI* BOOK, there are pictures of the Devi holding a little drum.* It is shaped like an hourglass and has a string tied around the middle. A seed is tied to the end of the string so that it can strike one end or the other of the drum. The purpose of this drum is to create vibration.† It takes time to learn to use the drum properly. You have to flip it with the wrist very, very fast.

The drum is an element of time. How much time do you spend on this end of the drum? How much on the other end? When you think of time, you think of clock time, calendar time, years of your life, centuries. I call this "small time." You can also think of "great time," like millennia, eons, eternity. Then you can go into a different level of time—your estimation of time. How much time does it take you?

In your time of reflection, you should think about what time means to you. This reflection may clarify something because your attitude and your action often determine how much time you have already let pass by

---

* This drum is pictured in Radha, *Kundalini Yoga for the West,* Plate VI, Svadhisthana Chakra; and Plate XVII, Ajna Chakra.

† Drums create vibrations and reactions in the human body. Big drums, for example, have their effects mainly in the region of the stomach and abdomen, creating thereby a different mood.

without awareness, and you really don't know how much more time you have left to do what you ought to do, to fulfill the purpose of your life.

The first four words I got from my Tibetan Guru were *God, Guru, prayer*, and *time.* These words have to be investigated. How long does it take you to know God? How long does it take you to know the Guru? How much time does it take until the Guru accepts the prayer? How much time until your prayers reach God? How many lifetimes have you already wasted? The time element is extremely important. When you reflect on these questions, you will see that you are really forced into a deep level of thinking.

The drum itself is symbolic for the womb. The seed that penetrates the one end of the drum or womb is connected with procreation. The seed that goes into the human womb creates another human being. The other end of the drum is the cosmic womb, or your own consciousness. The seed which penetrates this womb is the seed of knowledge, and when it penetrates, it produces your own spiritual being, your own spiritual baby.

You may need time to make a decision about which end of the drum your life is going to be—which seed in which womb, how it will be received, and how it will be nourished.

The penetration of either seed produces something else. When we think about which choice to make, we are dealing with the two selves: the human self, and the eternal Self—the Self of the Light that you are. The human part of you is symbolized in your tangible physical body, but you have also an intangible mind, an intangible consciousness, that you can't take in your hand and have a look at. So you live in two worlds, and that is symbolized also in the two halves of the hourglass shape of the drum. The hourglass has grains of sand which run downward when you turn it over, so you can measure a certain length of time. What is your time? Your own time? No one knows how much time is left in our lives. People get old, but people die young, some *very* young.

Time should become a new concept to you. You can stretch your time by just being leisurely about it, or you can be concerned about time and say, "I don't know how much time is left, so I had better make use of every day *as if* that were my last day."

What have you done with the time you have already had? If you realize that it is time-consuming to make significant changes in thinking, significant changes in attitude, in putting what you understand intellectually into practice, then time becomes something extremely precious.

We sometimes do a workshop at the Ashram where we ask, "If you had only three months to live, what would you do with your life? What if you had only three weeks?" Make up your mind to make the best of the time that is in your hands. Turn all action into spiritual practice. When you wash dishes, see that they are clean. Hold a glass up and say, "I would like one day, with the help of the Mantra and the Divine Light Invocation, to be as transparent as this glass." You must be transparent to the Divine. There is a saying, "Naked and unafraid you must come." The word transparent is just another word for that.

Never talk to anybody without also wrapping him or her in a spiral of Light. In other words, you don't need to set time aside to put people in the Light. Practice it at any moment. You live in this world, you have to act. You live near the beginning of the twenty-first century, so you cannot live as if you were in medieval times, or prehistoric times. Things have to be adjusted according to the time in which you find yourself.

Find out how you can let the Light penetrate all the work that you do. Otherwise you will become very unhappy and frustrated, and wonder what you are doing here. There is no time that cannot somehow get a ray of the Light if we let it in.

New Year's Resolutions

GURUDEV SIVANANDA had a New Year's tradition that people made resolutions about what they wanted to accomplish in the new year. He asked them also to write down the resolutions they had failed to carry out in the previous year or years. Then for the next year, their daily reflection was geared to all this.

I had been at Swami Sivananda's Ashram two or three days when Swami Paramananda told me, "Swamiji has granted you an interview."

I was thrilled, but I was also a little fearful to be meeting my Guru in a very personal setting in his kutir.

When I arrived, Gurudev said to Swami Satchitananda, "Bring me Mrs. Hellman's papers, her files."

I said, "Oh, no, what's going to happen now?" I was terribly worried. A big pile of papers arrived. Gurudev watched me very carefully, from the moment I entered the door to see what I would do, how I would act, how I would handle things. My heart was almost jumping out of my throat because I had no idea what to expect. I was in such a state as he went through the papers that I had blurred vision and couldn't recognize my own handwriting on them.

He took up one of the papers and he looked at it. Then he put it down, and took up another paper, and looked at this, turning several pages, and then he said, "Hmm, hmm," and put that one down. He went through all the papers, separating them into little piles. Then he looked at me very kindly, but in my excitement and fearfulness I didn't even see the kindness. After a little while I calmed down because he hadn't cut my head off, and he hadn't accused me of anything terrible.

Then he said something in Tamil or Hindi to Swami Satchitananda, who handed me a big sheet of paper. It had a title, "My Resolutions for the New Year," and about twenty-five questions.

Holding this paper in front of me and looking down at it was a tremendous relief, because it helped me to collect my high-flying emotions and to calm down so I could see what all this was about.

There were questions on the paper: How many times have you lied? How many times did you get up late? How many times did you go to the movies? How many times did you not fulfill your duty? How many times did you criticize your Guru? How many times did you criticize your gurubhais?* How many times did you *voice* your criticism?

Then there was another paper with more questions: What do you want to do? To do your practice, to get up in time, to do charity work, to be helpful? What do you want not to do? Not to lie, not to criticize? What are you going to do beyond the duties that you are requested to

---

* Gurubhais are disciples who have the same Guru.

do? What will you give up? Going to the movies, smoking, playing cards? (Playing cards was a big thing in India.)

Then came another question with a huge list: What are you going to do beyond and above all of that? How many malas of Mantra are you going to chant? How many Mantras are you going to write? How many prostrations are you going to do? How many hours of meditation? How many of Hatha Yoga? How many of chanting?

It was quite an undertaking. I read this and I said to Gurudev, "You want me to give this paper back?"

He said, "If you want to fill it out, and *then* give it back to me. That will be just right."

I said, "Do I have to do this right now, here?"

He said, "No, you can give it to me tomorrow." That was a great relief. I wanted to think about it, because if I made these promises, I would have to sign my name on the bottom, so I wanted to be sure that I could keep them.

These papers were not entirely new to me because Gurudev had sent papers like this to me every month in Montreal, so I had had some preparation. Except for this very first interview, I was always very easy with Gurudev. But sitting in front of him with these papers, I didn't know how I could say how many Mantras I would recite. I didn't know what my life would be like when I got back to Canada, or how much time I would have. I had given up my job. Would I have any money at all? I didn't know where my next meal would be coming from, or even if there would be anybody at the airport to meet me. All these things raced through my head, so you can imagine the great inner turmoil I was having.

But then Gurudev smiled at me and said, "Now, would you like some coffee or some milk?"

A few days later, Gurudev folded a piece of paper down the middle and made a plus at the top on one side and a minus sign on the other. He gave it to me and said, "Now you can sit over there on the veranda and write down all your shortcomings on the minus side, and on the other side, all the things that you can do well." It was very strange. I could find lots of shortcomings but I couldn't think of anything I could do well. So I handed him this, and I have to say that in my naivete and ignorance, there was probably some sense of pride: "See? I am courageous. I can tell you all these shortcomings."

But when he didn't see anything on the plus half of the page, he just tore it up, and said, "You say you know all these shortcomings but you don't know any good things. This is inverted ego. Try again."

It is not easy—it is really not easy—to know precisely where you are. It is not easy even to do your daily reflections correctly, because you have to zero in on all the things that you have missed in manifesting your spiritual ideals, otherwise nothing is going to happen. You can spend ten years, fifteen years, twenty years in an ashram without moving very much if you don't investigate everything. You may be a little bit more friendly after all that time, you may offer more of a hand to people, but beyond that you will not really advance. The daily reflection means asking, "Have I done my quota of work, spiritual work? Have I done my duties within the center or ashram with the proper attitude? Was it a giving of myself, an offering to Divine Mother?" If you can answer, "Yes," then you can sleep well, because so far as you can see, you have done everything necessary.

But what happens if you haven't? If you feel you can't get out of your critical nature, you can't get out of your emotions, then you have to do something more drastic. One of Gurudev's suggestions was, "If you like food, have no dinner. And, if necessary, do that for a whole week." Not as a punishment, but as a reminder. I have not observed many people who feel that they have failed again, and again, and again, in correcting their shortcomings. They are still quick-tempered, quick to judge, quick to condemn, still condemning others in their absence. They do not seem to notice any of this.

Even if you have failed in conquering a shortcoming for the fifth time, the tenth time, the twentieth time, you won't know about your failures if you don't put them down in your diary and examine them in your daily reflection. Then keep reading over the past months in your diary, and you will see a lot of things coming together.

There are little helpful hints that I can give you. For example, you can buy a whole bunch of highlighters and make your own color code: this color for lying, that one for criticism, another for condemning, another for emotional upheavals, one for missing your practice, one for being mechanical in your practice or your reactions. Backbiting is another thing to watch out for, and hitting back: "You criticized me. Now I will find out what I can do to you." It can be very subtle. And sometimes not so subtle. From all this, you can get a list together of what you should be paying attention to—not to tear yourself down, but to be very clear where you fall short.

Unless you put all this down in your daily reflection, you will not be inclined to do much about it. Read your reflections every week, and use your color code to highlight your shortcomings. Then if you see that one color is becoming a bit overwhelming, you had better get to work. Put your color code on the inside cover of your diary so you don't forget what it is.

I repeat: you can live what you call a spiritual life for five years, ten years, fifteen years, twenty years, but if you are only going through the motions, and your mind, your soul, your heart are not really in spiritual life, nothing happens.

Then you have to ask yourself the question, "Why am I doing this?" For some people there is a certain glorification in spiritual life: "I'm different. I'm better than you. I have chosen *this* life, but you? Hmm!" Self-importance is such a monster. We can all be very subtle about these things: "Oh, you eat meat? I'm a vegetarian." Jesus said that it's not what goes *into* the mouth, but what comes out that matters.* Think about that. You can become very proud: "*I'm* not a meat eater. *I* don't smoke."

This is what Gurudev meant by "inverted ego." You can be proud of anything: "I'm a renunciate, and a *great* one. Don't you see? And see my *humility*. I *never* miss satsang without at least three prostrations." But can you be sure you're not being a hypocrite? That you're not covering up something? Your resentment, your desire to get back at somebody? That is the point. That is what really matters.

I recognized this years ago when the Ashram began. We used to follow some of the Indian traditions, with prostrations and other ritu-

---

* Matthew 15:11.

als, but after about three or four years, I became aware that people were being hypocritical. They were just pretending a humility or devotion or surrender which was really not in their hearts, because it wasn't in their minds. So what was the point? These traditions mean something only when there is sincerity in people's hearts.

I have received wonderful papers from people—ready to publish without even editing. But the daily actions of the people who wrote them don't reflect what's in those papers. And that's what counts. I have met many great scholars, too, but their lives seem to be completely disconnected from what they write about. It is in the practice, and only in the practice, that change comes. People say to me, "I'm truly a seeker, you know, and I hope you will give me all the guidance and help that I need." But how shall I know that you are truly a seeker unless I can see it in your actions?

And they say, "Now I am here. I have changed things in my life. I have given up a relationship. I have given up my plans for a life in the future, a career. Now, are you going to make me a sanyasi? Can I be a swami and teach others? I want to give back to the world!"

Sure, you can, if you have the qualifications. But the qualifications I require are probably much different from what your expectations are. If I see backbiting and hypocrisy, I will have very little inclination to let you teach. I may not even seek your companionship. I may let you come to arm's length, but that's about all.

How quickly you get initiated depends on what you bring. I will tell you an Indian story, one that Gurudev himself told.

A great Indian king decided one day he would renounce everything. His Guru told him what this would mean. He said, "Look, you have to give up your kingdom."

The king said, "You know, it's just lots of worries and trouble. I don't think that will be such a big deal."

Then the Guru said, "And you have to give up your wife."

That was a little more difficult. He didn't answer too quickly. He thought about it, but then he agreed.

Then came the major thing: "You will have to give up your sons and your daughters." Sons are meant to light the funeral pyre when the father dies. Daughters are most of the time undesirable, but they can come in very handy if you want to give one to your neighboring king as a gift so that he won't invade your country. There are some great valuables that you really have to think about before you give them up.

Finally the king won the battle within himself and he said, "Okay, here it is. I give it all up. Where do you want me to go?"

The Guru said, "There is a little hut in the forest where you can stay." He told him precisely what the hut looked like among all the other little huts, so the king could find it, and the king retired to this little hut in the forest. The Guru told him, "The Divine will look after you." The king had no idea how that would take place.

In a hut nearby there lived a merchant. The king asked, "Are you a renunciate, too?"

The merchant said, "Yes, and really you know it wasn't all that difficult. Business goes up, business goes down, one day you have money, the next day you haven't. Then come customers who want their money back. It's a lot of headache. I'm glad I'm here."

The king said, "What about your family?"

He said, "Oh, you know, I have been married for thirty years. And there's not much left. My children are all married and they can take care of the grandchildren. I've had enough of all that."

Then a divine messenger came with two trays of food, one for the merchant and the other for the king. The merchant got his tray and looked at the food. Then he said, "Let me see, what do you have on yours?" He counted, "One, two, three, four, five, six, *seven* items. I have only three. Now this is not justice. I have renounced everything to become realized so I should be given the same. Aren't we all the same before the Divine?"

The divine messenger said, "Yes, the only difference is this man was a king and he has renounced a little more than you."

What this story tells us is not to make any comparisons. Not to be on the spiritual path in competition for whatever is given. We can't know if it is just. We can't know whether it is wrong. We can't measure those things. If somebody has waited a long time, and somebody else arrives and is given something right away, that's all within the karmic relationship. It all depends on the amount of karma that you bring into this life. It's often not entirely just the decision of a Guru.

A spiritual teacher gets certain pronounced intuitive insights in regard to spiritual life, and it is that inner command which decides what the teacher will do for an individual seeker. To explain this, I will tell you another story.

Lord Krishna plays the flute, and he plays very beautiful alluring melodies. There were about half a dozen devotees of Lord Krishna who got the idea that perhaps if they sang to him with all their hearts, with all their minds, in front of a temple door which had been closed for a hundred years and which nobody had been able to open, maybe the Lord would open the door and they would be able to meet him. They started, one by one, sitting in front of the door and singing their hearts out, putting everything they had into their singing.

One sang for two weeks. And then, lo and behold, the door opened. He entered and had his union with Lord Krishna. But the door immediately closed. So here was an indication that each person has to chant individually with all his or her heart to open the door. The next devotee came and it took five or six weeks, but then the door opened. The devotee was overjoyed because she had been wondering if the door really would open, and she had almost doubted her own sincerity. So she went into the temple. The door closed immediately again. So it became very obvious that each disciple had to chant to open the door to Lord Krishna's temple for himself or herself.

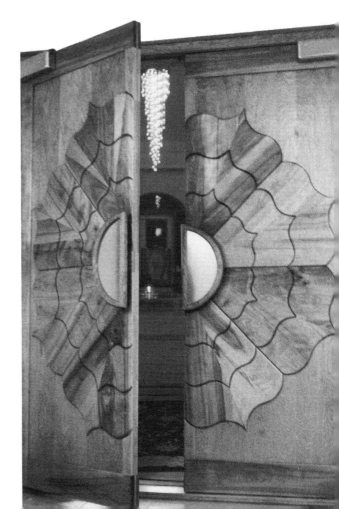

So the third devotee came, and the fourth, and the fifth. Then the sixth came. He sat in front of the door and chanted. One month passed, the second month passed, the third month passed, the fourth month passed, the fifth month passed—the door didn't open. Six months passed. It still didn't open. A year ended, and the poor disciple was thinking, "What have I done? What have I done wrong? Am I insincere? Am I hypocritical? Have I such bad karma?"

When he was almost ready to give up, both doors opened! And the disciple said to Lord Krishna, "I thought you had given up on me. You kept me waiting for such a long time."

Lord Krishna said, "No, I was listening very attentively to every minute of your chanting. It was so beautiful, I just forgot to open the doors." Then the disciple had a very beautiful embrace from Lord Krishna.

The New Year can be a very important warning to you to remember what you have undertaken to do. You must win this battle. Don't risk this life, because there may be no other one. This Earth will be eradicated, sooner or later, and the opportunity to make up for one's karma for many past lives, and for this one, may not be given again. At the end of the Mahabharata Lord Krishna says he will destroy the world.

I asked my Guru, "What does that mean?"

He said, "You become pure energy. And you may begin all over again. You may start off as a piece of rock, and go through this whole path of illusion and evolution again."

Put that in your diary as a good reminder.

Index

About the Author

Swami Sivananda Radha began her spiritual journey in 1955 on the basis of a vision and a longing. By the time of her death on November 30, 1995, at the age of 84, she had become one of the world's most highly respected spiritual teachers. She was a rare and courageous Yogini who realized her spiritual potential within her lifetime.

Swami Radha was the first Western woman to be initiated into sanyas. Although she was a swami, trained in Eastern yoga and philosophy, she never lost sight of the fact that she was a Westerner first. Her task, as her teacher, Swami Sivananda of Rishikesh, presented it to her, was to update the Eastern teachings of yoga for the Western mind.

She lectured all over North America and internationally at universities, colleges, churches and psychological institutes and is one of the most widely-known spiritual teachers today.

Her Ashram, on the shores of Kootenay Lake, British Columbia, Canada, is one of the most enduring spiritual teaching centers in North America. Her books, including *Kundalini Yoga for the West, Hatha Yoga: the Hidden Language, Mantras: Words of Power* and *Realities of the Dreaming Mind*, have become classics in the field and have been published in several languages. Swami Radha's teachings are considered by many to be the most sophisticated, practical approach to yoga available today.

Swami Radha worked unceasingly to fulfill the promise she had made to her guru so many years ago. She has deeply influenced the lives of many people, showing by her example how to live a life of purpose and quality.

Classes and Workshops

Workshops and classes based on Swami Radha's teachings are available at Yasodhara Ashram and at affiliated centers called Radha Houses located in urban communities internationally.

For further information (including details about a vacation and yoga retreat center in Mérida, Mexico) write: The Program Secretary, Yasodhara Ashram, PO Box 9 TH, Kootenay Bay, BC, Canada, V0B 1X0, phone 1-800-661-8711.